CIVIL LIABILITY ISSUES
IN CORRECTIONS

CIVIL LIABILITY ISSUES IN CORRECTIONS

Darrell L. Ross

CAROLINA ACADEMIC PRESS
Durham, North Carolina

Library of Congress Cataloging-in-Publication Data

Ross, Darrell L. (Darrell Lee), 1951–
  Civil liability issues in corrections / By Darrell L. Ross.
    p. cm.
  Includes index.
  ISBN 1-59460-083-X
  1. Correctional personnel--Malpractice--United States. 2. Prisoners--Legal status, laws, etc.--United States. 3. Torts--United States. I. Title.

  KF9730.R67 2005
  344.7303'56--dc22

                                                      2005002079

Carolina Academic Press
700 Kent Street
Durham, NC 27701
Telephone (919) 489-7486
Fax (919) 493-5668
www.cap-press.com

Printed in the United States of America

Prison and jail personnel around the country who daily pound the rock, maintaining the security of correctional institutions and thus providing for our community protection. I thank them for their tireless efforts. I dedicate this book to them.

Contents

Preface

Having worked in a close-custody prison with over 5,000 prisoners, I have an appreciation and understanding of what correctional officials and officers face on a regular basis. Daily, correctional staff must make decisions which affect the lives of prisoners. Frequently such decisions can have consequences that disturb the equilibrium of the facility, resulting in riots, disturbances, escapes, hostage taking, and/or violence directed at staff. The recent spotlight on the abuse of some detainees at a military prison in Iraqi as a result of improper decision making by a few soldiers should remind the astute correctional practitioner that the proper use of authority and decision making are instrumental in operating the correctional facility.

Working in the contemporary correctional facility requires that officers and administrators possess a fundamental knowledge of the constitutional rights of prisoners and how the courts apply the Constitution to the confined. This book has been written with this primary objective in mind. Since the emergence of prisoner litigation, numerous United States Supreme Court decisions have been issued. Frequently the Court establishes for the first time, or refines a standard of review, regarding a constitutional issue. Such legal standards are then applied by a lower court to a myriad of correctional topics. The resulting case decisions frequently create policy implications for the correctional agency which require a change in correctional procedures and practices. A lower court=s decisions force correctional practitioners to change how they make decisions which involve prisoner rights. Failing to follow these court-mandated standards of review heightens the risk of their liability.

Correctional liability is a dynamic area of constitutional law, and although the number of prisoner lawsuits have significantly decreased with the passage of the Prison Litigation Reform Act (1996) by Congress, prisoners still file about 25,000 Section 1983 lawsuits annually and file over 25,000 habeas corpus petitions. Keeping abreast of these standards of review and how lower courts apply them, can be a full-time endeavor for the correctional practitioner.

This book addresses the predominant liability issues which correctional officials routinely encounter. While the book focuses on Section 1983 liability decisions, cases reflecting state tort standards of review are also presented. A unique aspect of the text is that combines a multifaceted approach to the subject. The book not only presents an analysis of case law, but it combines current scholarly legal research specific to corrections with research on current trends in correctional liability. It also presents recommendations for reducing liability by examining components of risk management and by building defenses to counter prisoner litigation. Further, the book uses examples of cases in which I have participated as an expert witness, underscoring how lower courts apply Supreme Court standards to varying correctional issues.

Liability issues stemming from jail and prison circumstances comprise the bulk of the text. First, it presents an overview of the trends in correctional litigation. The next chapter addresses the court system, law making, and how to brief a case. Then a chapter outlines the evolution of prisoner litigation, followed by a chapter on the mechanics of Section 1983 prisoner litigation. Subsequent chapters follow, which apply specific constitutional amendments to specific correctional liability issues.

The book has been particularly structured to identify United States Supreme Court decisions on the more prominent issues in corrections, the appropriate constitutional amendment which addresses the issue, the applicable standard of review, and a review of how lower courts apply the standard. Reviewing cases in this manner allows students to study the laws regarding prisoner litigation more effectively and can assist the correctional official and line officer in applying the courts' decisions to the various facets of operating the jail or prison. One chapter addresses specific administrative liability concerns and provides proactive recommendations for reducing the number of lawsuits as well as suggestions for preparing to defend a prisoner or employee lawsuit.

It is hoped that the text will not only be useful in the college or university classroom but will also benefit detention and prison personnel and jail and prison administrators. It applies to correctional academies for new recruits or to in-service training for veteran correctional personnel. The main goals of the book are for the student to comprehend more fully how the courts apply constitutional amendments to the incarcerated in order that he or she can be better prepared to enter the field of corrections, and for veteran correctional employees to enhance their performance regarding these issues.

Darrell L. Ross, Ph.D.

ACKNOWLEDGMENTS

This book could not have been written without the assistance of others, and to the following individuals I would like to express my sincere appreciation for their suggestions:

Marvin Zalman, Wayne State University. I first was exposed to the study of correctional litigation in graduate school at Michigan State University. I am grateful to Professor Zalman and his teaching strategies, which influenced my interest in the field, including researching and teaching correctional law, and writing this book.

Jack Leonard, Carl Brannan, Melissa Webster, and Louis Titus Elliot. I appreciate their cooperation and long hours of review of the text and the many suggestions they gave which enhanced its readability.

CIVIL LIABILITY ISSUES
IN CORRECTIONS

CHAPTER 1

OVERVIEW OF THE TRENDS AND IMPACT OF PRISONER LITIGATION

Suing correction officials has become a popular sport!

Rolando del Carmen

Filing a civil lawsuit to resolve a dispute has become a common practice in American society. The United States has become a "litigious society"—ready, willing, and able to sue someone without hesitation. Litras and DeFrances (1999) conducted a study for the United States Department of Justice from 1967 to 1997 on the trends of 500,000 citizen civil-tort claims. They reported that almost $3 billion was awarded in combined compensatory and punitive damages involving claims of medical malpractice, personal injury, product liability, and property damage. They also reported that 75 percent of the cases were settled out of court.

del Carmen (2001) suggests that suing police officials has become a popular sport in the United States since they are vulnerable to civil rights violation claims. Silver (2003) also comments that it is highly popular to file civil liability actions against varying criminal justice agencies, and he estimates that approximately 30,000 claims are filed against the police by citizens annually.

Correctional officials are also easy targets for civil rights actions filed against them by prisoners claiming their rights were violated while under their supervision. Managing and operating a contemporary prison system within professional and state standards, and within the boundaries of the law, is a significant challenge for correctional personnel. Among the many job functions that correctional personnel perform, proper decision making regarding the safety of the confined is essential. Correctional personnel must exercise a high degree of skill in using their authority and discretion when implementing departmental policy and enforcing various aspects of the law. Frequently legal actions have arisen out of specific policies or practices which restricted services or constitutional rights of the prisoner population. Legal actions filed by prisoners have also emerged from allegations that correctional officials failed

3

to perform their legally assigned duties, performed them in negligent fashion, misused their authority, used excessive force, or deprived the prisoner population of certain constitutional rights.

Because of sweeping decisions by the United States Supreme Court since the 1960s, prisoners have been granted the right to file legal actions against their keepers. While habeas corpus actions have been accessible to prisoners since the 1800s for challenging the legality of their confinement, it was not until the 1960s that prisoners won the right to file lawsuits in federal and state courts under the Civil Rights Statute, Title 42 United States Code, Section 1983. State and jail prisoners have made increasing use of Section 1983 lawsuits (Turner 1979; Thomas, Keeler, and Harris 1986; Champion 1988; Bennett and del Carmen 1997; Ross 1997a). In these lawsuits, the prisoner complains generally about the manner in which he or she has been treated by correctional personnel or challenges the constitutionality of the treatment or the conditions of confinement. Other prisoners may file lawsuits to break up the monotony of prison life or to seek an opportunity to leave the prison facility for an appearance in court. A proliferation of Section 1983 lawsuits has inundated the court system as a result, and it has been characterized by various scholars as an "explosion," "an avalanche," a "deluge," "legal pollution," "hyperlexis," "excessive litigation," and an "epidemic" (Turner 1979; Bronstein 1987; Manning 1977; Galanter 1983).

However one characterizes the number of prisoner lawsuits filed annually, the legal decisions which have emerged have made a profound impact on the correctional system. Prisoner litigation and judicial intervention have directly affected a wide range of prisoner issues, including health care services, access to courts, food services, religious practices, conditions of confinement, sanitation standards, the disciplinary process, policies and procedures, and officer training, to identify a few (DiLulio 1991).

This chapter examines the prevalence of civil liability in corrections. Prisoner litigation is frequently targeted against prison/jail administrators, sheriffs, correction officers, detention officers, parole and probation officers, and other positions within the correctional system. The trends and the subject matter of these lawsuits are still emerging, and identifying past trends and patterns of prisoner litigation can aid in a better understanding of the various issues which generate frequent litigation.

TRENDS IN CORRECTIONAL LITIGATION

The United States Supreme Court established in *Cooper v. Pate* (1964) that state prisoners could bring lawsuits against correctional officials under Title

42 United States Code, Section 1983. The case dealt with the issue of access to religious literature while in prison. The Court's decision was narrow in scope, ruling that Muslim prisoners had standing to challenge religious discrimination in accordance with the First and Fourteenth Amendments under Section 1983. While prisoners prevailed in the case, the triumph for prisoners rights was not merely that correctional officials were forbidden to discriminate regarding religious issues but that prisoners, according to the Court's determination, have constitutional rights regardless of their convicted status. This decision established a forum for which prisoners in the future could confront correctional officials.

Since *Cooper*, prisoner litigation has flooded state and federal courts. Despite the quantity of prisoner lawsuits over the years, only a limited number of studies have examined the longitudinal trends of prisoner litigation. Turner (1979) examined 664 cases litigated between 1960 and 1977 in the federal districts of Virginia, Vermont, and the Northern and Eastern districts of California. He examined the increase of prisoner civil-rights suits, the treatment of these cases by the federal courts, the grievances alleged in Section 1983 complaints, factors affecting the volume of prisoner litigation, and alternative methods for both courts and prisons to resolve prisoner grievances. Turner found that a high proportion of these cases was filed *forma pauperis* (without legal counsel) and that a significant percentage (68 percent) of prisoner cases was disposed of at the pleading stage. The most prevalent issues raised were that of medical care, property loss/damage, and access to the courts. The size of the prison population had some relation to the volume of prisoner lawsuits, both nationally and within a particular jurisdiction, but the relation was found not to be significant.

McCoy (1981) analyzed 527 court records of the Southern District of Ohio from 1975 to 1980, which included all cases filed by prisoners. She found that the change in the court's philosophy regarding the acceptance of prisoner lawsuits resulted in an increase of Section 1983 suits filed by prisoners from 11 in 1975 to 87 in 1979. The data, however, also revealed a marked decrease in both Section 1983 suits and habeas corpus petitions filed between 1979and 1980. A high proportion of cases sought monetary damages and a significant number were dismissed.

Thomas, Keeler, and Harris (1986) compared the filings of habeas corpus petitions with Section 1983 lawsuits in the Northern District of Illinois from 1977 to 1984. They reported that prisoners filing civil rights complaints were more likely to be "repeat filers," while habeas corpus suits tended to be filed by "one-shotters." On the whole, prisoners who filed habeas corpus suits were not likely to file civil rights complaints, but a high proportion of prisoners were multifilers. Moreover, prisoners were more likely to file a civil-rights lawsuit than a habeas corpus petition. The authors concluded that prisoners who file either type of suit do so for specific reasons, not simply to harass correctional officials.

In a second study, Thomas, Keeler, and Harris (1986) compared state and federal prisoner civil lawsuits to the filing of civil rights complaints by the general population. They showed a steady but slow increase of prisoner filings of lawsuits from 1960 to 1984. This finding, however, failed to show strong evidence that prisoners are more likely than civilians to take complaints to court. They reported that as the national prison population was increasing, prisoners actually filed proportionately fewer lawsuits. In 1964, one prisoner filed two lawsuits on the average per 100 prisoners. The ratio reached its peak in 1981, when seven suits per 100 prisoners were filed. By 1984, approximately one prisoner in 20 filed a lawsuit, the lowest ratio since 1969.

Champion (1988) performed a content analysis of state and federal prisoner litigation trends for six southern states to determine the number and nature of civil filings by prisoners. State records were reviewed for five time periods: 1975, 1978, 1981, 1984, and 1987. The study revealed a decline in the filing of habeas corpus petitions and a decrease in the number of filings under the Federal Tort Claims Act, but an increase in Section 1983 lawsuits filed by state prisoners. His findings were consistent with other studies on the topic (Thomas, Keeler, and Harris 1986; Singer 1980; Turner 1979).

In a study of jail prisoners filing legal actions in 71 jails in six states, Champion (1991) found that between 1981 and 1985, 826 lawsuits were submitted. He found that 73 percent of all filings were civil rights actions, of which 42 percent were filed in federal court and 31 percent in state court. The remaining filings were classified as "other," which included mandamus and tort actions. Petitions of habeas corpus declined over the study period and by 1985 accounted for 6 percent of the total filings. Overall, Champion found an inverse relationship among prisoners filing legal actions. As Section 1983 litigation increased, petitions for writs of habeas corpus decreased.

Hansen and Daley (1995) researched 2,700 Section 1983 lawsuits from nine states during 1992. They found that the aggregate profile of Section 1983 prisoner litigation most frequently involved issues of physical security, medical treatment, and due process violations. The largest number of Section 1983 lawsuits named correctional officers (26 percent), followed by administrators (22 percent), medical personnel (9 percent), elected officials (7 percent), and the arresting officers (6 percent), as defendants. The overwhelming majority (94 percent) of the prevailing prisoners won little or nothing in terms of actual dollars. Virtually all prisoners acted as their own attorney (96 percent).

Hansen and Daley (1995) also found that jail prisoners filed lawsuits at one-half the rate of prisoners in state or federal prisons.

They further reported that prisoner lawsuits comprised three distinct gradations. First, lawsuits were dismissed owing to an inadequate basis of law. Second, cases that survived court review for six to twelve months, depending on the issue , were less likely to be dismissed. The final gradation consisted of cases that took up to two years, owing to the complexity of the legal issue and the greater likelihood an attorney was representing the prisoner.

Using a content analysis, Ross (1997a) conducted a 25-year assessment of 3,205 published jail and state prisoner Section 1983 litigations. In 1970 the national prisoner population was 176,391 and 2,030 lawsuits were filed (1.2 percent of the population filing). By 1994 the prisoner population was 992,000 and 36,318 lawsuits were filed (3.7 percent of the population filing). For the 25-year period 3.6 percent of the prisoner population filed Section 1983 lawsuits During that time, state correction officials prevailed in 57 percent of the cases. Since 1989, however, correction officials have been prevailing in approximately 80 percent of the cases litigated in court.

The Ross study also revealed 16 common types of cases filed by prisoners (Figure 1.1). Some of the more prevalent issues included medical care, access to courts, discipline, administrative liability, conditions of confinement, failure to protect, use of force, and issues of classification. In 92 percent of the cases the prisoner filed *pro se*, without legal counsel. When a prisoner prevailed (43 percent), equitable relief was awarded in 87 percent of the cases. Equitable relief is a nonmonetary judgment whereby the court, through what is termed "declaratory relief," declares to the defendant that a regulation is unconstitutional. The court, through "injunctive relief," may also prohibit specific practices of the defendant, as well as require certain measures to be taken or practices to be instituted to avoid further violation of the Constitution. Monetary damages were awarded in 13 percent of the cases and averaged $43,488 per case, while punitive damages averaged $30,667 per case. The total compensatory award per litigated issue ranged from $4,500 to $5.2 million during the study period. Punitive damages ranged from $414,000 to $12,345 per litigated issue. Nominal damages of $1.00 were awarded to prisoners on an infrequent basis. Cases involving issues of failure to protect, medical care, administrative liability, prisoner searches, conditions of confinement, and use of force all resulted in significant compensation and punitive damages and attorney's fees when a prisoner prevailed. These costs are estimates, since only 440 published decisions reported costs awarded to a prevailing prisoner.

These trends are consistent with other studies performed on prisoner lawsuits. The Administrative Office of the United States Courts (AOC) (2003) re-

Figure 1.1   Types of Section 1983 Correctional Litigation Filed
and Prevailing Party

Type of Case	# Studied	% Studied	Prisoner Prevailed (%)	Corrections Prevailed (%)	Jail Case	Prison Case
Medical care	362	11.3	164 (45.3)	198 (54.6)	212	150
Access to courts	337	11	120 (35.6)	217 (64.4)	256	81
Discipline	267	8.3	105 (39.3)	162 (60.7)	199	68
Administrative liability	241	7.5	130 (53.9)	111 (46.1)	121	120
Conditions of conf.	236	7.4	118 (50)	118 (50)	136	100
Failure to protect	218	6.8	105 (48.1)	113 (51.8)	118	100
Use of force	215	6.7	106 (49.3)	109 (50.7)	112	103
Classification	185	5.8	64 (34.6)	121 (65.4)	96	89
Religion	177	5.5	65 (36.7)	112 (63.3)	138	39
Searches	171	5.2	71 (41.5)	100 (58.5)	82	89
Admin. segregation	152	4.7	60 (39.5)	92 (60.5)	111	41
Cruel and unusual punish.	142	4.3	67 (47.2)	75 (52.8)	102	40
Mail	139	4.2	45 (32.4)	94 (67.6)	90	49
Speech	137	4.2	45 (32.4)	94 (67.6)	91	46
Mental health	125	3.9	67 (53.6)	58 (46.4)	59	66
Facilities	101	3.2	52 (51.5)	49 (48.5)	41	60
Total	3,205	100	1,392 (43.4)	1,813 (56.6)	1,864 (58)	1,341 (42)

Ross, D. L. 1997a.

ported that from 1970 to 2001, 96 percent of prisoner litigation was processed without the assistance of an attorney. Those cases which proceeded with counsel were three times more likely to be settled out of court, two-thirds more likely to go to trial, and two-and-a-half times more likely to end in a plaintiff's victory at trial (Eisenberg 1996). In 1995, prisoner civil litigation accounted for 15 percent of all civil trials held in federal district court. From 1998 to 2002 that percentage has declined to slightly over 10 percent.

Financial awards have been difficult to determine since not all cases where awards were granted were necessarily published. A limited number of studies have reported estimates of awards granted to a prevailing prisoner. Schlanger (2003) reported that in 1993, when a prisoner prevailed in a case, the average compensatory damages were $18,800 and the average punitive damages were $5,000. The average monetary award was around $24,000. This figure is considered low and factors out a few enormous awards that were awarded in the past, amounting to millions of dollars. Also, when compared to other areas of civil litigation such as medical malpractice, personal injuries, product liability, and auto accidents, prisoner litigation payouts are considerably lower. Thomas, Keeler, and Harris (1986) estimated that 15 percent of all prisoner litigation is filed by jail detainees, and jails spend less than half as much as state prisons on prisoner litigation. Jails house half as many detainees as prisons on any given day. In a separate study Ross (1997b) reported that prisoners in jails/detention facilities were less likely to prevail in a civil lawsuit than their prison counterparts. Jail officials lost 56 percent of the detainee litigation. Study results indicated that jail prisoners were more likely to prevail in cases involving administrative liability (63 percent) such as hiring and training of personnel, supervision of officers, and deficient or nonexistent policies and procedures, conditions of confinement (62 percent), deficient facility (i.e., overcrowding and defective building (60 percent), medical care (60 percent), mental health (58 percent), use of force (55 percent), and access to courts (52 percent).

The trend in filing Section 1983 civil rights claims reached a record high in 1996, when 41,952 claims were filed by state and jail prisoners. By 1998, prisoner filings had decreased to 25,479—half of those in 1996. While prisoner civil litigation has declined, appeals filed by prisoners to the federal civil appellate courts have increased. Miller (1999) reported that the filings of prisoner petitions rose nearly 94 percent between 1987, when filings numbered 8,774, and 1996, when filings increased to 16,996. In 1996, 33 percent of all federal court appeals were filed by prisoners. These trends appeared to be influenced by the Prison Litigation Reform Act (PLRA). In response to the increased number of lawsuits filed by prisoners and in an effort to reduce the number of baseless prisoner lawsuits, Congress passed the PLRA. This act established mandatory filing fees, restricted the filing of successive petitions, and required that prisoners exhaust administrative remedies before filing petitions. It also increased the ability of the courts to dismiss immediately any lawsuit that is frivolous or malicious, that fails to state a claim upon which relief can be granted, or that seeks monetary relief from a defendant who is immune from such relief. After the act went into effect, filings of civil rights prisoner

Figure 1.2   A Comparison of Prisoner Section 1983 Lawsuits, Habeas Corpus Petitions, and State Prisoner Populations

Year	Population	Section 1983 Lawsuits Filed	% Change	Habeas Corpus Petitions Filed	% Change
1970	176,391	2,030	—	9,088	—
1975	216,462	6,128	+202	7,943	-13
1980	295,363	12,397	+102	7,091	-11
1985	447,873	18,491	+49	8,534	+20
1990	689,577	24,843	+34	10,823	+27
1991	732,914	25,048	+1	10,331	-5
1992	781,565	28,308	+13	11,087	+7
1993	803,397	32,369	+14	11,411	+3
1994	992,000	36,318	+12	11,836	+4
1995	989,004	40,211	+11	13,275	+12
1996	1,032,440	41,952	+4	14,591	+10
1997	1,074,809	28,635	-32	21,858	+50
1998	1,113,676	26,462	-8	21,159	-3
1999	1,159,212	26,993	+2	24,089	+14
2000	1,381,892	25,505	-6	25,219	+5
2001	1,247,039	24,118	-5	24,684	-2
2002	1,277,127	25,964	+8	23,863	-3

Scalia (2002); Beck and Harrison (2003); Administrative Office of the United States Courts (2003).

petitions dropped by 20 percent from 1996 to 1997 and then declined by 12 percent from 1997 to 1998. While Section 1983 lawsuit filings have been declining, writs of habeas corpus and appeals have been increasing (Figure 1.2). Since 1996, habeas corpus petitions have increased by approximately 60 percent and have surpassed the number of Section 1983 filings (Administrative Office of the United States Courts [AOC] 2003; Scalia 2002). During 2001 and 2002, however, the number of Section 1983 prisoner filings was the same as that of habeas corpus petitions.

Since its establishment, the PLRA has had a marked impact on the number of civil actions filed by prisoners. Section 1983 prisoner litigation increased from 2,030 cases filed in 1970 to 41,952 in 1996 (AOC, 2003). After implementation of the PLRA, the number of civil actions filed by prisoners decreased precipitously. By 1997, Section 1983 actions had dropped to 28,635, a 32 percent decrease, and the largest decline since the AOC has recorded prisoner filings. By the end of 1999, there were 25,694 prisoner civil actions filed, a decline of approximately one-third from 1997. Habeas corpus petitions increased from 14,591 filings in 1996 to 24,089 in 1999, an increase of 14 percent. In one year (1996–1997), habeas corpus petitions increased by 50 percent, their largest increase to date. Since 1996, Section 1983 prisoner actions have decreased to an annual average of approximately 26,000 filings, while habeas corpus petitions have steadily increased despite the passage of the PLRA. While Congress passed one action to curb frivolous prisoner lawsuits, the use of another provision allowing prisoners to petition the court about prison conditions and sentencing appears to be increasing. (For a more detailed discussion on the PLRA, see Chapter 4.)

CASE EXAMPLES

As discussed above, correctional facilities have become easy targets for prisoner litigation. Over the years there have been a number of high-profile cases which illustrate this point. Chen (2000) reported in the *New York Times* that more than 500 former prisoners and relatives who were beaten during the 1971 Attica prison riot would share $8 million as part of a settlement with the State of New York. The plaintiffs each received payments ranging between $6,500and $125,000. Survivors of the 13 correction officer hostages who were killed by the New York National Guard during the five-day siege were allowed to collect only minimal death benefits provided by the state. The officer hostages were disallowed overtime payment by the state, since authorities ruled that they could sleep at varying intervals throughout the riot.

In *Gregory v. Shelby County* (2000), a jail prisoner filed a Section 1983 lawsuit for a detention officer's failure to protect him. The prisoner, Gregory, was returning to his cell from the evening shower when he was jumped by another prisoner, sexually assaulted, and beaten. As a result of the beating, Gregory sustained brain damage and injuries to his eyes. Testimony in court revealed that a detention officer purposely unlocked the attacking prisoner's cell door, knowing that the attacker would seek a victim for sexual assault. Further testimony revealed that Gregory lay in his cell for approximately ten hours before any detention officer discovered him. The evidence showed that medical attention was delayed for an extended period of time. The jury awarded Gregory $3 million, and the Sixth Circuit Court of Appeals affirmed the decision and award. The conduct of the detention officer was so egregious it was determined as "shocking to the conscience." The court found a reasonable relationship between the compensatory and punitive damages and concluded the award was not excessive. The officer was terminated from his position since his action was not the first in which he had violated jail policy.

In Texas, a privately operated jail incurred litigation stemming from a shakedown where officers were alleged to have used excessive force and physically abused prisoners, thereby violating their constitutional rights. The actions of the "shakedown" were videotaped and later shown across the country on *Dateline NBC* in 1997. The videotape revealed that officers and command personnel ordered prisoners to crawl across the floor nude, while officers kicked and pepper-sprayed them, prodded them with stun guns, and used a canine to move them out of their cells. On several occasions the video showed the canine biting various compliant prisoners. The incident resulted in civil litigation claim against the sheriff, the chief deputy, and a county official in charge of the detention center's emergency response team (*Kesler v. King* 1998). The claim alleged the use of excessive force, as well as the failure to train, supervise, and screen prospective officer candidates prior to employment. The court ruled against the county, holding that it was not objectively reasonable to use force or the canine when the prisoners were compliant.

In 1996 a former prisoner of a county correctional facility in New York was awarded $250,000 in compensatory damages and $500,000 in punitive damages in a sex abuse case (*Mathie v. Fries* 1996). The court found sufficient evidence that the director of the facility repeatedly sexually abused the prisoner while he was handcuffed to pipes in the security office. The court called the director's conduct an outrageous abuse of power and authority. A prisoner in Pennsylvania was awarded $36,000 in compensatory and punitive damages from four correction officers after they had beaten him on four separate occasions (*Giroux v. Sherman* 1992). The prisoner sustained internal injuries, including kidney damage. One correction officer beat the prisoner in the hospital, reinjuring his kidney while he was recuperating from kidney surgery. After a ten-year civil rights action in Texas (*Ruiz v. Estelle* 1980), a federal district court awarded $1,600,000 in attorney's fees to the attorneys who had brought the action to court. The case challenged the constitutionality of prison conditions in the Texas prison system.

Female prisoners in the District of Columbia prison system won a judgment against correctional officials in a class action lawsuit (*Women Prisoners v. District of Columbia* 1996), claiming violations in equal protection, discrimination, sexual harassment, and conditions of confinement. The District court found, first of all, that the Eighth Amendment was violated in physical ways—by sexual harassment and assault, by substandard living conditions, and by lack of proper medical care and access to personal hygiene. The court concluded that the sexual harassment by correctional officers amounted to wanton and unnecessary subjection to pain and was so malicious that it violated contemporary standards of decency. The court also found that the Eighth Amendment was violated by psychological injury to women prisoners—in the form of vulgar sexual remarks from prison officials, a lack of privacy within cells, and the refusal by some male guards to announce their presence in the living areas of the women.

Further sexual abuse of female prisoners by correction officers has continued within the District of Columbia's prison system, as illustrated in *Daskalea v. District of Columbia* (2000). At trial, Daskalea testified that she and female prisoners were sexually abused and exploited by male and female correctional staff. The jury awarded the prisoners $350,000 in compensatory damages, and the Circuit Court of Appeals affirmed the award. The Department of Corrections in Michigan (2000) settled out of court several civil lawsuits involving sexual abuse of female prisoners by male officers.

In a New York case, a prisoner was awarded $125,000 in compensation and $25,000 in punitive damages for a claim involving medical care and the Americans with Disabilities Act (ADA) (*Beckford v. Irvin* 1999). The prisoner required a wheel chair and was placed in a bigger cell than usual so that the wheel chair could fit inside. But shortly after placement in the cell, the wheel chair was removed and then denied him after he requested it several times. The jury concurred that the actions of prison supervisors constituted deliberate indifference to the prisoner's serious medical needs.

In *Madrid v. Gomez* (1995), prisoners at the maximum custody Pelican Bay State Prison in California filed a class action lawsuit claiming excessive force, failure to train officers, and delay of medical and psychiatric care. The court found in favor of the prisoners, determining that the officers' use of force and its frequency of use were deliberately indifferent to prisoners and posed a substantial risk of harm to them. The court found that the delivery of physical and mental health services was constitutionally inadequate and therefore violated the prisoners' Eighth Amendment rights. Moreover, the court found that the staffing levels were insufficient and that the training and the supervision of medical staff were almost nonexistent. Finally, the court concluded that the correctional officials had already known for certain that the conditions in the prison presented a risk of harm to prisoners and that therefore the officials acted wantonly in violation of the Eighth Amendment.

Jails and prison systems have also sustained many consent decrees as a result of prisoner litigation. In response to a filed civil action, a consent decree is a formal agreement out of court, between the parties, to correct some correctional practice within a specified time in lieu of proceeding to trial. Frequently this decree has been applied to improving conditions of confinement, to building additional facilities, to stopping or starting certain practices, to hiring more personnel, or to initiating certain rehabilitative programs. Koren (1994) reported that the number of correctional systems under court order/consent decree increased from 11 in 1988 to 39 in 1994, largely because of prisoner litigation. Camp and Camp (2002) reported that 20 states reported that they were operating under a consent decree, which involved 229 prisons. Camp and Camp (2002) also reported that 9 states were under court order, which involved 144 prisons.

IMPACT OF COURT INTERVENTION

Legal decisions by the courts have brought about numerous changes within the American penal system. One of the primary changes is reflected in the bureaucratization of the prison (Jacobs 1977). For years prison systems operated without policies and procedures, or with limited ones. This lack of bureaucratization allowed wardens to run an institution as they saw fit. Decisions regarding early cases illustrated that correctional officials could not justify many of their practices, which, according to the courts, violated prisoners' constitutionally protected rights. As a result of many case decisions involving correctional practices, correctional management has been forced to change prior practices. Hence, institutions are becoming more bureaucratic, requiring the documentation of official policies regarding the actions, the decisions, and the direction of correctional personnel.

Procedural protections for prisoners have emerged as a second outcome of prisoner litigation. Procedural due process regarding discipline, transfers to mental health facilities, and forfeiture of earned "good time" has been instituted. Most prison systems have also instituted a grievance system, which affords protections to prisoners regarding various decisions made by correctional personnel.

Third, society has become more aware of prison conditions and program services as a result of much of the prisoner litigation. This new awareness is highly evident since many communities have experienced an increase in prisoner population, resulting in overcrowded prisons. Court decisions have forced most states to build more prisons in order to meet constitutional standards of confinement. When taxes are increased and start-ups of prison construction are initiated, the media have a field day reporting the system's response.

Fourth, prisoner litigation has made it increasingly more difficult to control prisoners. Limitations on punishment of recalcitrant prisoners have made prison sentences less of a deterrent for some criminals. While correctional officers are now less likely to engage in misconduct and brutality, prisoners are more likely to challenge correctional officers' authority as a result of favorable case decisions. As a consequence, the ability of officers to enforce the law and prison policies has eroded over time. This erosion has resulted in the demoralization and increased insecurity of officers. Many of them resent court decisions which favor prisoner rights—decisions which, in their view, undermine their authority when they are supervising prisoners and maintaining security throughout the prison.

Fifth, while court decisions have brought about more judicial intervention which appears to be negative in consequence, there have been positive benefits to the American penal system. Prison litigation has led to the building of more prisons, which provide newer and safer facilities for both prisoners and correctional personnel. Additionally, new technology has accompanied new prison construction, allowing increased safety and producing more efficient methods of prison operation. Case decisions have also helped professionalize corrections. More training of officers and administrators has been initiated, which enhances the operation of the agency. Newly developing policies and procedures, while cumbersome and increasingly bureaucratic, have been shown as positive benefits, since they communicate the overall mission of the prison and direct officers in their decision making and in their job performance. The new policies and procedures underscore and document the philosophy of a correctional department. Moreover, they have assisted in defending the lawsuits of prisoners who have challenged the rationale behind certain correctional practices. DiIulio (1987) suggests that prisons which are more formalized through a bureaucratic structure and management style are more predictable and stable; they increase officer morale, are more accountable, and provide better prisoner programs as well as a safer and more civilized prison environment.

Summary

As the above discussion indicates, correctional personnel and agencies continue to be targets of civil liability. While the number of prisoner filings has been high, correctional officials prevail in these actions more frequently than prisoners. Past research also reveals that a majority of lawsuits are settled out of court and that it appears this trend is increasing. Civil litigation is costly, but many of the judgments have been instrumental in providing jails and prisons with more resources for performing daily duties, expanding personnel training, and developing more efficient policies and procedures to guide officer decision making.

Civil lawsuits can be bothersome and stressful, and their outcomes can be unpredictable. Administrators must remain committed to providing personnel with training, guidance, and legal updates to more fully understand how to perform their sworn duties. Officers must also remain committed to performing their duties within the framework of the law. This continual commitment can assist in defending the next legal action the officer or the department faces.

REFERENCES

Administrative Office of the United States Courts, Statistics Division. 2003. Civil and trial statistics: Twelve-month periods (1996–2000), Table C-2A. *Annual report to the director*. Washington, DC: Administrative Office of the United States Courts.

Beck, A. J., and P. M. Harrison. 2003. Prisoners in 2003. *Bureau of Justice Statistics Bulletin*. Washington, DC: United States Department of Justice.

Bennett, K., and R. V. del Carmen. 1997. A review and analysis of Prison Litigation Act court decisions: Solution or aggravation? *The Prison Journal* 77 no. 4: 405–55.

Bronstein, A. J. 1987. Fifteen years of prison litigation: What has it accomplished? *Journal of National Prison Project* 11: 6–9.

Camp, C. G., and G. M. Camp. 2002. *The 2001 corrections yearbook*. Middletown, CT: Criminal Justice Institute, Inc.

Champion, D. J. 1988. Some recent trends in civil liability by federal and state prison inmates. *Federal Probation* 2: 43–47.

Champion, D. J. 1991. Jail inmate litigation in the 1990s. *In American jails: Public policy issues*, edited by J. A. Thompson and G. L. Mays. Chicago: Nelson-Hall Publishers

Chen, D. W. 2000. Awards after an uprising. *New York Times*, 3 September, 1A, 2A–3A.

del Carmen, R. V. 2001. *Civil liabilities and other legal issues for probation and parole officers and supervisors*. 3rd ed. Longmont, CO: United States Department of Justice, National Institute of Corrections.

DiLulio, J. J., Jr. 1991. *Courts, corrections, and the Constitution*. New York: Oxford University Press.

DiLulio, J. J., Jr. 1987. *Governing prisons: A comparative study of correctional management*. New York: The Free Press.

Eisenberg, T. 1996. *Civil rights legislation: Cases and materials*. 4th ed. Minneapolis, MN: West Law Publishers.

Galanter, M. 1983. Reading the landscape of disputes: What we know and don't know (and think we know) about our allegedly contentious and litigious society. *UCLA Law Review* 31: 4–71.

Hansen, R. A., and H. K. Daley. 1995. *Challenging the conditions of prisons and jails: A report on section 1983 litigation.* Washington, DC: Bureau of Justice Statistics, U.S. Department of Justice.

Jacobs, J. B. 1977. *Statesville: The penitentiary in mass society.* Chicago: University of Chicago Press.

Koren, E. I. 1994. Status report: State prisons and the courts—January 1, 1994. *The National Prison Project Journal* 9: 9–12.

Litras, M. F., and C. J. DeFrances. 1999. *Three out of four tort cases settled out of court.* Washington, DC: Bureau of Justice Statistics.

Manning, B. 1977. Hyperlexis: Our national disease. *Northwestern University Law Review* 71: 767–82.

McCoy, C. 1981. The impact of section 1983 litigation on policymaking in corrections. *Federal Probation* 45: 17–23.

Miller, J. M. 1999. *Changing trends in prisoner petition filings in the U.S. Court of Appeals: A fact sheet.* Washington, D.C.: Administrative Office of the Courts .

Ross, D. L. 1997a. Emerging trends in correctional civil liability cases: A content analysis of federal court decisions of Title 42 United States Code Section 1983: 1970–1994. *Journal of Criminal Justice* 25:501B515.

_____. 1997b. Section 1983 jail litigation: A twenty-five year content analysis. *Corrections Compendium* 22: 1–8.

Scalia, J. 2002. Prisoner petitions filed in U.S. District Courts, 2000, with trends 1980B2000. *Bureau of Justice Statistics, special report.* Washington, DC: Department of Justice.

Schlanger, M. 2003. Inmate litigation. *Harvard Law Review* 6: 1557–1706.

Silver, I. 2003. *Police civil liability.* Newark, NJ: Matthew Bender Publishers.

Singer, R. G. 1980. Prisoner's rights litigation: A look at the past decade and a look at the coming decade. Federal Probation 44: 3–11.

Thomas, J., D. Keeler, and K. Harris. 1986. Issues and misconceptions in prisoner litigation: A critical view. *Criminology* 24: 775–96.

Turner, W. 1979. When prisoners sue: A study of prisoner Section 1983 suits in the Federal Courts. *Harvard Law Review* 92: 610–63.

CASES CITED

Beckford v. Irvin, 49 F. Supp. 2d 170 (W.D.N.Y. 1999)

Cooper v. Pate, 382 F. 2d 518 (7th Cir. 1964)

Daskalea v. District of Columbia, 227 F. 3d 433 (D.C. Cir. 2000)

Gregory v. Shelby County, 220 F. 3d 433 (6th Cir. 2000)

Giroux v. Sherman, 807 F. Supp. 1182 (E.D. Pa. 1992)

Kesler v. King, 29 F. Supp. 2d 356 (S.D. Tex. 1998)

Madrid v. Gomez, 889 F. Supp. 1146 (N.D. Cal. 1995)

Mathie v. Fries, 935 F. Supp. 1284 (E.D. N.Y. 1996)

Ruiz v. Estelle, 609 F.2d 118 (5th Cir. 1980)

Women Prisoners v. District of Columbia, 93 F. 3d 910 (D.C. Cir. 1996)

CHAPTER 2

AMERICAN LAW
AND THE COURT SYSTEM

Our very freedom is secure because we are a nation governed by laws, not by men.
We cannot pick and choose the laws we will or will not obey.

Ronald Reagan

Corrections is that component of the criminal justice system which provides a wide range of programs, agencies, and institutions, and which encompasses a broad range of philosophies about crime and the criminal offender. Subunits of corrections include prisons, parole, probation, and jails. Corrections has a dual function. First, it controls offenders through their incarceration and through supervision by the communities to which the courts have committed them. Second, it attempts to rehabilitate offenders when possible. Other philosophies regarding corrections include punishment, deterrence, and reintegration of previously incarcerated prisoners back into the community. Punishment is one of the oldest rationales for incarceration. Criminal offenders are sentenced to prison as punishment for a criminal violation but are *not* to be punished by correctional personnel.

Each of the subunits and philosophies of corrections carry with it important decisions which impact the prisoner. Such decisions may include issues such as security and classification levels, discipline, medical care, religious practices, early release on parole, working assignments, prisoner programming, prisoner and facility searches, and seizing of property. But correctional personnel cannot make any decision they wish regarding the criminal offender. Their decisions must be made carefully and must be made within the purview of the law. The law sets forth standards and guidelines for performing correctional responsibilities and for providing protections for prisoners and employees. Because the law establishes the foundation of conduct, failing to perform correctional duties within the law heightens the potential for liability for the officer and the department. The court system examines violations of the law, interprets the law, and assesses legal sanctions for law violations.

Correction officers, administrators, and students studying correctional law should understand American jurisprudence. Before the text studies court decisions, this chapter will discuss the role of the law and the court system. The rule of law governs all phases of human enterprise, and its precepts control relationships between individuals and the public and relationships between individuals and the government. Acquiring a fundamental understanding of the dynamics of the law and the courts will be useful to those who examine court decisions and who work in the correctional arena.

CRIMINAL LAW VERSUS CIVIL LAW

In the American criminal justice system the law is divided into two broad categories: criminal law and civil law. Criminal law consists of the power of the state to punish those whose conduct has breached society's standards. Civil law is tort law, which pertains to wrongful actions committed against another, including personal injury or injury to one's property. The term *tort* comes from the Latin word *tortus* ("bent" or "twisted") and thus suggests an old English punishment of the injuring party. Tort law also pertains to contract and property issues. In the American criminal justice system each type of law is composed of distinct components and is procedurally treated separately from the other. Each type of law seeks to control an individual's conduct by preventing him or her from violating a law and by imposing a sanction for a violation.

Criminal Law

Laws are enacted as a formal means to control the behavior of members of society and comprise several objectives. The major objective of criminal law is to protect members of society from others who violate the law (Levenson 1997). Such conduct threatens or inflicts harm on individuals, or violates the public interest. Second, through society's political process, the law quantifies and specifies unlawful behavior collectively called "crimes." This process provides a formal means of identifying conduct unacceptable to society in general and distinguishes crimes from unwritten rules or ordinary customs. Third, criminal law is classified in terms of the severity of a crime and prescribes a punishment for an adjudicated violation. For example, felonies are serious crimes and include murder, rape, robbery, and so on. Felonies are punished by a sentence of at least a year in prison or probation. A convicted felon can receive a sentence for a number of years (often with probation), a life sentence (with or without probation), or a death sentence. Misdemeanors are less serious than felonies and include such crimes as disorderly conduct and disturbing the peace. Punishment for a misdemeanor can be a fine or a sentence of less than a year in jail. Finally, the publicizing of criminal laws and their established punishments for committing certain offenses serves as a deterrent to crime. The philosophy is that the law will deter crime through the strong likelihood that a criminal will be caught and a severe and appropriate punishment will be administered. The basic principle of the law, then, is to protect law-abiding citizens while maintaining social order through the conviction and sentencing of criminals. Moreover, according to Schmalleger (2002), the law functions to:

- protect members of the public from harm;
- preserve, maintain social order and support fundamental social values;
- distinguish criminal violations from civil wrongs;
- deter people from criminal activity;
- express communal condemnation of criminal behavior;
- punish those who commit crimes;
- rehabilitate offenders; and
- assuage victims of crime.

In criminal law, the state, on behalf of the victim, brings the case before the court for adjudication. The state (through one of its prosecuting attorneys) charges the accused (the defendant) with a criminal violation and bears the responsibility of proving its case "beyond reasonable doubt." While such proof constitutes a complex and high standard of evidence, the United States Supreme Court in *Jacobellis v. Ohio* (1964) determined that "guilt beyond reasonable doubt" should not be reduced to a definition. It does not mean guilt beyond doubt, or any doubt, or that a defendant is entitled to the benefit of any doubt, just guilt beyond reasonable doubt (Dershowitz 1997). In the case *In re Winship* (1970), the United States Supreme Court determined that the reasonable-doubt standard plays a vital role in the American criminal procedure. The standard provides concrete substance for the presumption of innocence—a basic principle whose enforcement lies at the foundation of the administration of our criminal law. In instructing the jury in the O. J. Simpson case, Judge Lance Ito stated: "It is not a mere possible doubt, because everything relating to human affairs is open to some possible or imaginary doubt. It is that state of the case which, after the entire comparison and consideration of all the evidence, leaves the minds of the jurors in that condition that they cannot say they feel an abiding conviction of the truth of the charge."

The state must prove that a crime was committed and that the defendant committed it. Should a judge or jury find the defendant guilty, the judge will determine an appropriate sanction. In a criminal case the defendant has numerous constitutionally protected rights. For example, the defendant has the right to appeal a conviction, the right to counsel (under the Sixth Amendment), and the right to avoid self-incrimination (under the Fifth Amendment). The state usually does not have the right to appeal an acquittal.

Civil Law

Civil law is distinct from criminal law in that it involves private wrongs, or torts, whereby an injury or harm was caused by another. In other words, civil law is tort law which claims that one party (the plaintiff) was injured by the action or the inaction of another party (the defendant). In civil law, the plaintiff seeks monetary damages for the harm incurred.

In a civil action, the plaintiff must prove that (1) the defendant owed some legal or contractual duty and that (2) some breach of duty by the defendant resulted in harm to the plaintiff. The standard of proof needed for a plaintiff to prevail in a civil action is "preponderance of the evidence," which is a lower standard than "guilt beyond reasonable doubt." This means that a jury reviewing the case and evidence needs only to be convinced by just over 50 percent of the evidence that the defendant did what had been claimed (Schmalleger 2002). In other words, the evidence needs to show only that it was more likely than not that the defendant had breached some duty, resulting in harm. In a civil case, the state does not represent either party; rather, one or both parties may be represented by retained counsel, or one or both parties may proceed *pro se* (without aid of counsel). A losing party may appeal the decision to the next higher court, including the United States Supreme Court.

The purpose of tort law is to compensate the plaintiff, provide justice, and deter others from committing harmful behavior. Should the plaintiff prevail, the defendant may have to pay monetary damages, including compensatory damages, punitive damages, court costs, and attorney's fees. The scope of the duty, the extent to which it was breached, and the nature of the harm that resulted will determine the size of the award of damages. In other cases, including prisoner civil lawsuits, the plaintiff may be granted injunctive relief, which is a remedy requiring the defendant to act in a specified manner.

Rule of Law

The basic purpose of law is to maintain social order. This implies that individual citizens must obey the law and that the law must be enforced by an authorized entity. This process must be carried out under the "rule of law, and not the rule of man." The rule of law, often known as the "supremacy of law," is based on the belief that an orderly society must be governed by established principles and known codes, which are applied uniformly and fairly to all of its members (Schmalleger 2002). President Nixon, during the Watergate investigations in 1973, stated that "no one is above the law, and no one is below the law," which implies that applying the facets of the rule of law must be fair and that those enforcing the law must also abide by the law.

The rule of law clearly acts as a limitation on executive agencies such as the police and the judiciary (Zalman and Siegel 1997). The rule of law gives legality to the law process and is designed to ensure that all branches of government act in accordance with legal rules. It provides a framework with which to direct lawful conduct (rules) and sanctions for misconduct (punishment). From the rule of law, attributes of the law are observed. Laws must be promulgated in written form and duly passed. Laws must be understandable to the average citizen in the United States and made public. Laws must be impartially, not arbitrarily, enforced, and they should not change too frequently. Frequent changes in laws can make the laws too difficult to follow and can demand what is impossible for citizens. Also, the practices of government must be congruent with the laws as written. And laws must not be retroactive in nature. In other words, legislatures cannot enact a law that can be enforced before its enactment. In fact, Article I, Sections 9 and 10, of the United States Constitution prohibits the federal government or the government of any state from passing ex post facto laws (i.e., retroactive laws).

The rule of law has been defined by the American Bar Association (1958) to include the following essential ideologies:

- freedom from private lawlessness provided by the legal system of a politically organized society;
- a relatively high degree of objectivity in the formulation of legal norms and a like degree of evenhandedness in their application;
- legal ideas and juristic devices for the attainment of individual and group objectives within the bounds of ordered society; and

- substantive and procedural limitations on government power in the interest of the individual for the enforcement of which there are appropriate legal institutions and machinery.

The American Bar Association's definition reflects that the rule of law provides each citizen with due process, guaranteeing procedural rights to those charged with a crime. Due process protects the legal proceedings of those charged with a crime and provides rules for conducting such proceedings. The guarantee for due process is contained in the Fifth, Sixth, and Fourteenth Amendments of the United States Constitution (see Figure 2.1). The Fifth Amendment applies to the federal government, while the Fourteenth Amendment applies to each state government. Hence, due process means that rules must be adhered to and not enforced in an arbitrary manner.

Sources of American Law

American law can be traced to the Babylonian Code of Hammurabi (2000 B.C.), the Mosaic Code of the Israelites (1200 B.C.), and the Roman Twelve Tables (Senna and Siegel 1993). The first codification of laws occurred in the sixth century under the Byzantine emperor Justinian. A body of civil law known as *Corpus Juris Civilis* constituted the system of Roman law that had gradually developed for over a thousand years. To ensure the safety of the state and the individual, rules were organized into a code which served as the basis for future civil and criminal legal classifications. Using Justinian's code as a model, Napoleon I, the French emperor, developed the French civil code centuries later. France and other countries which designed their legal systems around French and Roman law have what is known as the civil law system.

Common Law

The status of the legal system in Europe, prior to the Norman Conquest in 1066, was decentralized. There were no written laws, except those covering crimes, and they varied from country to country. Crimes were viewed as personal wrongs, violent crimes were punished by death, and property crimes were frequently punished by requiring payment of compensation to the victim.

After the Norman Conquest, the English legal system developed and became a primary source for American law. During the reign of King Henry II, from 1154 to 1189, common law emerged from unwritten laws in England. Common law then replaced local customs with national law. Royal judges, known as circuit judges, were appointed by the King and traveled a specific route (circuit), hearing cases across England. As these judges heard cases in court and made a court decision, the decision became law that was "common" for the entire country. Common law developed over time and evolved to fit specific situations that judges encountered in court. As cases were decided, other judges would look to a previous decision to aid them in deciding a similar case that was before them.

Over time, common law decisions produced a body of rules and legal procedures about crime and punishment and formed the basis for the American legal system. In the American colonies the common law was the law of the land. After the War of Independence, many state legislatures integrated the common law into standardized legal codes.

Case Law

Components of common law developed into what is now known as "case law" in the United States. Case law is developed through judges' decisions. Through interpreting the law and applying it to various circumstances, judges create new laws or modify existing ones. These "judge-made" laws become binding on other courts in subsequent cases. For example, if a judge hears a case on theft, the judge, in making the ruling on the case, develops law for dealing with theft in the future.

As a body of case law was developed, these cases set the "precedent" for other cases. This legal principle, known as "stare decisis," originated in England and is used as the basis for deciding future cases. Stare decisis comes from the Latin phrase *stare decisis et non quieta mouere,* meaning to "stand by precedent and not to disturb settled points." Stare decisis is a basic principle in the American legal system since it provides a guide to judges in deciding similar cases. The United States Supreme Court is the ultimate authority for creating and determining precedent (Kappeler 2002). The doctrine of stare decisis is binding on lower courts once a higher court makes a case ruling. The use of case precedents in judicial decisions provides consistency and stability in the law and thus provides for equitable application of the law to individuals who find themselves in similar situations. This practice of judicial decision making results in predictability and uniformity. The legal principle, however, does allow judges to change laws over time. As technology, economics, and political and social conditions change in society, courts can refine legal traditions and depart from former decisions. The law is dynamic in nature and provides for change over time when former legal decisions are no longer appropriate. Thus, when new decisions are made by the courts, they become new case precedents and serve to keep the principle of stare decisis entrenched in the American legal system.

At the federal level, the United States Supreme Court, through judicial decision making, establishes case precedents which are applicable to and binding in all fifty states. State supreme courts establish case precedents which are binding to a particular state. This text will focus on case precedents which apply to correctional issues that have emerged from the federal courts.

Constitutions

Constitutions are the foremost authoritative sources of rights (del Carmen 2001). Constitutions of states and the United States Constitution provide fundamental laws, power for the government, and individual protections from the government. Ratified in 1788, the United States Constitution explains the powers and structure of Congress (Article I), the executive power of the president (Article II), and the judicial power of the Supreme Court (Article III). While there are 26 amendments in the United States Constitution, the Bill of Rights (ratified in 1791), which contains the first ten amendments, provides safeguards for the individual rights of citizens. These amendments also provide a focus for examining legal issues as they apply to prisoners' rights. The Fourteenth Amendment, ratified in 1868, contains additional rights which provide for due process and equal protection of the laws. The United States Constitution is the highest source of law in the country. Article VI, Section 2, of the U.S. Constitution provides that:

> This Constitution, and the Laws of the United States, which shall be made in Pursuance thereof; and all Treaties made, or which shall be made, under the Authority of the United States, shall be the supreme Law of the Land; and the Judges in every State shall be bound thereby, any Thing in the Constitution or Laws of any State to the Contrary notwithstanding.

Figure 2.1 illustrates selected constitutional amendments which apply to correctional legal issues. The application of the First Amendment to correctional issues involves five elements: freedom of religion, freedom of speech, freedom of the press (and publications), freedom of assembly (visitation in prison), and freedom to petition the government for redress of grievances (access to courts). Generally, under the Fourth Amendment correctional concerns include individual, cell, and facility searches; seizures of property and contraband; and privacy issues. Concerning corrections the Fifth Amendment generally applies to matters of due process of law. The Eighth Amendment applies to issues which may be construed as "cruel and unusual punishment." This may involve conditions of confinement, the kind of force used by offi-

Figure 2.1   Selected Constitutional Amendments

The First Amendment: "Congress shall make no law respecting an establishment of religion, or prohibiting the free exercise thereof; or abridging the freedom of speech, or of the press; or the right of the people peaceably to assemble, and to petition the government for a redress of grievances." If criminal justice personnel violate First Amendment rights in their official capacity, they are subject to Section 1983 litigation (*Alliance to End Repression v. City of Chicago* 1982).

The Fourth Amendment: "The right of the people to be secure in their persons, houses, papers, and effects, against unreasonable searches and seizures, shall not be violated, and no Warrants shall issue, but upon probable cause, supported by Oath or affirmation, and particularly describing the place to be searched, and the person or things to be seized." This Amendment restricts the state and its officers (*Wolf v. Colorado* 1949).

The Fifth Amendment: "Nor shall any person be subject for the same offense to be twice put in jeopardy of life or limb; nor shall be compelled in any criminal case to be a witness against himself, nor be deprived of life, liberty, or property, without due process of law." State and local officers must follow this requirement (*Benton v. Maryland* 1969).

The Eighth Amendment: "Excessive bail shall not be required, nor cruel and unusual punishments inflicted." This is another restriction binding on the states (*Robinson v. California* 1962).

The Fourteenth Amendment (in part): "No state shall make or enforce any law which shall abridge the privileges or immunities of citizens of the United States; nor shall any state deprive any person of life, liberty, or property, without due process of law; nor deny to any person within its jurisdiction the equal protection of the laws." This amendment, according to its terms, applies to the states (*Powers v. Lightner* 1987, cert. denied).

cers, and medical and mental health care concerns, to mention a few. The Fourteenth Amendment applies to matters concerning due process of law and equal protection of the law. These may include issues of discrimination, disciplining prisoners, granting and/or revoking parole, and transfers of prisoners to various correctional institutions. Correctional personnel and students should become familiar with these amendments since they provide the framework for protecting the constitutional rights of prisoners and employees within the system.

Each of the fifty states has its own state constitution. A state's constitutional provisions must comply with the United States Constitution. State constitutions are similar to the federal Constitution in that they provide safeguards and protections from the government and explain powers vested in the government. Generally, a state's constitution describes the state legislative body and the office of governor, explains state law, and includes a bill of rights. Provisions in a state's constitution or a state law often grant more protection than what is allowed in the federal Constitution. As a general rule, if a state constitution or a state law provides less protection than the United States Constitution, such limitations would be ruled as unconstitutional, since the federal Constitution prevails. Conversely, if more protections are granted to individuals in a state constitution or a state law than the Federal Constitution, the state prevails. For example, the United States Supreme Court has ruled that under the Eighth Amendment the death penalty for capital murder is not considered "cruel or unusual punishment" (*Gregg v. Georgia* 1976). A state, however, is not required to implement the death penalty in capital murder convictions and can implement a life sentence instead. Conversely, the United States Supreme Court ruled in 2002 that sentencing convicted murderers to death row is a matter for a jury rather than a judge to decide. Hence, states which had allowed judges to sentence convicted murderers to death row were required to change their laws to be consistent with the Supreme Court's ruling.

Statutes

While case law establishes case precedents through judicial decision making, statutes are laws enacted by legislatures at the state, local, and national levels. Congress is responsible for enacting laws applicable to the entire nation, while state legislatures enact laws applicable to the state. A state legislature possesses the power to make law through enacting statutes. It defines crimes and punishments within its respective state and its statutes apply only to that state. State and local law enforcement and correctional agencies are responsible for enforcing state statutes. Congress defines federal crimes and appropriate punishments, which are enforced by federal law enforcement and correctional agencies.

Administrative Rules

Some federal and state governmental agencies possess authority to develop rules which control conduct within society. These are called administrative rules and they provide definitions of conduct and describe appropriate sanctions. For example, the Internal Revenue Service is a federal agency which regulates taxation. Failing to pay income taxes can result in fines, loss of property, and/or imprisonment. Similar state agencies develop rules at the state level. For example, a state parole board performs an administrative function: It controls the behavior of criminal offenders who are released on parole after a period of imprisonment. These administrative rules have the force and authority of law.

The same philosophy applies to rules, regulations, directives, and policies and procedures of a governmental agency. Employees failing to adhere to agency regulations may be faced with administrative disciplinary action—and potentially with civil liability. Compliance with agency rules, however, will normally show reasonable or good-faith actions by an employee, thereby eliminating his or her civil liability.

THE UNITED STATES COURT SYSTEM

The American system of jurisprudence comprises a "dual" court system: federal and state courts. Each state, the District of Columbia, and the federal government operate their own court systems in accordance with state and federal laws. A brief overview of the two systems is discussed below.

State Courts

While each state operates its court system within the boundaries of the state, most state court systems have the same structure, with few exceptions. The Tenth Amendment of the United States Constitution authorizes the states to operate their own state court systems:

> The powers not delegated to the United States by the Constitution, nor prohibited by it to the States, are reserved to the States respectively, or to the people.

Each state has a tiered court structure which normally comprises four levels. Courts with magistrates generally comprise the lowest level of many state courts. A magistrate's duties include hearing misdemeanor charges, authorizing warrants, ruling on traffic charges, and trying civil cases involving amounts under $10,000. Above the magistrate courts, many states have a level of courts called district courts, superior courts, or circuit courts, which normally conduct arraignments on felony charges and try felony cases as well as civil cases involving amounts over $10,000. In many states such courts are responsible for overseeing the supervision of probationers. Some states have another court level called drug courts, which try only drug related offenses.

Appellate courts hear legal matters, without a jury, which are appealed from the lower courts. Appeals are legal petitions claiming that a lower court or a jury made an error when reviewing a case. The highest court within the state

Figure 2.2   The Dual Court System in the United States

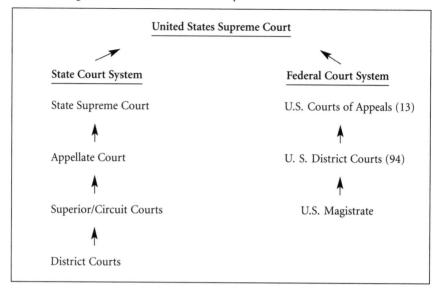

system is the supreme court. This court is normally referred to as the court of final resort on state legal matters. While a decision of a state supreme court is binding within the state, the decision may be appealed to the United States Supreme Court for possible review.

Federal Courts

Article III, Section 1 of the United States Constitution grants authority for the federal court system as follows:

> The judicial Power of the United States shall be vested in one supreme Court, and in such inferior Courts as the Congress may from time to time ordain and establish.

This excerpt means that federal courts have jurisdiction over the laws of the United States, treaties, cases involving maritime jurisdiction, as well as disputes between two or more states and between citizens of different states. The excerpt also means that the federal courts have jurisdiction over federal criminal statutes, over civil disputes between citizen and citizen, and over civil disputes between a citizen and an agency of the government.

Three levels of courts comprise the federal court system. All judges in the system are appointed by the president and confirmed by the Senate. The 94 district courts form the basis of the federal system across the country. The federal district courts were established by Congress in the Judicial Act of 1789, and in 1999 the courts contained 646 judges. Each state has at least one federal district and normally has more than one judge; the districts do not cross state lines. The federal district courts are considered the "workhorse" of the federal system since they have trial authority. They have jurisdiction over violations of federal law, such as bank robberies, terrorist crimes, crimes involving interstate trafficking, kidnappings, and civil rights violations. Civil cases involve those claiming that a constitutional right was violated by another individual or entity, or by a governmental agency. Prisoners' rights claims are tried in federal district courts. These courts also oversee the United States marshals and the federal probation services.

To assist in case load relief, Congress has created an adjunct court to the district courts comprised of magistrates. A magistrate oversees preliminary proceedings in criminal cases, such as issuing arrest or search warrants, setting bail, and conducting preliminary hearings. In some jurisdictions, a magistrate performs an initial screening of Section 1983 civil actions. These include actions filed by prisoners claiming that their constitutional rights were violated.

The second level of courts in the federal system are United States Courts of Appeals. These courts are divided into 13 circuits dispersed across the country and cover a multistate territory, with the exception of the Court of Appeals for the District of Columbia. These courts are frequently referred to as "U.S. circuit courts of appeals" since during early English and American history, judges traveled throughout regions of the country to hear cases. Today, appellate court judges are not required to travel from circuit to circuit, but they may sit in more than one court. Each circuit is numbered and comprises several states. For example, the U.S. Court of Appeals for the Fourth Circuit hears appeals only from Maryland, Virginia, West Virginia, North Carolina, and South Carolina. An individual filing an appeal must do so within the circuit in which they reside.

The appellate courts are authorized to examine constitutional rights issues stemming from federal and state appellate court cases. The circuit courts assess judicial interpretations of the law of the lower courts to determine whether the law was applied properly. This assessment may include examining jury instructions in lower-court cases and ensuring that constitutional protections were followed as they applied to the facts of the case. Normally a panel of three judges decides a case. When a case involves a special or complex legal matter, all members of that circuit court will sit to hear the case. This procedure is known as "sitting en banc." Cases are decided by a majority of the judges who have heard the case. The appellate court may affirm a lower court's decision, reverse the decision, and/or affirm the decision in part and reverse it in part,

Figure 2.3   Article III Section 2 of the United States Constitution

"The Judicial Power shall extend to all Cases, in Law and Equity, arising under this Constitution, the Laws of the United States, and Treaties made, or which shall be made, under their Authority;—to all Cases affecting Ambassadors, other public Ministers and Consuls;—to all Cases of admiralty maritime, Jurisdiction;—to Controversies to which the United States shall be a Party;—to Controversies between two or more Citizens of different States;—between Citizens of the same State claiming Lands under Grants of different States, or Citizens thereof, and foreign States, Citizens or Subjects.

"In all Cases affecting Ambassadors, other public ministers and Consuls, and those which a State shall be Party, the Supreme Court shall have original jurisdiction. In all the other Cases before the mentioned, the Supreme Court shall have appellate jurisdiction, both as to Law and Fact, with such Exceptions, and under such Regulations as the Congress shall make."

depending on the court's interpretation. The appellate court's decision then becomes the case precedent for that circuit. One judge will write the majority opinion of the case, and other judges who disagree with the opinion may write a dissenting opinion. While the decision is not binding on other circuits, it may be reviewed by other courts and may guide them when they are faced with a similar issue. Should the losing party disagree with the appellate court's decision, they may appeal the case to the United States Supreme Court.

United States Supreme Court

The Supreme Court is the highest court in the country and the court of last resort for all cases which have been tried in lower state and federal courts. Article III, Section 2, of the United States Constitution provides authorization for the Supreme Court (Figure 2.3). The power of judicial review, however, was not confirmed until the decision in *Marbury v. Madison* (1803). In this case, Chief Justice John Marshall held that the Court's responsibility to overturn unconstitutional legislation was a necessary consequence of its sworn duty to uphold the Constitution. He declared that it is the responsibility of the judicial department to define the law.

The Court is exclusively an appellate court, but in a few exceptions it may hear cases of original jurisdiction. The Court is a "term" court, which means that it is in session for a period of time—from the first Monday of October to the end of June. All other federal courts operate full-time through the calendar year. The Court is made up of nine justices appointed by the president and confirmed by the Senate. They serve for life and may be removed from office only by impeachment.

A party desiring to appeal a lower court's decision may file a petition for a writ of certiorari, which is a discretionary procedure requesting appellate review. Sitting in chambers, the Court will decide whether to grant the writ of certiorari; at least four justices must vote in favor of granting the writ. Each year the Court reviews 6,000 to 7,000 petitions and usually grants certiorari in 100 to 150 cases, or in about 5 percent of the petitions. In 2000, the Court received 7,337 case filings, a 6 percent increase over those received in 1999. The Court argued 86 cases and disposed of 83; 77 cases were signed opinions. All nine justices sit to hear the arguments as one body (en banc). The Court may affirm a lower court's decision, reverse the decision, and/or affirm the decision in part and reverse it in part. The decision of the Court is final and becomes the case precedent, or landmark decision, on a specific issue.

GUIDE TO CASE AND STATUTORY CITATIONS/LEGAL RESEARCH

The reference to a legal case is called the case citation and follows a system for citation. Consider the following example: *Burdeau v. McDowell*, 256 U.S. 465, 41 S. Ct. 574, 65 L.Ed. 1048 (1921). The first named party is considered the plaintiff or petitioner, and the second named party is the defendant or respondent. The parties' names should be italicized or underlined. The example above was a case decided by the United States Supreme Court (S. Ct.), and the case can be found in one of three sets of books: volume 256 of the United States Reports (the official case reports of the Court) on page 465; in volume 41 of the Supreme Court Reporter on page 574; and in volume 65 of the Lawyers Edition on page 1048. The date in parentheses (1921) indicates the year in which the U.S. Supreme Court decided the case.

The decisions of the United States District Courts and the United States Circuit Court of Appeals are published by West Publishing Company in the Federal Supplement and Federal Reporter, respectively. The citation, *Thomas v. Kaufman*, 436 F. Supp 293 (W.D. Pa. 1977), indicates that the case will be found in volume 436 of the Federal Supplement on page 293 and that the case was decided by the Federal District Court for the Western District of Pennsylvania in 1977. The case citation, *United States v. Maddox*, 492 F. 2d 104 (5th Cir. 1974), indicates that the case was a Fifth Circuit Court of Appeals decision reported in volume 492 in the second series of the Federal Reporter on page 104. The Federal Reporter also reports decisions from the Court of Claims and the Court of Customs and Patent Appeals.

In general, state cases are reported in official state reporters as well as in a series of regional reporters. For example, a court of appeals case arising in North Carolina would be reported as *State v. Powell* 109 N.C. App. 1, 426 S.E. 2d 91 (1993). This citation indicates the case can be found in volume 109 of the North Carolina Court of Appeals Reports on page 1, as well as in volume 426 of the second series of the South Eastern reporter on page 91. The case was decided in 1993.

The following represents a listing of regional state reporters:

Reporter	States
Atlantic	CT, DL, ME, MD, NH, NJ, PA, RI, VT, as well as D.C. (Decisions of the Court of Appeals for D.C. are reported in the Federal Reporter series) (__A. ____A. 2d)
Southern	AK, AL, FL, LA, MS (___So. ___So. 2d)
Pacific	AZ, CA, CO, HW, ID, KS, MT, NV, NM, OK, OR, UT, WA, WY (P.__P.2d)
South Western	AK, KT, MO, TN, TX, (___S.W. ___S.W. 2d)
North Eastern	IL, IN, MA, NY, OH (__N.E. ___N.E. 2d)
North Western	IA, MI, MN, NE, ND, SD, WI (__N.W. ___N.W. 2d)
South Eastern	GA, NC, SC, VA, WV (__S.E. ___S.E. 2d)

In addition to the seven reporters above, the West Publishing Company National Reporter System includes the Supreme Court Reporter, the Federal Reporter, the Federal Supplement, Federal Rules Decisions, the New York Supplement, and the California Reporter. The United States Code Annotated (U.S.C.A.) is an unofficial edition, which presents the federal statutes as well as notes of cases which have applied or interpreted the statutes.

BRIEFING A COURT CASE

In order to fully examine the contents and impact of a case, a procedure known as "briefing" has been developed. Briefing a case is essential to learning the law, as well as how a court makes a decision, how the courts apply the law and legal standards, and how the decision may impact a particular legal area. While there are several ways to brief a case, any brief has fundamental components which should be addressed—preferably in the following order, since a well-structured brief is essential to the audience's understanding:

1. name of the case, citation, and year decided;

2. facts of the case;

3. issue (or issues) of the case;

4. court decision (opinion and rationale);

5. dissenting or concurring opinions;

6. comments/case significance (analysis); and

7. standard or test developed/relied upon.

First, it is important to read the case in its entirety. The reader should understand that the court rendering the opinion did not write its decision for the enjoyment or entertainment of the reader, but to communicate a point of law central to the decision. Second, one should read the case a second time, taking notes which correspond to the seven items cited above. When reading a decision, one should highlight passages which reveal the issues of the case, the court's holding, the standards the court relied upon, and the important points of law regarding the case.

Case Citation

Providing a full case citation is a simple task. Include both parties' names, the reporter citation, and the year of the citation, as in the following example: *Hudson v. Palmer*, 468 U.S. 517 (1984). Here, Hudson is the plaintiff and Palmer is the defendant. The case was brought before the United States Supreme Court and can be found in volume 468 of the Supreme Court Reporter, starting on page 517. The case was decided in 1984.

Case Facts

Next, in two to three paragraphs, describe the important facts of the case. Here, you write a case synopsis. It should provide enough information so that a person who has not read the case will be able to understand it. Decide what facts are important about the case and what are not. Clearly articulate the claim(s) the plaintiff is asserting. As you read about the case, ask what specifically the plaintiff is claiming, protesting, alleging, or challenging so that you can obtain the central facts.

Identify the classification of the case (i.e., state tort, Section 1983, habeas corpus, class action, and so on) and what amendment (s) is/are applicable. For example, a prisoner may have challenged a policy on the use of force in a prison and has brought to the court a Section 1983 action under the Eighth Amendment.

Issue/Issues

You should write out the issue(s) in question format and then answer the question(s) either "yes" or "no." Your question should address the legal issue as it was examined by the court, and the issue should be presented succinctly enough to capture the essence of the allegations. Consider the following example:

> Does a prisoner have a reasonable expectation of privacy in his cell entitling him to the protection of the Fourth Amendment against unreasonable searches and seizures? No.

Frequently, the court will state what the question of law is. To discover it, review the holding and simply turn it into a question. This process can be the most problematic part of briefing a case, but it is the most important. Your success in discovering the question of law depends on how the issue is framed by the court. Pay attention to phrases like "the question is/are before us;" "we hold;" and "we decide."

In this section of the brief you should also identify the question of law. In assessing the case you should be able to determine the argument(s). Frequently, a case will have more than one issue. The number of issues can be determined if you focus on the facts of the complaint. Your guiding principle should be the question, Is the case simple enough to be boiled down to just one issue, or is it so complex that it would be better to see it as having two or more issues? You should also identify the appropriate amendment which applies to the issue(s).

Court Decision

The court's decision answers the question posed in the issue section of the brief. Determine whether the court affirmed, reversed, or modified the decision of a lower court. When dealing with a lower court, explain briefly how the court decided the case and how the question posed in the issue section was answered.

In this section you should discuss just the essence of the majority opinion. Do not quote everything that the court states. Instead, explain in your own words what the court says, and discuss briefly the rationale behind the court's decision. You may want to include the procedural history for future reference.

Dissenting or Concurring Opinions

Appellate court cases will frequently have both dissenting and concurring opinions. In your own words, state the dissent and the concurrence, emphasizing how they differ from each other. Capture only the essence of the concurring or dissenting opinion instead of merely quoting the full opinion. When there is no dissenting opinion, simply state so.

Comments/Case Significance (Analysis)

In this section of the brief, you evaluate the impact of the case on the field of corrections. Here, you should (1) evaluate the significance of the case; (2) describe how the case relates to other cases; (3) assess the impact of the case on the specific component of the criminal justice system; (4) evaluate the quality of the opinions and give any other opinions you consider important; (5) discuss how the decision impacts liability for the agency, officer(s), and/or administrator(s); and (6) describe any policy, training, or procedural issues which may be relevant.

Standard/Principle of Law

Frequently, a standard will be identified in the case decision. In your brief, identify the standard or test which the court relies on or develops as a result of the decision. Standards and tests developed by the court are used to evaluate future claims in similar cases. You should state the standard or test briefly, clearly, and precisely. The decision of the court may appear at the beginning or toward the end of the case report.

SUMMARY

This chapter has provided an overview of the significant differences between criminal law and civil law. The distinction is important in that when a prisoner files a lawsuit claiming that a constitutional right has been violated, he is submitting a civil complaint. The procedures for processing and hearing such a complaint are different from those followed in criminal court. A major distinction is the standard of evidence that is applied in civil cases. This standard, preponderance of evidence, requires only enough evidence to convince jury members that an officer or correctional department should be liable. Also, the sanctions in a civil case are different from those in criminal court. In civil cases the plaintiff is primarily seeking monetary damages or some form of relief.

The sources of law were also discussed. Students should be familiar with how and where laws are made. A significant number of cases presented in this text are United States Supreme Court decisions which establish case precedents requiring lower courts to adhere to the landmark rulings when deciding similar cases. In fact, an examination of these Supreme Court decisions and how lower courts apply these rulings to various correctional issues is the primary focus of this text.

In the chapter, state and federal court systems were also contrasted. This text's major focus is on the the federal court system, since most prisoner lawsuits are filed in a federal court and a number of cases have been decided by the United States Supreme Court. Therefore, students must become aware of how a case progresses and the responsibility of each court when hearing a prisoner complaint. Finally, in this chapter, students were exposed to the processes of researching and briefing cases. Case law can be difficult to comprehend at first, and briefing cases takes a considerable amount of time. Following a structure such as the one explained in the chapter can assist the student in assuring that he or she covers the essential facts and legal issues in order to analyze case decisions more fully.

References

American Bar Association Section of International and Comparative Law. 1958. *The Rule of law in the United States*. Chicago: American Bar Association.

del Carmen, R. V. 2001. *Criminal procedure: Law and practice*. 5th ed. Belmont, CA: Wadsworth Publishers.

Dershowitz, A. M. 1997. *Reasonable doubts: The criminal justice system and the O. J. Simpson case*. New York: Simon and Schuster.

Kappeler, V. E. 2002. *Police civil liability: Supreme Court cases and materials*. Prospect Heights, IL: Waveland Press.

Levenson, L. L. 1997. *Criminal law*. New York: Aspen Publishers, Inc.

Schmalleger, F. 2002. *Criminal law today*. 2nd ed. Upper Saddle River, NJ: Prentice-Hall.

Senna, J. J., and L. J. Siegel. 1993. *Introduction to criminal justice*. 6th ed. Minneapolis, MN: West Publishing Company.

Zalman, M., and L. J. Siegel. 1997. Criminal procedure: Constitution and society. *2nd ed. Belmont, CA: Wadsworth Publishers*.

Cases Cited

Alliance to End Repression v. City of Chicago, 561 F. Supp. 537 (N.D. Ill. 1982)

Benton v. Maryland, 395 U.S. 784 (1969)

Burdeau v. McDowell, 256 U. S. 465 (1921)

Gregg v. Georgia, *428 U.S. 153 (1976)*

Hudson v. Palmer, 468 U.S. 517 (1984)

In re Winship, 397 U.S. 358 (1970)

Jacobellis v. Ohio, 378 U.S. 184 (1964)

Powers v. Lightner, 820 F.2d 818 (7th Cir. 1987)

Robinson v. California, 370 U.S. 660 (1962)

State v. Powell, 109 N.C. App. 1, 426 S. E. 2d 91 (1993)

Thomas v. Kaufman, 436 F. Supp. 293 (W.D. Pa. 1977)

United States v. Maddox, 492 F. 2d 104 (5th Cir. 1974)

Wolf v. Colorado, 338 U.S. 25 (1949)

CHAPTER 3

THE EVOLUTION
AND RESTRICTION
OF PRISONER RIGHTS

> *There is no "iron curtain" drawn between the Constitution*
> *of this country....A prisoner is not wholly stripped of*
> *constitutional protections when he is imprisoned for a crime.*
>
> Justice Byron White

Correctional law is a body of law which applies the United States Constitution to issues germane to the correctional field. This accumulation of court opinions is primarily decisions of the United States Supreme Court and also includes decisions of the lower federal courts. Decisions of the courts generally revolve around four basic areas: prisoner rights cases (pretrial detainees, convicted prisoners, probationers, and parolees), liability of correctional employees, organizational administrative liability, and employee rights.

As heretical as it may sound, individuals under some form of correctional supervision possess certain constitutional rights regardless of their criminal status. The epigraph for this chapter, taken from the Supreme Court decision *Wolff v. McDonnell* (1974), may solicit responses such as, "Prisoners should not possess any rights; after all, they were charged with a crime and convicted!" Yet the *Wolff* decision may create more questions than it can answer, and two central questions emerge: (1) What is the scope of prisoners' rights?, and (2) How do these rights impact correctional personnel charged with supervising the confined?

Prisoners did not always possess the safeguards of the Constitution. Not until the 1960s did the Supreme Court begin to take a more activist stance on prisoners' rights issues. Correctional law is less 40 years in age, yet numerous court decisions have been penned that have changed the legal landscape in corrections. This chapter will trace the evolutionary development of prisoners' rights issues and conclude with a discussion on the current status of correctional law.

THE HANDS-OFF DOCTRINE (1789–1964)

Punishment and Discipline in the Penitentiary

Americans' understanding of deviant behavior led to the invention of the penitentiary (Rothman 1971). With the development of the prison system in the United States in the 1820s, the prevailing ideology was that prisoners could be reformed from their deviant and corrupt ways through isolation from the community and a period of punishment. In New York, the Auburn prison system became the paradigm for other states to follow in terms of prison design, correctional management, and philosophy. That is, during their incarceration, prisoners were to be subservient to their keepers. Correctional officials organized their early correctional philosophy around the doctrines of separation, obedience, and labor (Rothman 1971). They were careful to inform prisoners that they were to labor diligently, to obey all orders, and to do so without uttering a word. A strict adherence to silence was a key component to reforming the deviant prisoner (Morris and Rothman 1998).

In order to accomplish the above, prison officials developed a strict regime of prison rules, discipline, and a variety of sanctions for disobedient prisoners. Prison systems across the country developed numerous measures to punish prisoners. At the prisons of Sing Sing and Auburn, prison officers relied primarily on whipping prisoners to enforce rules. The Maine system used the ball and chain, while the systems in Massachusetts, Virginia, Maryland, and Pennsylvania used solitary confinement and small provisions of bread and water (Morris and Rothman 1998). The system in Connecticut used multiple measures to discipline prisoners, including the whip, solitary confinement, chains, and borderline starvation.

Various measures of torture were also created to instill discipline in prisoners. The Pennsylvania system used the iron gag, on the notion that prisoners were men of idle habits, vicious propensities, and depraved passions. A warden in Ohio justified the use of the whip by stating that whenever a prison becomes a place for relaxing or a pleasant place to reside, it loses its influence and the minds of men become disposed to evil. Kansas prison officials used the "box." Shaped like a coffin, an unmanageable prisoner was placed inside, with the lid secured and a water hose inserted through a small hole in the top of the box. Water would slowly fill the box until the prisoner, begging for his life, agreed to abide by prison rules.

As evidenced by the prevailing ideology, prisoners were treated as if they were devoid of rights, and prison officials operated the penitentiary as they saw fit. While reforms were attempted through different prison acts, state legislation, and the federal government in the late 1800s and the early 1900s, little actual change occurred. Changes that were instituted did not afford prisoners constitutional right protections.

Reluctant to intervene at the state level, the federal government maintained a "hands-off doctrine" in state correctional matters. The hands-off doctrine is not an historical document like the Constitution or the Monroe Doctrine, but a court attitude or an abstention philosophy regarding the operation of state prisons and prisoners' rights. In *Prevar v. Massachusetts* (1866) the underlying philosophy of the hands-off doctrine was first articulated by the courts. A prisoner attempted to challenge the conditions of the Massachusetts prison, claiming under the Eighth Amendment that the totality of the conditions violated the "cruel and unusual punishment" clause. The United States Supreme Court determined that the Eighth Amendment did not apply to prisoners in state prisons and that the federal government did not have a legitimate interest in the operation of state penal institutions.

Legal Status of Prisoners

In *Ruffin v. Commonwealth* (1871) the Court of Appeals in Virginia stressed a strict approach concerning the hands-off doctrine by declaring that prisoners, by their very status of conviction, were "slaves of the State," a condition of penal servitude to the state. Ruffin, while serving a prison sentence, was contracted by the prison to work for the railroad. He attempted to escape during work and killed a prison officer. Ruffin was found guilty of murder, sentenced to hang, and filed an appeal to the Virginia Court of Appeals. He sought a change of venue for trial, which he contended was a state constitutional right of those criminally charged. The Virginia court, however, somewhat deemphasized its earlier reference, "slaves of the State," stating that the Bill of Rights applied to freemen and not convicted felons. The court ruled that the proper place for the trial of a prisoner was the prison and not another location.

Even though the U.S. Constitution had contained the Bill of Rights since 1789, the court-based attitude of denying prisoners' rights dominated the court's philosophy. Prisoners were unable to redress a grievance outside the confines of the prison walls. The Supreme Court also maintained a hands-off attitude through its constitutional interpretation of their own powers to intervene in state prison matters. Moreover, prisoners were considered *"Civiler Mortus,"* or civilly dead, that is, dead under the law and therefore unable to perform legal actions. Later, in *Illinois v. Russell* (1910) a court concluded that as a result of having been convicted, prisoners lose civil rights, a condition which practically deprives the convict of his citizenship. The court further held that a prisoner became "an alien in his own country."

The idea that prisoners were slaves of the state was not totally correct under common law. Prisoners were not entirely stripped of their rights. Prisoners could still own property and could still be sued, although they could not bring a legal action. In *Anderson v. Salant* (1916) a court in Rhode Island concluded that a prisoner's rights were broader than a slave's. A slave had no property rights but a prisoner could have an interest in property. In *Anderson*, a prisoner sought to recover damages from a prison contractor, claiming he was illegally compelled to work for the contractor.

Further, not all courts embraced an abstention position regarding prisoner lawsuits. In many jurisdictions, the courts applied the Constitution to several prisoner legal claims (Wallace 1992). In the case *In re Bird Song* (1889) a federal district court found that correctional officials had violated the constitutional rights of a prisoner: They had demonstrated cruel and unusual punishment by forcing him to stand up in his cell for several days with chains around his neck. The court noted that correctional officials had no arbitrary and unreviewable power to choose any method of discipline that would be deemed appropriate. In *Kusah v. McKorkle* (1918) the Supreme Court of Washington determined that a custodian may be liable if he failed to protect a prisoner. A county jail prisoner claimed that he was attacked and stabbed by a mentally disordered prisoner who had been placed in his cell without having been searched. The court held that correctional officials could be held liable for failing to keep the prisoner free from harm.

Prisoner discipline by administrators was an issue in which judicial review was limited unless there were gross violations of prisoner rights. In *Topeka v. Boutwell* (1894) a prisoner was beaten and treated with harshness and cruelty after having been subdued and placed in custodial control. Correctional officials were held liable for damages for needless sufferings inflicted on prisoners. In a Tennessee case, *Peters v. White* (1899), the administrator of a county workhouse was held liable for using unauthorized corporal punishment against a prisoner. The administrator had secured the prisoner to a "whipping post" and delivered several lashes on the prisoner's back. The court ruled that the county commissioners lacked statutory authority to delegate permission to deliver corporal punishment to prisoners-an authority which had been abolished in Tennessee.

The North Carolina Supreme Court, in *North Carolina v. Nipper* (1914), upheld the prior decision in criminal court that correctional officials were guilty for flogging a prisoner. The Supreme Court ruled that there was no statute or court decision that allowed flogging as a part of prison discipline.

A court in Illinois upheld damages awarded to a prisoner held in jail because a grand jury determined that it was absolutely cruel and inhumane to confine a human being for any length of time (*Stuart v. LaSalle* 1876). Later, the Illinois Supreme Court dismissed the suit by finding an adequate remedy in the statute and not because prisoners were "slaves of the State."

These limited number of cases indicate that some courts were willing to hear prisoner claims and found that officials did violate prisoners' rights. These cases illustrate that there were a limited number of courts willing to hear prisoner complaints during this period and that prisoners were not totally stripped of all constitutional rights or completely became "slaves of the State."

Gradual Erosion of "Hands-Off"

A crack in the foundation of the hands-off doctrine created a shift in the court's thinking in the 1940s. In *Ex Parte Hull* (1941), the United States Supreme Court held that the state and its officers may not abridge or impair a petitioner's right to appeal to a federal court for a writ of habeas corpus. Hull's submission of a writ of habeas corpus to the Supreme Court was denied by Michigan prison officials, as was a later letter to the Court. A regulation in the Michigan prison system required prisoners to submit all legal documents to the mail room for review prior to being mailed to the court. If the documents were properly drafted, they would be forwarded to the court; if not, they were rejected. Hull, however, somehow sent the document to his father and he submitted the document to the court clerk. The court struck down the regulation and did provide relief on Hull's habeas corpus petition. This landmark case established the principle that prison officials may not screen, censor, or interfere with the mail of prisoners. Prisoners also won the right to court review and gained access to the courts, but much did not change in the hands-off approach.

Another shift in the hands-off doctrine was also observed in *Cochran v. Kansas* (1942), when the United States Supreme Court recognized that prisoners could appeal conditions of their original conviction. Finally, a major crack was evidenced in *Coffin v. Reichard* (1944), when the court concluded that prisoners retain all the rights of an ordinary citizen except those expressly or by necessary implication taken from him by law. This decision was a 180-degree-turn from the decision in *Ruffin*. Prisoners were no longer considered slaves of the state, but the decision ostensibly created more questions than it answered. What specific rights the prisoner possessed remained a mystery, and it would take another twenty years before the mystery was solved.

The rationale behind the hands-off doctrine can be analyzed according to four fundamental factors. First, the courts were concerned with maintaining a separation of powers between the branches of government-the judicial, the executive, and the legislative branches. There was a concern on the part of the courts that judicial intervention regarding prisoners' rights would interfere with the operation of state institutions. Second, the courts expressed concern that their involvement with prisoner claims would violate the basic constitutional principle of federalism. The concern was that if the courts began to routinely command state officials to afford constitutional rights to prisoners, the courts would, in essence, encroach on the authority of the states to operate their prisons.

Third, the courts recognized their lack of expertise in running prisons. Therefore, the courts were concerned that such judicial intervention would likely jeopardize prison operations and security within the prison (Call 1995). Finally, the courts maintained the hands-off doctrine because they were concerned that once prisoners began filing lawsuits, the litigation spigot would open, flooding the courts not only with a deluge of claims but with a number of frivolous actions (Branham 2002). The courts were not only concerned about the number of prisoner lawsuits that could emerge, but they also feared that the court system would become clogged, thereby impeding the courts' ability to handle legitimate claims.

PRISONER RIGHTS ERA (1962–1979)

Rationale for Granting Rights to Prisoners

Approximately twenty years after the *Ex Parte Hull* decision, the courts reversed their philosophy regarding prisoner rights by determining that they had a duty to resolve the constitutional discrepancies concerning prisoners. Several factors underscored this 180-degree turnabout. First, and foremost, was the change in composition of the United States Supreme Court. During the tenure of Chief Justice Earl Warren, the Court became more of an activist court as compared to previous years (Alexander 1993). The "Warren Court" became known for its broad interpretation of the Constitution, particularly concerning politically disadvantaged individuals, persons accused of crimes, and prisoners. For example, in 1965, the Court decided *Miranda v. Arizona*, which provided for warnings prior to custodial interrogation, and *Mapp v. Ohio* (1961), which held that the exclusionary rule applied to the states.

Second, turmoil filled the country during the 1960s. Protests and demonstrations against the Vietnam war and marches regarding advances in civil rights were frequent. Assassinations of President John F. Kennedy, Robert Kennedy, and Reverend Martin Luther King, Jr., as well as citizens rioting in many large U.S. cities, underscored the tumultuous 1960s. Behind prison walls, prisoners became more militant and assertive in pushing for constitutional protections which became more difficult for the courts to ignore. Of significance was the prison riot at Attica (NY) in 1971. Militant prisoners took control of the prison and held officers hostage for five days. They complained about a lack of prisoner programming and about the conditions of the prison. On the fifth day of the siege, the National Guard and state police troopers stormed the prison, killing forty-three people, including the officer hostages.

Third, the legal profession developed more "public interest lawyers" who were willing to take cases and causes on behalf of the prisoner population, either pro bono or through government or private aid. As these lawyers brought prisoners' claims before the courts, the judiciary became more responsive to the legal problems of prisoners. Cases which illustrated horrendous conditions of confinement called for the court to provide some sort of remedial action (Call 1995).

Collectively these developments helped to set the stage for court intervention regarding prisoners' rights. A significant United States Supreme Court decision was instrumental in creating a favorable climate for prisoners to bring legal actions into the federal court system. In *Monroe v. Pape* (1961) the Court's decision gave life to a barely living civil-rights statute known as Title 42 U.S.C. Section 1983. The statute had lain dormant for ninety years after its enactment by Congress in 1871 (see Chapter 4). In this case the Court ruled that state officials acting "under color of law" could be held liable for violating a citizen's constitutional rights. In *Monroe*, Chicago police officers entered a residence and searched the occupants without a search warrant, in violation of the Fourth Amendment. The Court noted that Section 1983 was enacted to provide a federal remedy for the violation of constitutional rights and it therefore held the errant officers liable for the misuse of their authority.

Prior to *Monroe*, it was extremely difficult to hold individual police or correction officers liable under Section 1983 because they had to be performing actions under color of law. Before 1961, the accepted interpretation of Section1983 was that a state official who acted in violation of state law was not acting under color of state law. *Monroe* changed and expanded this concept of acting under color of law to include actions of the police or correction officials who were authorized by state law and by department policy. As a result, correctional officers can be held liable for actions or omissions under Section 1983.

Prisoners Possess Constitutional Rights

The United States Supreme Court ruled in a series of cases that the Due Process Clause incorporated most of the rights contained in the Bill of Rights into the Fourteenth Amendment. This meant that the first ten amendments were made applicable to the states via the Fourteenth Amendment. On the heels of *Monroe*, the Court ruled in *Robinson v. California* (1962) that the Eighth Amendment's prohibition against cruel and unusual punishment clause applies to the states. This marked the first time that the Court associated the Eighth Amendment with the Due Process clause of the Fourteenth Amendment. This association was a complete reversal of the Court's former opinion approximately one hundred years earlier in *Prevar v. Massachusetts* (1866). After the *Robinson* decision, the Court for the first time held, in a per curiam opinion, that a state prisoner could file a Section 1983 lawsuit in federal court (*Cooper v. Pate* 1964). Cooper, a prisoner in an Illinois prison, brought a Section 1983 civil action, claiming that his First Amendment right to freedom of religion was violated by the refusal of prison authorities to allow him to purchase religious literature. Prisoners were thus granted an explicit and direct access to federal courts. This case expanded religious freedoms and extended the Bill of Rights protections to prisoners. It was not the breadth of the ruling in *Cooper* that mattered but the Court's determination that prisoners have constitutional rights and that correctional officials were not free to do with prisoners as they pleased (Jacobs 1977).

The *Cooper* decision ushered in an era known as the "halcyon days of prisoners' rights" (Branham 2002). The 1960s and 1970s have been characterized as the "hands-on-doctrine," "judicial activist," and/or "interventionist" era (Kutak 1976; McCoy 1981). Correctional case law began to develop during this time and was focused primarily on reform at the jail and prison level.

From 1966 to 1979 the United States Supreme Court ruled in a number of prisoner cases-rulings which developed an early baseline for later decisions. The Court ruled in *Coleman v. Peyton* (1966) and in *Johnson v. Avery* (1969) that under the First Amendment access to courts is a fundamental right which may not be denied or obstructed by correctional officials. Johnson was a "writ writer," a prisoner who assisted other prisoners in submitting before the courts writs of habeas corpus which challenged their convictions. In the prison vernacular, Johnson was known as a "jailhouse lawyer," one who is self-taught in legal matters. Correction officials disciplined Johnson for this activity. The Court decided that the constitution does not prohibit even convicted persons from gaining access to the courts. Unless the state could devise alternatives which would reasonably assist prisoners in postconviction relief, it could not deny prisoners from assisting one another in petitioning the courts.

Johnson represented the Court's first full written opinion on prisoners' rights issues and established the attitude toward prisoner cases during this period. The Court also determined in *Younger v. Gilmore* (1971) that correctional regulations which limited access to law books, legal materials, and lay assistance on preparing documents for courts were unconstitutional. Prisoners incarcerated in California correctional institutions challenged prison regulations which limited access to legal materials. The Court upheld that prison law libraries must have sufficient legal materials to enable prisoners to have reasonable access to the courts. Moreover, the Court further expanded the fundamental right to access to courts in *Bounds v. Smith* (1977) by requiring the states to establish methods for assisting prisoners in submitting petitions to the courts through the development of law libraries or persons trained in the law.

The courts addressed other First Amendment rights. In *Palmigano v. Travisono* (1970) the court established restrictions on correction officials censoring prisoner mail. In *Procunier v. Martinez* (1974) the United States Supreme Court held that prison authorities could not censor outgoing mail in which prisoners were complaining about prison life or expressing views contradictory to the prison administration. Censorship of mail between prisoner and attorney was prohibited on the grounds of client-attorney relationship. Prison officials censoring other mail were required to notify the prisoner and must afford him or her the opportunity to object. In *Cruz v. Beto* (1972) the Supreme Court addressed the issue of religious worship while a prisoner was incarcerated. Cruz, incarcerated in Texas, was a practicing Buddhist and claimed that his First Amendment right to freedom of religion was denied. He alleged that correction officials allowed other faiths to exercise their religious beliefs but that he was denied the opportunity because he practiced the Buddhist religion. The Court determined that correction officials must provide all prisoners a reasonable opportunity to exercise their religious beliefs. Less than four years after the *Johnson* decision, the National Advisory Commission on Correctional Standards and Goals (1973) identified eighteen issues regarding prisoners' rights, most of which had not existed prior to 1969.

Prisoners continued to prevail in civil litigation throughout the 1970s. The United States Supreme Court held in *Haines v. Kerner* (1972) that prisoners in forma pauperis petitions (waivers of filing fees for indigent prisoners) had to be treated in a manner most advantageous to prisoners. Their cases could not be dismissed. In *Wolff v. McDonnell* (1974) the Court examined the issue of disciplinary proceeding protections for prisoners and applied the Due Process Clause of the Fourteenth Amendment to serious misconduct infractions. The Court held that state-created "liberty interests" were connected to earning good-time credits, which allowed prisoners to be considered for early release on parole for maintaining good behavior while incarcerated. Accumulating serious misconduct reports could forfeit good-time credits, thereby increasing the likelihood a prisoner would not be considered for early release. The Court held that denying good-time credits without holding a hearing violated the prisoner's Due Process Clause of the Fourteenth Amendment and thus required correctional officials to first conduct a hearing. The decision applied only to serious institutional misconduct, and the Court enumerated five required components to be considered when conducting such disciplinary hearings.

Two years later, in *Meachum v. Fano* (1976), the Supreme Court concluded that prisoners had no liberty interest under the Due Process Clause relative to prisoner transfers to another prison where the conditions may be considered harsher. The Court ruled that a transfer to another facility was within the "range of normal custodial limits," which is part of the conviction which the state imposes. In *Estelle v. Gamble* (1976) the Court examined under what circumstances prisoners may prevail in a medical care claim under the Eighth Amendment's cruel and unusual punishment clause. The Court established that correctional officials may be held liable by being "deliberately indifferent to a prisoner's serious medical need."

In two North Carolina cases the United States Supreme Court further examined prisoner rights claims. First, in *Jones v. N.C. Prisoners Labor Union* (1977), the Court held that prisoners did not have the right to form unions for the purpose of negotiating the conditions of their confinement. Prisoners' First Amendment rights were not violated by the ban on membership, solicitation, and group meetings, since prisoners do not retain First Amendment rights that are inconsistent with their prisoner status or with the legitimate goals of the correctional system. In *Bounds v. Smith* (1977) the Court addressed another issue relating to access to courts by examining the adequacy of law libraries in prison. The Court ruled that prison authorities were required to assist prisoners by providing meaningful access to courts. This ruling may be interpreted to mean the development of prison law libraries, as well as the availability of paralegal assistants, law students, paraprofessionals, jailhouse lawyers, and writing materials.

The United States Supreme Court examined legal claims stemming from parole and probation revocations during this period. In *Morrissey v. Brewer* (1972) and *Gagnon v. Scarpelli* (1973) the Court set forth a more elaborate set of due process procedural protections than the set which had been established in *Wolff*. Minimum due-process requirements must be afforded to persons on either probation or parole prior to revoking the person's probation or parole status.

From a review of these cases it is clear that the attitude of the courts dramatically changed regarding the legal status of prisoners. The courts reversed their prior position and adopted a presumption that prisoners retained certain fundamental constitutional rights unless there were sufficient reasons for restricting them. Almost overnight, prisoners, probationers, and parolees went from legally disenfranchised persons to those possessing legal clout. Then the very thing that the courts had been wary about occurred. Prisoners began to flood the court system with one civil claim after another. Further, the courts, in essence, began to control the prisons from the bench, by handing down case decisions in which prisoners prevailed.

RESTRAINED APPROACH/DEFERENCE ERA (1979 TO PRESENT)

Deference to correctional officials emerged in 1979 as a third period in which a number of cases have been decided by the United States Supreme Court. The legal ground that prisoners gained during the 1960s and 1970s has slowly been lost to correctional authorities through a number of case decisions by the Court. In *Bell v. Wolfish* (1979) the Court addressed constitutional rights of pretrial detainees for the first time. While the case involved numerous claims (double-bunking, cell searches, and possessing hardback publications), the primary claim dealt with body cavity searches after contact visits. The purpose of the searches was to discover the possession of contraband and to deter prisoners from smuggling drugs or weapons into the facility. The Court held that such searches under the Fourth Amendment were not unreasonable, since the security needs outweighed the privacy interests of prisoners. The other issues involving legitimate rules and order maintenance were also upheld by the Court. Moreover, the Court applied the case decision to convicted prisoners.

Commencing with *Parratt v. Taylor* (1981), the United States Supreme Court decided a series of cases which weakened the ability of prisoners to prevail in Section 1983 actions. Prison officers had lost hobby-craft property of a prisoner worth $23.50 and failed to follow prison regulations. Taylor filed a Section 1983 action claiming that he had suffered a deprivation of his property under the Fourteenth Amendment. The Court held that the actions of the officers amounted to negligence which is not actionable under Section 1983. A prisoner must prove more than negligence to prevail in a constitutional case.

Similarly the Court ruled on jail prisoners' claims which addressed negligent actions of correction officers in *Daniels v. Williams* (1986). In *Daniels* a jail prisoner filed a Section 1983 action claiming that an officer negligently left a pillow case on a flight of stairs, causing the prisoner to slip and injure himself. He allegedly sustained ankle and back injuries. The Court held that the Fourteenth Amendment protects individuals from "intentional" deprivations of life, liberty, or property by governmental officials. Prisoners are prohibited from bringing negligence claims to federal courts under Section 1983. Negligent acts, no matter how harmful, can never violate the Fourteenth Amendment.

The United States Supreme Court addressed the issue of prison cell searches in *Hudson v. Palmer* (1984). The Court determined that prisoners do not have a reasonable expectation of privacy in a prison cell under the Fourth Amendment and that therefore the amendment ostensibly does not apply to cell searches in the correctional setting. In another case addressing pretrial detainees, the Court, in *Block v. Rutherford* (1984), ruled that such detainees have no due process rights to observe a correction officer's search of a prisoner's cell.

Perhaps the most significant case decided by the United States Supreme Court pertaining to prisoners' rights issues is *Turner v. Safely* (1987). Prisoners incarcerated in the Renz Correctional Institution in Missouri filed a class action lawsuit seeking injunctive relief and damages challenging two prison regulations: (1) correspondence between prisoners at different institutions and (2) permission of the warden for prisoners to marry. The Court struck down the regulation requiring prisoners to seek permission from the warden. The regulation pertaining to prisoner correspondence was constitutionally valid under the First Amendment, since it was "reasonably related to legitimate penological objectives," namely the maintenance of security and order maintenance at the institution. The decision provides a standard with which all prison regulations must be written and grants more authority to correctional officials.

A second decision, in *Thornburg v. Abbott* (1989), illustrates another conservative shift in the Court's philosophy concerning prisoners' rights. Prisoners housed within the Federal Bureau of Prisons challenged a regulation which censored or rejected various outside publications, claiming the regulation violated their First Amendment constitutional rights. Prison officials maintained that the regulation was necessary in order for the warden to reject such publications which threatened the security and good order of the institution. Relying on the *Turner* decision, the Court expanded the "legitimate penological objectives" standard to include all incoming correspondence, not just publications. The Court further added that this standard is the applicable one to use when assessing whether a prison regulation allegedly deprived a prisoner of his constitutional rights. In *O'Lone v. Estate of Shabazz* (1987), the Court determined that prison authorities did not have to allow a prisoner to return to the prison for a religious service because that would have created a security risk. Shabazz was a Muslim and his security classification required him to be on a work detail outside the prison. The Court again applied the *Turner* standard to regulations which underscore legitimate prison security objectives which may restrict the religious observance of prisoners.

The Court further gave deference to prison officials in three decisions affecting the Eighth Amendment rights of prisoners. First, in *Whitley v. Albers* (1986), the Court held that it is not cruel and unusual punishment for a prison response team to employ lethal force in a disturbance or emergency situation when prisoners are rioting and have taken officers as hostages. A prisoner was shot in the knee and filed a Section 1983 action. The Court determined that the prisoner must prove the state of mind of the officer at the moment the officer used force. This means that the officer must have acted wantonly with obduracy (hard heartedly and without remorse). In a second case (*Wilson v. Seiter* 1991) the Court further expanded the state-of-mind standard and applied it to the condition of confinement cases. In cases of overcrowding and deplorable institutional conditions, prisoners must prove that correctional officials acted wantonly and with deliberate indifference to some basic human need of prisoners.

In *Farmer v. Brennan* (1994) the Court further expanded the definition and application of deliberate indifference in cases of failing to protect prisoners. Farmer claimed that he had been sexually assaulted by another prisoner and that prison officials knew his sexual orientation created a safety risk which they had deliberately ignored. The Court applied the criminal law definition to deliberate indifference and stated that officers' actions must be "reckless" to be considered as an Eighth Amendment violation. The Court concluded that prison officials could be held liable only for those risks of which they are actually aware.

In three cases, prisoners prevailed regarding Eighth Amendment issues. In *Hudson v. McMillian* (1992) a prisoner filed a Section 1983 action claiming that an officer beat him, causing facial swelling, minor bruising, and a cracked dental plate. Correctional officials maintained that in order for force to be considered an Eighth Amendment violation, a prisoner must sustain serious injury. The Court disagreed, and determined that the degree of injury is not the applicable standard but that excessive force claims must be evaluated by determining whether the officer used force in a "sadistic and malicious" manner. In *Hudson*, the Court ruled that the officer had acted with malice, particularly because the prisoner had been compliant. The Court adopted a different standard of review in use-of-force cases which excluded cases arising from a prison disturbance.

Second, in *Helling v. McKinney* (1993), a prisoner complained of environmental health risks from being forced to inhale secondary smoke from a cell mate and other prisoners incarcerated in the housing unit. McKinney complained that prison officials were deliberately indifferent to his medical health, thereby violating his Eighth Amendment rights. The Court agreed with McKinney, concluding that cruel and unusual punishment could be demonstrated by being exposed to conditions that pose an unreasonable risk of harm to the prisoner's current or future health concerns. Finally, the Court addressed whether the Americans with Disabilities Act (ADA) applied to incarcerated prisoners. In *Pennsylvania Department of Corrections v. Yeskey*, (1998) a prisoner filed a civil action against correctional authorities who denied his admission into a boot camp program based on a past medical history of hypertension. The prisoner's position was that under the ADA he should be allowed to participate in the boot camp. The Court agreed and held that Title II of the ADA applies to all citizens, including prisoners.

This discussion of selected United States Supreme Court decisions reveals the historical evolution of varying subject matters which comprise prisoner rights issues. The combination of cases and their time periods in which they were decided, as illustrated in Figure 3.1, reveals three unique cycles or phases. The evolution of correctional law closely resembles a conceptualization model comprised of three phases which explain the emergence of all ideas: thesis, antithesis, and synthesis (Archambeault and Archambeault 1982). The first cycle, thesis, reveals the hands-off doctrine period in which a significant number of prisoner civil claims were rejected by the courts. The courts maintained that prisoners were slaves of the state, possessing no rights, although not all courts completely embraced this philosophy. The antithesis phase reveals a reversal in the courts' philosophy in the 1960s and through the 1970s. The courts began intervening on behalf of prisoners and granted constitutional rights to prisoners. These decisions established varying legal standards, decreased correctional officials' scope of authority, and forced them to make policy and operational changes consistent with court rulings. The synthesis phase exists during the restrained/deference era. This phase marked the courts' philosophy that prisoners still retain fundamental constitutional rights, but the courts developed higher legal standards than in the preceding era, making it more difficult for prisoners to prevail. The majority of case decisions since 1979/1980 have restored more decision-making authority to correctional officials.

ESSENTIAL DEVELOPMENTS IMPACTING CORRECTIONAL LAW

From the discussion above, it should be recognized that the law is dynamic in nature. Since the *Cooper* decision in 1964, the legal status of prisoners has

Figure 3.1   Evolutionary Stages of Correctional Law

Stage	Legal status of prisoner	Correctional authority	Liability
"Hands-off" (1786-1962)	"Slave of the State"	Total	None
Court intervention (1962 to 1979)	Convicted with rights	Reduced/restricted through case decisions	Civil/criminal
Court deference (1979 to 1995)	Modification of Constitutional rights	More discretionary power	Civil/criminal
PLRA (since 1996)	Restrictions on filing legal actions	Broader use of administrative remedies	Civil/criminal

(modified from Archambeault and Archambeault 1982)

been drastically changed and the number of resulting lawsuits has increased, as indicated in Chapter 1. Some of these lawsuits have assisted in bringing about certain reforms and have aided in establishing correctional standards, but much of the prisoner litigation has been frivolous and baseless in nature.

There have been a number of various legislative, judicial, and executive attempts to constrain prisoner litigation. For example, the "exhaustion of state court remedies doctrine" existed before its codification in 1948. Federal and state courts are bound to protect rights secured under the constitution. In *Rose v. Lundy* (1982) the United States Supreme Court held that state prisoners must exhaust state court remedies prior to filing for a writ of habeas corpus in federal court. Both state and federal habeas corpus petitions are available to prisoners for postconviction relief. In *Rose* the prisoner mixed state- and federal-court concerns and filed them before a federal court. The Court decided that 28 U.S.C. Section 2254 requires a federal court to dismiss a writ of habeas corpus containing any claims that have not been exhausted in state courts. The implication is significant since it lengthens the time for potential relief in these proceedings.

In 1980, Congress passed the Civil Rights of Institutionalized Persons Act (Section 1997e) to restrict the use of Section 1983 by state prisoners. Section 1997e requires prisoners to first exhaust state administrative remedies prior to filing a Section 1983 action. This measure authorizes district courts to stay a state prisoner's Section1983 action for a period not to exceed 180 days while the prisoner exhausts available administrative remedies. This act, however, only applies when such grievance systems within a state institution meet minimally accepted standards. Section 1997e denies state prisoners direct access to the courts by first requiring that they explore alternative remedies. Section 1997e, however, failed to decrease the number of Section 1983 lawsuits since prisoners filed more civil rights actions than before the act, averaging 28,000 annually between 1985 and 1996. The actual enforcement of the act by the courts was, in large part, discretionary.

The Prison Litigation Reform Act, and the Antiterrorism and Effective Death Penalty Act

In an effort to constrain the massive amount of prisoner litigation and to more carefully define a legitimate lawsuit, Congress enacted the Prison Litigation Reform Act Title VII in 1996 (PLRA) and Title I of the Antiterrorism and Effective Death Penalty Act (AEDPA). It was signed into law as part of HR 3019, the Omnibus Appropriations Bill, and was codified as 18 U. S.C. Section 3626. The PLRA pinpoints actions addressing conditions of confinement, and the AEDPA focuses on state and federal habeas corpus prisoner petitions (Bennett and del Carmen 1997).

Habeas corpus prisoner actions are petitions contesting the legality of a prisoner's confinement. In *Coffin v. Reichard* (1944) the Sixth Circuit Appellate Court expanded a prisoner's use of habeas corpus actions to include suits challenging the conditions of his confinement beyond the legality of a sentence. The United States Supreme Court in *Preiser v. Rodriguez* (1973) clarified a writ of habeas corpus, ruling that prisoners may only contest the legality of his or her confinement and not the validity or the duration of the confinement. Prisoners may not use a habeas corpus action to appeal the loss of good time. The AEDPA mandated substantial changes to habeas corpus procedures in federal court. Time limits for filing petitions were established, as was the requirement to consolidate all issues into one petition. Prior to filing second or successive petitions in the federal courts, prisoners must first obtain permission from the courts of appeals. The AEDPA also limited the scope of federal court review of the claims of state prisoners by requiring these prisoners to exhaust all state remedies first and obtain certificates of their ability to file habeas petitions in U.S. courts of appeals.

The PLRA did not curtail the right of a prisoner to file a lawsuit. The purpose of the new legislation was to limit the ability of prisoners to complain about prison conditions and to limit the jurisdiction of the federal courts to issue orders relieving conditions of confinement that allegedly violated the constitutional rights of prisoners (Palmer and Palmer 2004). Certain provisions were designed to discourage "abusive" filers from bringing suits against their keepers (Inmate litigation and the PLRA 1996; Schlanger 2003). The act also was intended to grant more authority to the states to manage their correctional systems and, at the same time, to limit the federal courts "hands-on" intervention of managing prisons from "the bench." The days of the courts' holding correctional administrators accountable for requirements not mandated by the Constitution and continuing to maintain some level of oversight for many years may be ending. There are numerous sections of the PLRA and only six will be discussed.

Section 1915 A(a) requires a federal court to screen all prisoner claims prior to docketing a case as soon as is reasonably feasible. Under this provision, the court is required to identify legitimate claims and dismiss all frivolous and malicious claims, as well as those claims failing to state a claim. This requirement applies to any civil lawsuit filed by a pretrail detainee or confined prisoner, adult or juvenile.

Section 802 of the act addresses appropriate remedies with respect to prison conditions and seeks to resolve these actions in the least intrusive means necessary to correct the violation. This section ostensibly pertains to consent decrees. A consent decree is a binding court agreement made outside of court between two conflicting parties and established with time limits. For example, correctional officials would agree to build more prisons to alleviate prison overcrowding within five years.

For years many correctional systems have entered into consent decrees (sometimes involuntarily), primarily owing to overcrowding, as one alternative in resolving a prisoner lawsuit. This provision of the act terminates existing court-ordered consent decrees, unless the court finds continuing constitutional violations. This section of the act mandates that courts shall not enter or approve consent decrees unless the decrees correct a harm found by the court and the court requires preliminary relief to correct such harm. This mandate can create a double-edge sword. On the one hand, terminating a consent decree requiring a population cap on a crowded prison population may appease legislatures. On the other hand, it may create a whole new set of problems for correctional personnel. The impact of this provision is observed as violating the separation of powers clause of the Constitution. At least one legal scholar states that consent decrees constitute final judgments which cannot be reopened by Congress (Alexander 1993).

Even though the PLRA terminates consent decrees, an Arizona district court refused to resolve a consent decree in *Taylor v. Arizona* (1997). The decree had been in effect since 1972, involving mainly overcrowding issues. The court held that such a provision by Congress was unconstitutional and was inimical to separation of powers. Compare, however, the ruling of the appellate court in *Ruiz v. U.S.* (2001). Texas prison officials moved to terminate a consent decree existing from the 1980s, which alleged numerous Eighth and Fourteenth Amendment violations. The lower court denied the motion, stating the PLRA was unconstitutional. The appellate court reversed the ruling, finding that the PLRA provisions did not violate separation of power principles or the due process clause. The court also found that the Final Judgment requiring population caps on the number of prisoners allowed to be housed in special groups of Texas prison units was a "prisoner release order" within the meaning of the act.

Iowa correctional authorities moved to terminate consent decrees that had regulated prison conditions for numerous years in *Hazen Ex Rel. LeGear v. Regan* (2000). The district court terminated the decrees and the prisoners appealed. The appeals court affirmed the district court's ruling, finding that it was within the power of Congress to remove state court jurisdiction to enforce consent decrees that were subject to termination under the PLRA. Contrast, however, the appellate court's decision in *Gilmore v. People of the State of California* (2000). Correctional officials sought to remove a consent decree governing prison conditions in accordance with the PLRA. The federal district court granted the motion for termination and the prisoners appealed. The appeals court held that the PLRA's termination provision is not a unilateral mandate to the courts to unconditionally prescribe the rule of decision. The appeals court further stated that the lower court should have examined the court record on the matter more closely.

Under Section 1983, there is no requirement for prisoners to first exhaust administrative remedies prior to filing under state law (Silver 2003). **Section 803** of the act, however, states that lawsuits brought by prisoners alleging conditions of confinement may not be filed until available administrative remedies have been exhausted. This means that grievances in the grievance system within the institution (or detention center) must first be exhausted before prisoners can file a lawsuit. Prior to the act, the federal courts could require prisoners to pursue internal remedies if such a system was certified by the Department of Justice or a federal district court. There appear to be at least two potential problems with this provision. First, the U.S. Supreme Court held in *McCarthy v. Madigan* (1992) that federal prisoners need not exhaust the prison grievance procedures prior to filing a Bivens action for damages. The Court did not believe that policy reasons required judicial imposition of an exhaustion requirement. Moreover, the Court also held that a nonprisoner plaintiff bringing suit under Section 1983 need not first exhaust available state judicial or administrative remedies (Patsy v. Florida Board of Regents 1982). The Court, however, in Farmer v. Brennan (1994) did indicate that prisoners bypassing "adequate" internal prison procedures might be denied injustice relief. The Court emphasized that "an inmate who needlessly bypasses such procedures may properly be compelled to pursue them" (at p. 1984).

In *Morgan v. Arizona Dept. of Corrections* (1997) the district court addressed the issue of exhausting the prison system's grievance procedures prior to a prisoner's submission of a Section 1983 action alleging an assault by other prisoners. The district court dismissed the action, finding that the prisoner failed to file an initial grievance under the corrections department's procedures, thereby depriving the court of jurisdiction because he had failed to exhaust his administrative remedies. According to the court, the PLRA has made exhaustion provisions mandatory rather than discretionary, and courts no longer possess the discretion in the absence of exhaustion. The prisoner had requested a thirty-day continuance to amend his complaint to prove he had exhausted his administrative remedies.

Requiring exhaustion of administrative remedies has created a second potential problem. Maahas and del Carmen (1995) reported that in 1995 few states had a certified grievance system in place-primarily because of the slow and cumbersome certification process. Theoretically, a grievance provision appears to assist in reducing the number of actions that can be filed by a prisoner, since it requires conflicts to first be presented at the institutional level. Further examination, however, reveals that requiring a prisoner first to file a grievance may be unconstitutional since the Supreme Court has traditionally held that such remedies need not first be exhausted. Also, if an institution does not have such a system in place, a lack of internal remedies may create more administrative problems than the act was intended to resolve. Additionally, this section of the act limits the awards for attorney fees and the recovery of damages.

Luong v. Hatt (1997) illustrates how a federal district court in Texas dismissed a prisoner civil action and denied the recovery of damages in conjunction with the PLRA. A prisoner brought action against prison officials alleging that they failed to protect him from an assault by other prisoners. The court dismissed the case, finding that the prisoner failed to demonstrate violations of his rights sufficient to support an order from the court requiring his transfer to another institution. The court also held that the prisoner could not recover damages in the absence of any indication that he suffered a "physical injury" within the meaning of the PLRA. According to the court, cuts, scratches, and minor bruises suffered by the prisoner did not constitute the requisite level of physical injury. In *Santiago v. Meinsen* (2000) the court concluded that a failure to protect from prisoner assault claim was subject to Section 1997e and that therefore exhaustion of administrative remedies was required even though monetary damages were not available.

The United States Supreme Court held in *Booth v. Churner* (2001) that Congress did indeed intend for prisoners to exhaust available administrative remedies prior to filing a civil action. Before submitting his civil action, Booth only exhausted step one of the institutional remedies of the Pennsylvania grievance system. He failed to complete steps two and three. The Court concluded that completion of every step is required by the statute. It is not enough to file a grievance only at the jail or institutional level: If further appeals are available, they must be completed prior to filing the action in federal court. Secondly, prisoners are not allowed to bypass the grievance system merely because they believe that doing so is an exercise in futility.

In a second case, the United States Supreme Court unanimously put the exhaustion requirement to rest in *Porter v. Nussle* (2002), ruling that prisoners (in jail and in prison) should not bring any action in federal court until such administrative remedies as are available have been exhausted. Nussle, a prisoner incarcerated in a Connecticut prison, bypassed the institution's grievance process and filed a Section 1983 claim of excessive force, alleging that several correction officers threw him up against a wall, kneed him in the back, struck him with their hands, and pulled his hair. He further claimed that one officer threatened to kill him should he report the beating. The district court dismissed the case, relying on the exhaustion of administrative remedies language of the PLRA. The Court of Appeals for the Second Circuit reversed the lower court's ruling, holding that exhaustion of administrative remedies was not required in prisoner claims of assault or excessive force under Section 1983. In making its decision the Court of Appeals made a distinction between excessive force claims and conditions of confinement claims. The Supreme Court granted certiorari in order to determine how the term "prison conditions" should be defined under the PLRA.

Relying on their former decision in *McCarthy v. Bronson* (1991), which authorized district judges to refer to magistrate judges to assess prisoner challenges to prison conditions, the Court determined that Congress did not intend to divide prisoner petitions into subcategories for judicial review (i.e., civil actions and habeas corpus petitions). The Court concluded that Congress did not intend to exempt use of force cases from prison condition cases under the PLRA and that, therefore, prisoners could not "skip" the administrative remedy process at the institutional level. Further, the Court concluded that it was unlikely that Congress, when it included in the PLRA a firm exhaustion requirement, meant to leave the need to the pleaders' option. Finally, the Court determined that the exhaustion of administrative remedies was important so that correctional administrators could know of correction officers' misconduct. Authorizing prisoners to bypass the internal grievance process excluded the possibility that administrators would take corrective actions when they might be warranted. The Court ruled that PLRA's exhaustion requirement applied to all prisoner suits about prison life, whether they involved general circumstances or particular episodes, and whether they alleged excessive force or some other wrong.

Section 804 of the PLRA addresses the issue of filing fees. Generally, the filing fee of a civil action is approximately $150.00, and previously the fee had been waived for prisoners. The law now requires prisoners to pay the full filing fee, and it requires institutional officials to verify the funds that the prisoner may have at his/her disposal. Additionally, this section provides the appointment of an attorney if any person is unable to afford one. Bonafide indigent prisoners will not be affected by this stipulation and they may still proceed in forma pauperis. The court shall dismiss the action at any time if it determines that the poverty claim is untrue. The lower courts have begun to rule on this provision. In Hampton v. Hobbs (1997) and Roller v. Gunn (1997) both courts found that the PLRA filing fee requirement was rationally related to curtailing prisoner litigation without merit and did not violate the equal protection clause of the Fourteenth Amendment.

Under **Section 807** of the act, fee awards to counsel representing a prisoner must be proportional to relief, and a portion must be derived from any monetary award (Silver 2003). The PLRA strictly limits attorneys fees to 150 percent of the total judgment, should the prisoner prevail. Generally, if an attorney brings the action on behalf of the prisoner, he/she will receive approximately $169.50 per hour for his/her work on the case (Schlanger 2003).

In *Boivin v. Black* (2000) fees of almost $8,000 were held proportionate to a $10,000 damages award. The award for attorney's fees was limited to the PLRA's requirement that it be no more than 150 percent of that established under 18 U.S.C. Section 3006A. In *Morrison v. Davis* (2000) the court awarded compensatory damages of $12,000 and punitive damages of $3,000 to a prisoner claiming that officers used excessive force, but it reduced the attorney's fees in accordance with the PLRA. The court found that awarding attorney's fees of $53,000 was not inherently disproportionate to the prisoner award. The court noted that the prisoner had vindicated a significant Eighth Amendment right and obtained a judgment that would arguably have a deterrent impact on others who might violate the same right.

In *Wolff v. Moore* (2000) a prisoner prevailed in an excessive force claim and sought attorney's fees. The court found the PLRA's cap on attorney's fees violated the equal protection rights of prisoners and was not rationally related to the PLRA objective of reducing frivolous lawsuits. The court held that the award of $29,840 that was based on an hourly rate of $225 and $135 for the attorneys involved was reasonable and would not be reduced.

A federal district court in Michigan ruled in *Spruytte v. Hoffner* (2001), that pursuant to the PLRA, attorney fees were limited to 150 percent of the total judgment award. Prisoners prevailed in a case challenging their transfer to other institutions within the state and filed a motion to recover fees and costs. The court awarded $8,450 in attorney fees and $3,474 in costs.

Section 809 provides for the revocation of earned good time or early-release credit of a federally incarcerated prisoner, should that prisoner file a malicious or false civil action. It is, however, not definitive what characterizes a "malicious" civil action. Some guidance is given in this section because the PLRA has its own version of the "three strikes and you're out" law. States that have legislated the three-strikes law place a prisoner in prison for life who has three convictions of the same type of crime or for violent crimes. The PLRA version provides that a prisoner who has had three previous lawsuits dismissed for failing to state a claim as frivolous or malicious is banned from filing further lawsuits without further paying the full filing fee in advance. The exception to this is if the prisoner is under "imminent danger or serious physical injury." Reaction by the courts to this provision appears to be split. In Lyon v. Vande Krol (1996) the court found the provision to be unconstitutional. In Abdul-Wadood v. Nathan (1996), however, the court upheld the provision.

Moreover, in its decision in *Lewis v. Casey* (1996), the United States Supreme Court added its own limitations to prisoner litigation. Arizona prisoners had filed an action claiming inadequate libraries at the prisons in violation of their First Amendment right to access to courts. The Court ruled that the constitution does not guarantee a "freestanding" right to a law library or legal assistance. It held, rather, that a constitutional right is violated when a prisoner can show that an "actual injury" hindered his ability to pursue a legal claim. Under *Lewis*, only when a lack of library services has caused the injury, will the prisoner have a valid claim. This decision has resulted in a marked decline in the availability of law libraries and other legal services to prisoners (Schlanger 2003).

Summary

This chapter has outlined the evolution of prisoners' rights, tracing their roots back to 1871 and the *Ruffin* decision. Since the *Cooper v. Pate* (1964) decision, prisoners have won the right to file civil lawsuits against their keepers for a host of alleged constitutional violations. Rulings in the 1960s through the early 1980s were generally decided in favor of prisoners' rights. Since the 1980s, prisoners have prevailed less in their civil rights violation claims, and their overall constitutional rights are now more restricted.

Judicial intervention regarding prisoners' rights issues has made a significant impact on the field of corrections. Correctional officials' practices and procedures were required to change in concert with the legal decisions. In the contemporary correctional arena, the astute executive and officer must show a legitimate penological objective in restricting a right of a prisoner to prevail in most prisoner civil actions. Many decisions discussed in this chapter underscore that correctional officials are operating their prisons within the legal framework and prevailing in a higher percentage than in past years.

While prisoners still possess the right to file a civil lawsuit, the passage of the PLRA by Congress, has made a profound impact on prisoner litigation, paralleling the significance of many Supreme Court decisions. Since its implementation, the number of civil actions filed by prisoners has dramatically decreased. The passage of the act however, appears to have raised some constitutional questions other than those it was designed to resolve. The Supreme Court has thus far supported the intentions of Congress, making it quite clear that all prisoners must first exhaust administrative remedies in all circumstances involving prison life prior to filing a civil action in court. The *Porter* (2002) and the *Booth* (2001) decisions underscore the intentions of Congress. Continued observation is required of the legal landscape to keep abreast of further developments which may either erode the PLRA or support it.

References

Archambeault, W. G., and B. J. Archambeault. 1982. *Correctional supervisory management*. Englewood Cliffs, NJ: Prentice-Hall.

Alexander, R., Jr. 1993. Slamming the federal courthouse door on inmates. *Journal of Criminal Justice* 21: 103–16.

Bennett, K., and R. V. del Carmen. 1997. A review and analysis of Prison Litigation Reform Act court decisions: Solution or aggravation? *The Prison Journal* 77: 405–55.

Branham, L. S. 2002. *Sentencing, corrections, and prisoner's rights.* 6th ed. St. Paul, MN: Thompson Publishing Co.

Call, J. E. 1995. The Supreme Court and prisoners' rights. *Federal Probation* 59: 36–46.

_____. 1996. Inmate litigation and the PLRA. *Corrections Compendium* 22: 1–3.

Jacobs, J. B. 1977. *Stateville: The penitentiary in mass society.* Chicago, IL: University of Chicago Press.

Kutak, R. J. 1976. Grim fairy tales for prison administrators. In *Issues in corrections and administration: Selected readings,* edited by George G. Killings, Paul F. Cromwell, Jr., and Bonnie J. Cromwell. St. Paul, MN: West Publishing Co.

Maahas, J. R., and R. V. del Carmen. 1995. Curtailing frivolous Section 1983 inmate litigation: Law, practices, and proposals. *Federal Probation* 59: 53–61.

McCoy, C. 1981. The impact of Section 1983 litigation on policymaking in corrections. *Federal Probation* 45: 17–23.

Morris, N., and D. J. Rothman. 1998. *The Oxford history of the prison: The practice of punishment in western society.* New York: Oxford University Press.

Palmer, J. W., and S. E. Palmer. 2004. *Constitutional rights of prisoners.* 7th ed. Cincinnati: Anderson Publishing.

Rothman, D. J. 1971. *The discovery of the asylum: Social order and disorder in the new republic.* Toronto: Little Brown and Co.

Schlanger, M. 2003. Inmate litigation. *Harvard Law Review* 6: 1557–1706.

Silver, I. 2003. *Police civil liability.* Newark, NJ: Matthew-Bender Publishers.

Wallace, D. H. 1992. *Ruffin v. Virginia* and slaves of the state: A nonexistent baseline of prisoners' rights jurisprudence. *Journal of Criminal Justice* 20: 333–42.

CASES CITED

Abdul-Wadood v. Nathan, 91 F. 3d 1023 (7th Cir. 1996)

Anderson v. Salant, 38 , 463 A. 425 (R. I. 1916)

Bell v. Wolfish, 441 U.S. 520 (1979)

Block v. Rutherford, 468 U.S. 576 (1984)

Boivin v. Black, 235 F. 3d 36 (1st Cir. 2000)

Booth v. Churner, 532 U.S. 731 (2001)

Bounds v. Smith, 430 U.S. 817 (1977)

Cochran v. Kansas, 316 U.S. 255 (1942)

Coleman v. Peyton, 302 F. 2d 905 (4th Cir. 1966)

Coffin v. Reichard, 143 F.2d 443 (6th Cir. 1944)

Cooper v. Pate, 378 U.S. 546 (1964)

Cruz v. Beto, 405 U.S. 319 (1972)

Daniels v. Williams, 474 U.S. 327 (1986)

Estelle v. Gamble, 429 U.S. 97 (1976)

Ex Parte Hull, 312 U.S. 546 (1941)

Farmer v. Brennan, 511 U.S. 825 (1994)

Gagnon v. Scarpelli, 411 U.S. 778 (1973)

Gilmore v. People of the State of California, 220 F. 3d 987 (9th Cir. 2000)

Hampton v. Hobbs, 196 F. 3d 1281 (6th Cir. 1997)

Haines v. Kerner, 404 U.S. 519 (1972)

Hazen v. Ex Rel. LeGear v. Regan, 208 F. 3d 697 (8th Cir. 2000)

Helling v. McKinney, 509 U.S. 25 (1993)

Hudson v. Palmer, 468 U.S. 517 (1984)

Hudson v. McMillian, 503 U.S. 1 (1992)

In re Birdsong, 39 F. 599 (S. D. Ga. 1889)

Johnson v. Avery, 393 U.S. 483 (1969)

Jones v. North Carolina Prisoners' Labor Union Inc., 433 U.S. 119 (1977)

Illinois v. Russell, 245 Ill. 268, 91, 1075 (N. E. 1910)

Kusah v. McKorkle, 318, 170 P. 100, 1023 (Wash. 1918)

Lewis v. Casey, 516 U.S. 804 (1996)

Topeka v. Boutwell, 20, 35 P. 819 (52 Kan. 1894)

Turner v. Safely, 482 U.S. 78 (1987)

Whitley v. Albers, 475 U.S. 312 (1986)

Wilson v. Seiter, 501 U.S. 294 (1991)

Wolff v. McDonnell, 418 U.S. 539 (1974)

Wolff v. Moore, 104 F. Supp. 2d 892 (S.D. Ohio 2000)

Younger v. Gilmore, 404 U.S. 15 (1971)

CHAPTER 4

CIVIL LIABILITY
AND THE MECHANICS
OF SECTION 1983 ACTIONS

*While persons imprisoned for crime enjoy many protections
of the Constitution, it is also clear that imprisonment carries
with the circumscription or loss of many significant rights.*

Bell v. Wolfish 1979

Federal civil lawsuits arising from allegations of constitutional rights deprivations by correctional officials are filed in accordance with Section 1983. It provides remedies for violations of federal rights. Section 1983 lawsuits may include claims of correctional personnel, prisoners' claims of abuse by authorities, issues of school desegregation, and other institutional reform litigation. Since the 1960s, these actions have comprised the majority of civil litigation against correctional personnel and entities. This chapter will provide an overview of the historical and contemporary use of Section 1983 and the various methods used to bring a constitutional claim before the courts.

HISTORY OF SECTION 1983

At the conclusion of the Civil War, Congress enacted the Civil Rights Act (Title 18 U.S. Code, Section 242, April 9, 1866) to put an end to lawless activities of the Ku Klux Klan. The act provided federal criminal penalties for state and local officials who violated guaranteed rights of citizens (Esienberg and Schwab 1987; Gressman 1992). In April 1871, Title 42 United States Code, Section 1983, was passed by Congress, which provided a vehicle for citizens to file suit against violations of guaranteed constitutional rights. Section 1983 added civil remedies to the criminal penalties which had been established in 1866.

Prior to Reconstruction, there existed only a handful of constitutional provisions which afforded protections against actions by state and federal governments. State courts and the common law were virtually the only protections for citizens' pursuits of life, liberty, and property. The conclusion of the Civil War changed this. Between 1866 and 1870, Congress enacted three constitutional amendments: the Thirteenth Amendment (the abolition of slavery), the Fourteenth Amendment (Due Process and Equal Protection clauses), and the Fifteenth Amendment (the right of freedom from discrimination in voting). In 1866, Congress enforced the Thirteenth Amendment by passing a civil rights statute guaranteeing the rights to African-American citizens. In 1867, congress enacted a habeas corpus statute which gave those held in state facilities the right to challenge in federal court the constitutionality of their incarceration. Section 1983 came at the end of a five-year period when Congress was moving quickly to pass and enforce provisions for protecting constitutional rights of citizens and for providing remedies for violations of those rights.

Prior to the enactment of Section 1983, the only option for redressing a violation of a constitutional right was through provisions of the common law, and those actions were heard in state courts. Section 1983 allowed constitutional violations to be heard in federal court. From its enactment in 1871 to 1961, Section 1983 lay virtually dormant, since it was used in only twenty-four cases.

For ninety years Section 1983 lawsuits were rarely filed against governmental officials since they were immune from suit. In two famous cases, however, the United States Supreme Court began to expand their interpretation of who could be sued under Section 1983. In *United States v. Classic* (1941), the Supreme Court held that officials acting under color of law, as election officials had done in Louisiana when they rigged an election, could be held liable for misuse of power by virtue of state law. Further interpretation of Section 1983 was expanded in *Screws v. United States* (1945), when the Court ruled that acting under color of law also meant acting under pretense of law. In *Screws*, Robert Hall, an African-American, was beaten to death by officers who arrested him for theft. The officers were prosecuted under Section 242 for criminal violation of civil rights, and the Court stated that "acts of officers who undertake to perform their official duties are included whether they hew to the line of their authority or overstep it" (at pg. 111).

ESSENTIAL COMPONENTS OF SECTION 1983

Title 42 U.S.C., Section 1983, is primarily known today as Section 1983 litigation. It was enacted by Congress for three primary reasons: (1) to redress unconstitutional laws; (2) to provide a federal forum absent a state court remedy; and (3) to provide a federal remedy when the state court remedy was available in theory but not in fact. According to Section 1983,

> Every person who under color of any statute, ordinance, regulation, custom, or usage, of any State or territory, subjects, or causes to be subjected, any citizen of the United States or other persons within the jurisdiction thereof to the deprivation of any right, privileges, or immunities secured by the Constitution and laws, shall be liable to the party injured in an action at law, suit in equity, or other proper proceeding for redress.

Section 1983 itself does not create substantive rights or jurisdiction in the federal courts (*Chapman v. Houston Welfare Rights Organization* [1979]) and is therefore procedural. The plaintiff suing under Section 1983 must specifically plead federal jurisdiction under the appropriate jurisdiction statute (*Monroe v. Pape* 1961). Under the precedent set by *Monroe*, the plaintiff need not first bring separate actions under state and federal law.

This law has four important components. First, the term "every person" has been defined twice by the Untied States Supreme Court. In the landmark decision, *Monroe v. Pape* (1961), the Supreme Court established the foundation for federal civil liability. In *Monroe* the Court defined a person within the meaning of Section 1983 as an individual officer. A governmental employee may be sued for monetary damages in his or her individual capacity for acts performed while discharging his or her duties. A suit against a state employee acting in his/her "official capacity" imposes liability against the entity the employee represents and therefore cannot be brought, since the Eleventh Amendment prohibits lawsuits against the state (*Brandon v. Holt* [1985]).

Prior to *Monroe*, it was extremely difficult to hold criminal justice officials liable under Section 1983 owing to the requirement of acting under "color of law." *Monroe* broadened the language of this concept. In the early morning hours, thirteen Chicago police officers broke into Monroe's house and rousted him and his family out of bed, made him stand naked in the living room, and ransacked the house. He was arrested and detained at the police department for ten hours and later released. Monroe was never prosecuted but did file a Section 1983 lawsuit for an illegal search and seizure and violation of his Constitutional rights. The United States Supreme Court granted certiorari to examine whether the Chicago police officers and the City should be liable under Section 1983 for the officers' actions. The Court ruled that the officers' actions, which were clothed in state law, constituted acting under color of law and that they misused their authority and power as police officers. The Court held that the officers' actions were "action under color of law" within the meaning of Section 1983, even if what they did also happened to be in violation of state law. The Court concluded that the City of Chicago was not liable as Congress had not intended to bring municipalities within the provisions of Section 1983.

Justice Douglas's opinion was significant for several reasons. First, the decision resurrected the rarely used Section 1983 after a lengthy period of disuse. Douglas stated that "Section 1983 makes a man responsible for the natural consequences of his actions." Prior to this decision it was difficult to hold public officials liable for their actions under Section 1983. Second, the case was a seminal one since it literally opened the floodgates of the courts, ensuring that citizens who claimed their constitutionally protected rights had been violated by public officer's actions could now bring a civil suit against that officer. Third, the decision interpreted the following language in Section 1983: "[E]very person acting under color of law...may be held liable." Every person was defined as "every officer." As a result, when officers perform their sworn duties by virtue of state law and misuse their authority, they may be held liable for such abuse of power. An officer will be held liable under Section 1983 when an officer misuses his/her authority and violates an individual's constitutionally protected rights.

The Court further concluded that Monroe did not have to first exhaust alternative remedies available in state court prior to lodging his claim in federal court. This decision, however, did not include liability against governmental entities, but only against individual officers. This case helped to pave the way for liability to be imposed against correctional officers.

In a second decision, *Monell v. Department of Social Services of the City of New York* (1978), the Supreme Court further expanded the definition of "person" to include local governments and their employees. Prior to *Monell*, local governments were held immune from Section 1983 liability under the rationale that they were not "persons" as defined by law. The Supreme Court concluded in *Monell* that municipalities, as well as other governing bodies, are defined as "persons" within the meaning of Section 1983 (Figure 4.1).

The Court in *Monell* held that governmental bodies may be held liable when an officer acts pursuant to a custom or official policy of the agency and the action violates the constitutional rights of a person. Plaintiffs may now sue for and recover damages from county, city, municipalities, and other units

Figure 4.1   *Monell v. Department of Social Services of the City of New York, et al.* (1978)

Female employees of the Department of Social Services filed a Section 1983 action against the Commissioner and the Department of Social Services, the Board of Education, its chancellor, the City of New York, and the mayor of New York. The action alleged that the policy of the department required pregnant employees to take unpaid leaves of absence before they were medically necessary. The plaintiffs sought injunctive relief and back pay for prior periods of leave.

Prior to the District Court's decision, the department changed the policy and the court ruled the issue of injunctive relief mute. Relying on *Monroe v. Pape* (1961), the court ruled against the plaintiffs on the back-pay issue. The plaintiffs appealed and the Court of Appeals affirmed the lower court's decision. The United States Supreme Court granted certiorari to determine if municipalities or local governments could be held liable under Section 1983 when an unconstitutional act is the result of a governmental policy or custom.

The Supreme Court ruled that governmental entities are "persons" that can be sued directly under Section 1983. They can be sued for monetary damages as well as injunctive and declaratory relief. Governmental entities may not be sued under claims of *respondeat superior* in Section 1982 actions. The prior decision in *Monroe v. Pape* was overruled to the extent that it included governmental departments within the definition of "every person" for purposes of liability.

The ruling expands the definition of "every person" under the language of Section 1983. Plaintiffs may sue governmental agencies for officer conduct pursuant to official policies and customs of the department. Governmental agencies are no longer immune from liability under Section 1983.

---

of local governments for the actions of their officers. A more detailed discussion of supervisory liability will be presented in Chapter 10.

However, the Supreme Court has narrowed the scope of liability under Section 1983. In *Quern v. Jordan* (1979) the Court held that states are not considered "persons" subject to suit under Section1983 and that local governments cannot be sued for punitive damages in Section 1983 actions (*City of Newport v. Fact Concerts*, 1981). Further, the Supreme Court ruled in *Will v. Michigan Department of State Police* (1989) that state officials cannot be sued for violating a person's constitutional rights when they act in their official capacity. The court emphasized that Congress did not intend to include states or state agencies within the definition of "person" for purposes of Section 1983 liability. Plaintiffs may, however, sue under Section 1983 a state and state agencies for prospective injunctive relief (*Kentucky v. Graham* [1985]).

State officials can be sued in their official capacity under Section 1983 for injunctive relief. When sued in their official capacity for damages, state officials are not considered "persons" in the legal sense, since the lawsuit, in effect, is one against the state. Any damages awarded would be paid by out by the state's treasury (Branham 1998).

Acting Under Color of Law

Second, in order to be held liable, a person must be acting under "color of law": The official must be acting within the scope of his authority at the time of the constitutional deprivation. This phrase normally means an officer or official has misused his or her official powers granted by virtue of the law in the office the officer or official was sworn to uphold (*Monroe v. Pape* 1961). The United States Supreme Court in *West v. Atkins* (1988) further stated that employees who carry out their official responsibilities act under color of state law and are state actors even when they act in violation of state law. The courts have broadened this phrase to include actions taken under auspices of state and local laws, ordinances, and agency rules. Actions which exceed the law and the scope of authority constitute acting under "color of law." For example, brutalizing a prisoner after a prison disturbance would constitute action outside the scope of the officer's authority.

Actions taken under color of federal laws by federal employees are excluded. *Bivens* actions are not incorporated under Section 1983. Off-duty actions of an officer cannot be the basis of litigation unless the officer uses police equipment or uses his authority as an "official" employee.

Inquiries by the courts for what constitutes acting under color of law require a determination of the "nature of the officer's act, not simply his duty status" (Vaughn and Coomes 1995). Using the totality of circumstances analysis, courts determine acting under color of law by examining if criminal justice personnel invoke power, if they discharge duties routinely associated with their work, or if they use their authority to lure plaintiffs into compromising positions. Further, courts hold that officers act under color of law if they wear their uniforms, draw their firearms, identify themselves correctional officers, place suspects under arrest, detain and confine them, file official reports, and otherwise hold themselves out as official personnel for a governmental agency (Vaughn and Coomes 1995).

In *Richardson v. McKnight* (1997) the United States Supreme Court expanded the language of "acting under color of law." The Court ruled that private correction officers working for privately operated state correctional facilities could be held liable in Section 1983 claims. This decision means that private individuals who are under contract with or performing public functions for a state agency can likely be sued under Section 1983.

The Thrust of Section 1983 Actions

Third, the alleged violation must rise to a constitutionally protected right violation. The plaintiff must show that the conduct of the defendant caused a violation of a constitutional right or federal law that can be enforced in accordance with Section 1983. Section 1983 creates no rights but is a vehicle to redress violations of the Bill of Rights and certain federal statutes. Only a person who "subjects" another to a constitutional violation or "causes" another to be subjected can be held liable under Section 1983 (Branham 1998).

Mere negligence is not actionable since a Section 1983 claim but must be brought in state court (*Daniels v. Williams* (1986)). In *Daniels,* the prisoner brought a claim of negligence against a detention officer for leaving a pillow case on a stairway, causing him to slip. The prisoner claimed he had a constitutional right to be free from injury under the due process clause of the Fourteenth Amendment. The United States Supreme Court ruled that prisoners may not use civil rights actions (Section 1983) to sue prison officials for negligence. In this decision, the Court overturned one part of a former decision which had suggested that negligence could constitute a claim under the due process clause when the plaintiff had no other effective state remedy (*Parratt v. Taylor* 1981). Further, violations of city ordinances or state laws are not actionable under Section 1983.

Using Section 1983

Finally, a person filing suit must be a protected person within the meaning of the act. This means that anyone under the jurisdiction of the United States may bring suit under Section 1983. Section 1983 provisions authorize any citizen in the United States to file a federal civil lawsuit. Pretrial detainees, probationers, convicted prisoners, and parolees may also file Section 1983 lawsuits. Corporations are excluded by law from filing Section 1983 lawsuits. The law also has been interpreted to mean that aliens legally in the United States may also file litigation under Section 1983 (*Graham v. Richardson* 1975). Some courts have extended the Fourteenth Amendment Due Process and Equal Protection Clause in Section 1983 cases to apply to illegal aliens.

A plaintiff may file a Section 1983 lawsuit in state and federal court simultaneously, although a majority of such suits are filed in federal court (*Maine v. Thiboutot* 1980). Plaintiffs are subject to statute of limitation requirements when filing a Section 1983 lawsuit. Statute of limitations are laws stipulating a certain time period required for the action to be filed in court from the date the action occurred. In *Wilson v. Garcia* (1985), the Supreme Court determined that Section 1983 cases are "personal injury" cases and that the same statues of limitations used in state courts be used. Generally speaking, the time period for such limitations is three years.

Bivens Actions

Section 1983 only authorizes actions for violations of protected constitutional rights that are incident to situations which occur under "color of state law." Federal prisoners may not file Section 1983 claims but must file legal actions under the Federal Tort Claims Acts (FTCA) (28 U.S.C. Section 1346 (b) and Section 2671-2680). The FTCA waives immunity of the federal government but not its employees. Federal employees are responsible for ensuring that the rights of individuals are protected just like their state and local counterparts.

A plaintiff files claims against federal employees under provisions established in the United States Supreme Court's decision in *Bivens v. Six Unknown Federal Narcotics Agents* (1971). Federal agents entered Bivens' apartment to search for evidence of drug violations. Bivens was restrained, searched, and arrested. The agents conducted the search without a warrant or probable cause, thereby violating his Fourth Amendment rights. Bivens sued the agents, claiming mental suffering and damages from the invasion of his privacy. The Supreme Court found in favor of Bivens and determined that the agents were acting within the scope of their employment, giving rise to a cause of action.

Plaintiffs may file FTCA claims only against federal employees and within two years of the alleged violation. The Supreme Court has specifically upheld filing *Bivens* actions for violations of the Fifth Amendment's due process clause (*Davis v. Passman* 1979) and for federal prisoners claiming Eighth Amendment violations (*Carlson v. Green* 1980; *Farmer v. Brennan* 1994).

In *Muhammed v. United States* (1998) a federal prisoner filed an action pursuant to the Federal Torts Claims Act for failing to transfer him to a medical facility. The court found that the Bureau of Prisons' employees were negligent in not assigning him to a medical facility during the two-and-half years following the prisoner's complaint that he had been unable to walk and had requested a wheel chair and a cane. The court awarded the prisoner $30,000 for physical pain and $15,000 for mental anguish.

In *Bultema v. U.S.* (2002) a federal prisoner brought an action against the warden under the FTCA claiming his rights were violated when he fell from an upper bunk, injuring his knee. He claimed that the bunks were defective and unsafe in that there were no guardrails or ladders to assist him in climbing to the top bunk or from falling out while sleeping. Medical personnel had cleared him to sleep on a lower bunk and not allowing him to do so was the proximate cause of his injury. The court granted summary judgment to the warden, ruling that the prisoner contributed to his own injury and that under the FCTA, the warden had discretion as to what bunk he assigned prisoners.

In *Papa v. U.S.* (2002) the widow of an alien who had been killed by another detainee while being held by the Immigration and Naturalization Service (INS) brought a *Bivens* action under the FTCA. The appeals court affirmed, ruling that the officer knowingly placed the deceased in a cell where harm was likely to occur to him, in disregard of, or with deliberate indifference to his, due process rights. The court noted that limited rights under the due process clause extend to detained aliens.

As previously mentioned, the United States Supreme Court held in the *Richardson v. McKnight* (1997) case that correction officers working in a private correctional facility may be sued for violations of a prisoner's protected right. The Supreme Court addressed a slightly different issue in *Correctional Services Corporation v. Malesko* (2001) when it reviewed the question of whether a prisoner could sue a private entity like a corporation for allegedly violating the prisoner's constitutional rights. Malesko, a federal prisoner, was serving a sentence of 18 months for federal securities fraud and was placed in a Federal Bureau of Prisons halfway-house operated by Correctional Services Corp (CSC). CSC is a private corporation, under contract with federal, state, and local governments to provide correctional supervision of prisoners. During his incarceration, Malesko was diagnosed with congestive heart failure and later assigned to the halfway-house. He was assigned to the fifth floor and allowed to use the elevator to gain access to his room. Soon after his assignment, CSC instituted a policy that only prisoners with rooms above the fifth floor could use the elevator. Malesko was still allowed by staff to use the elevator since they were aware of his heart condition. Allegedly, a CSC employee, however, prevented Malesko from using the elevator one day, even when Malesko reminded him of his medical condition. While climbing the stairs, Malesko experienced a heart attack, fell, and injured his ear, allegedly causing problems with his balance. Malesko also contended that ten days earlier he had run out of his prescribed medication and that CSC had failed to replenish it. Subsequently, he filed an action against CSC and individual defendants, claiming that they were negligent in refusing him the use of the elevator, and sought millions in damages.

The district court treated the complaint as a *Bivens* action. The court dismissed the suit, holding that *Bivens* actions may be filed against an individual, not a corporate entity. The Second Circuit Court of Appeals held that private entities should be held liable under *Bivens* to accomplish important goals of providing a remedy for a constitutional violation when they act under "color of law." The Supreme Court granted certiorari and reversed the appellate court's holding. In a 5 to 4 decision, the Court held that the *Bivens* remedy against individuals acting under color of law should not extend to allow recovery against a private corporation operating a half-way house under contract with the Federal Bureau of Prisons. The Court reasoned that prisoners may use *Bivens* to hold liable individual employees but not private entities. To do otherwise would allow claimants to focus their collection efforts on the entity and not on the individual directly responsible for the injury, which would undercut the deterrent effect of the *Bivens* remedy.

The Court made it clear that prisoners may only sue individual employees under *Bivens* but not the private company providing the service. This decision applies to state prisoners in the same position as Malesko. Hence, only the governmental employee/officer is subject to suit for alleged constitutional violations, not the governmental agency that employs the officer/employee.

Remedies under Section 1983

Filing a Section 1983 lawsuit in federal court allows the plaintiff a range of remedies should the plaintiff prevail. A prevailing plaintiff may be awarded monetary damages and injunctive or declaratory relief. As ordered by a court, injunctive relief prohibits a certain practice that a governmental entity may be performing which violates a constitutionally protected right of another. Declaratory relief, the court's opinion, may determine that a regulation or practice is unconstitutional without necessarily requiring anything be done.

Another benefit in filing a lawsuit in federal court is that the process of discovery (obtaining documents from the defendant) is more simplified than in state court. Since 1976, the prevailing plaintiff's attorney may be awarded attorney fees. These features make filing a Section 1983 lawsuit attractive and more likely that plaintiffs and their attorneys will file Section 1983 lawsuits against criminal justice personnel.

Damages awarded in Section 1983 litigation include nominal, compensatory, or punitive damages. Compensatory damages are awarded for an injury sustained, pain and suffering, loss of earnings, emotional distress, medical expenses, and loss of property (*Carey v. Piphus* [1978]). In *Carey* the United

States Supreme Court ruled that the cardinal premise in American jurisprudence is the awarding of compensatory damages for a violation of a constitutionally protected right.

In *Davis v. Moss* (1994) a prisoner brought a Section 1983 claim alleging cruel and unusual punishment in violation of the Eighth Amendment. During a riot a correctional officer shoved the compliant prisoner down a fire escape. The prisoner sustained two permanently damaged discs in his lower back, causing him to undergo surgery. The court determined the prisoner was entitled to $10,000 for pain and suffering and $25,000 in punitive damages. The imposition of punitive damages was necessary to deter the officer and other officers from using excessive and malicious force in the future.

A female prisoner in *Berry v. Oswalt* (1998) won a verdict claiming she had been raped by one correctional officer and sexually harassed by a second. The second officer was found to have harassed the prisoner by attempting to perform nonroutine pat down searches, propositioning the prisoner, and making sexual comments. The appeals court found that the officers violated her Eighth Amendment rights and awarded her $40,000 in compensation and $15,000 in punitive damages.

Punitive damages may be awarded for particular blameworthy conduct on the part of the defendant. In *Smith v. Wade* (1983) the Supreme Court held that actual malice is not necessary to recover punitive damages; reckless or callous indifference to constitutional rights is sufficient (Figure 4.2). The court in *Franklin v. Aycock* (1986) assessed $5,000 in punitive damages each against three detention officers. For eight minutes they had kicked a prisoner shackled in bed for no reason.

In *Lowrance v. Coughlin* (1994) a prisoner filed a Section 1983 action for being transferred from prison to prison and kept in segregation as retaliation for exercising his free expression of religious rights. The prisoner alleged he was subjected to retaliatory cell searches, spent 115 days in segregation, and had a knee surgery delayed for almost two years after the medical diagnosis. The court found evidence to support the prisoner's claim and awarded him $132,000 in compensatory damages and $25,000 in punitive damages.

Plaintiffs filing Section 1983 lawsuits may also seek declaratory and injunctive relief. When awarding a declaratory judgment, the court may declare a state statute or regulation unconstitutional. Declaratory relief in federal court is discretionary, since the court may award compensation for rights violated. For example, a court may examine a correctional department's policy on use of force, declare it unconstitutional, and require the department to rewrite it in accordance with constitutional provisions. When authorizing injunctive relief, a court goes further in providing redress to the plaintiff. The court may prohibit defen-

Figure 4.2   *Smith v. Wade* (1983)

Wade was voluntarily placed in protective segregation in a youthful correctional facility in Missouri since he complained of physical abuse by other prisoners. Classification officer Smith placed Wade in a cell with another prisoner and later placed a third prisoner in the same cell who had a history of fighting. Smith was aware of the third prisoner's assaultive history, ignored it, and failed to determine if other cells were available. Later Wade was sexually assaulted and filed a Section 1983 claim against Smith, other officers, and correctional officials, asserting his Eighth Amendment rights had been violated. Wade prevailed and was awarded $25,000 in compensatory damages and $5,000 in punitive damages. The appellate court affirmed the decision, and Smith appealed the punitive damage award to the United States Supreme Court.

The Supreme Court examined the issue of whether a jury could award punitive damages against an officer who acts with reckless disregard or indifference to the safety of a prisoner and his protected constitutional rights. The Court concluded that a jury is permitted to assess punitive damages in a civil action where an officer's action is motivated by malicious intent and if the defendant acted with callous indifference or reckless disregard to a prisoner's rights. Punitive damages may be awarded for particularly egregious and blameworthy misconduct marked by evil intent or motive, as demonstrated by the defendant's actions.

This case is significant since by awarding punitive damages, the jury is sending a message that such actions are outrageous and the award is meant to punish that officer for such actions. Punitive damages may be awarded when a defendant's actions were motivated by malicious intent and when the defendant acted in a callous, reckless manner without regard to the safety or rights of the prisoner. This decision makes it less difficult for a plaintiff to recover punitive damages.

---

dants from engaging in certain unconstitutional conduct in the future or mandate that they take certain steps to avoid further violations of the Constitution.

Injunctive relief may be afforded in the form of a temporary restraining order, a preliminary injunction, or a permanent injunction. Courts can grant a broad range of injunctive orders in Section 1983 lawsuits. In *Harris v. Angelina County, Tex.* (1994) prisoners filed a class action Section 1983 suit challenging conditions of confinement in a detention facility. The district court found in favor of the prisoners and issued injunctive relief in the form of a population cap. The county appealed and the Fifth Circuit Appellate Court upheld the lower court's decision, finding evidence that the population of the facility exceeded its capacity, which led to the denial of the basic human needs of the prisoners. The court further held that the county was aware of the overcrowding and the resulting conditions. In an effort to limit federal court intrusion into the state's operation of prisons and jails after a finding of unconstitutional conditions in a facility, the courts have normally afforded officials the opportunity to develop a plan to bring conditions into compliance with the Constitution (*Lewis v. Casey*, 1996).

Attorney's Fees

Section 1983 does not on its face require the awarding of attorney fees. Awarding of attorney fees is discretionary on the part of the court. Congress modified the American Rule in the Civil Rights Attorney's Fees Awards Act of 1976 (42 U.S.C.A. Section 1988). The "Rule" is a tradition in common law that each party pay for its own counsel costs, win or lose (*Alyeska Pipeline Service Co. v. Wilderness Society*, 1975). The statute provides a financial incentive to bring lawsuits which might not otherwise attract attorneys, either because only injunctive relief is sought or because the likelihood of substantial damages is uncertain. The Attorney's Fees Awards Act states (in part):

> [T]he court, in its discretion, may allow the prevailing party, other than the United States, a reasonable attorney's fee as part of the costs, except that in any action brought against judicial officer for an act or omission taken in such officer's capacity such office shall not be held liable for any costs, including attorney's fees, unless such action was clearly in excess of such officer's jurisdiction.

In order for an attorney to recover attorney fees, the plaintiff must obtain at least some actual relief on the merits of his or her claim. Plaintiffs who proceed in a Section 1983 lawsuit *pro se* (on their own behalf) are not entitled to attorney fees even when they prevail. Further, the Supreme Court has held that prevailing plaintiffs, not prevailing defendants sued under Section 1983, should recover attorney's fees (*Hughes v. Rowe* [1980]). There must be a trial to recover attorney's fees. In *Maher v. Gagne* (1980), the Supreme Court ruled that the plaintiffs were entitled to attorney's fees even though the case was settled through consent decree agreement. This ruling is significant in many prisoner rights suits that challenge conditions of confinement in prisons and jails and that are settled by a consent decree.

In determining the appropriate amount to award an attorney under Section 1988, the Supreme Court, in *Hensley v. Eckerhart* (1983), established a figure known as "lodestar." This figure is computed by multiplying the number of hours reasonably expended on the litigation by a reasonable hourly rate. This computation is completed at the end of the litigation. The following factors are normally considered in calculating the lodestar figure: (1) the time and labor required; (2) the novelty and difficulty of the questions; (3) the skill requisite to perform the legal service properly; (4) the preclusion of other employment by the attorney owing to the acceptance of the case; (5) the customary fee for similar work; (6) whether the fee is fixed or contingent; (7) time limitations imposed by the client or the circumstances; (8) the amount in dispute and the results obtained; (9) the experience, reputation, and ability of the attorneys; (10) the "undesirability" of the case; (11) the nature and length of the professional relationship with the client; and (12) awards in similar cases. In 1996, however, Congress placed a cap on the hourly rate utilized under Section 1988 in prisoner rights litigation. In accordance with the PLRA, the hourly formula used in determining the fee by federal judicial courts cannot exceed 150 percent of the total award.

Payment for Damages

Correctional personnel are generally represented by counsel provided by their employing agency in a civil lawsuit. Law or written policy in most state agencies provides for representation through the attorney general's office, which is the legal counsel of the state. As long as the officer acted within the scope of his or her authority, and held liable, the state will pay all or part of the award.

County sheriff's departments are different. The county's attorney's office normally will defend a civil lawsuit filed against the officer or governmental entity. In many jurisdictions across the country, local departments participate in a risk-management pool and retain legal counsel through this provision. Still other departments retain legal representation on their own to defend departmental personnel. Most agencies will provide an attorney for the officer, but such a decision is made by local administrators on a case-by-case basis. This policy may be addressed in the department's policy manual, and officers should investigate the current status of the policy at their local department. If the agency decides not decide to provide an attorney, the officer must provide one at his or her expense.

Should an officer lose a civil lawsuit, generally his or her employing agency will pay the award. Many states provide indemnification for state employees, and the amount varies. Most agencies will not indemnify blatant and outrageous actions outside the officer's authority. If the court awards more than the indemnification, the officer pays the difference. Indemnification also varies in local agencies. If the court also grants punitive damages, the individual officer must pay the amount on his or her own. The concept underscoring punitive damages is to punish the officer for blameworthy conduct, and payment by the agency would be contrary to public policy. Correctional personnel should be aware of how their agency provides legal representation in the event of a civil lawsuit and the arrangement for paying an award should the officer be liable.

OFFICIAL IMMUNITY

There are several types of defenses that can be asserted in Section 1983 claims. Only two will be addressed. One is absolute immunity and the other is qualified immunity. The purpose of either type of immunity is to prevent the fear of being sued as well as officials being hindered from performing their job functions.

Absolute Immunity

While Section 1983 authorizes legal actions against "every person" (officers and governmental agencies) while acting "under of color of law," it does provide for several defenses. For example, the Court ruled in *Tenney v. Brandhove* (1951) that state legislators possess absolute immunity from Section 1983 liability. Personal immunity defenses can be asserted by officials sued for damages while in their personal capacities. Such defenses cannot, however, be invoked by officials sued while in their official capacities (*Kentucky v. Graham*, 1985).

In *Cleavinger v. Saxner* (1985) the United States Supreme Court determined who could qualify for absolute immunity. Prisoners confined in a Federal Bureau of Prisons facility filed a *Bivens* action against three members of the disciplinary committee that had found them guilty of violating prison rules. The prisoners claimed their Fifth Amendment rights were violated and the district court agreed, awarding each prisoner compensation of $4,500. The appellate court affirmed the decision, and the United States Court granted certiorari to determine whether the disciplinary committee should be afforded absolute immunity.

The Court concluded that only certain types of "functional categories" possessed absolute immunity, such as the president, judges, prosecutors, and parole board members. Members of a prison disciplinary committee possessed only "qualified immunity." In determining who could be afforded absolute immunity, the Court reasoned that immunity analysis rests on functional categories, not on the status of the defendant. Absolute immunity is not dependent on the rank or title or "location within the government" but on the nature of the responsibilities of the individual official. The Court rejected the idea that the disciplinary committee functioned like a judge in court. The decision applies to all public officers and officials, such as corrections officers, police officers, probation and parole officers, juvenile officers, and supervisory and administrative personnel.

Qualified Immunity and Good Faith

Corrections personnel are afforded the affirmative defense of qualified immunity (*Procunier v. Navarette*, 1978). In *Harlow v. Fitzgerald* (1982) the United States Supreme Court established that the sole inquiry into an officer's entitlement to qualified immunity is whether the officer knew or should have known that he was violating the constitutional rights of the plaintiff. The Court held that a judge may determine whether a law was clearly established at the time an action occurred and whether the law forbade conduct not previously identified as unlawful. While *Harlow* did not involve correction officers (it involved aides in the Nixon White House), in *Anderson v. Creighton* (1987) the Court stated that the *Harlow* standard applied to public officers. In *Anderson*, federal and other law enforcement officers made a search of a home without a warrant, believing a bank robber to be hiding there. The home owners sued under Section 1983, claiming the officers violated their Fourth Amendment right against unreasonable searches and seizures. The Court of Appeals overturned the lower court's granting of summary judgment stating the officers did not have probable cause. The United States Supreme Court held that the proper inquiry is a matter of law, whether an officer reasonably believes his actions are lawful under the circumstances. If they are, then dismissal prior to discovery is required.

This decision has established the "good faith" defense. This defense is an affirmative defense and tied to the discretionary powers of the court. A defense of good faith means that the actions of the officer were in accordance with the established law at the time of the incident. The implications are important. First, an officer must know the basic constitutional and federal rights of prisoners. Acquisition of such knowledge can come from college courses, basic training, in- service training, and reading of case decisions. A good faith defense implies that officers must keep abreast of changes in the law in order to perform their legal duties. Officers must perform their duties within the parameters of the law. Secondly, administrators must keep officers updated with the law, revise their policies and guidelines, and inform officers of such revisions as they apply to changing court decisions.

In *Ralston v. McGovern* (1999) a prisoner alleged under Section 1983 that an officer denied him medical care in violation of his Eighth Amendment. The appeals court reversed the lower court's summary judgment for the officer, finding that the prisoner had made a valid claim. The court ruled that the officer was not entitled to qualified immunity since the officer's refusal to treat the prisoner bordered on barbarous and the officer's deliberate refusal of request for pain medication was gratuitously cruel and inhumane. Conversely, in *Montez v. Romer* (1999), prisoners with varying disabilities brought a class action suit claiming their Eighth and Fourteenth Amendment rights were violated under the American with Disabilities Act. The district court granted qualified immunity to the individual defendants, stating that it was clearly established at the time of the alleged discriminatory conduct that the act applied to corrections.

MECHANICS OF A SECTION 1983 LAWSUIT

Figure 4.3 illustrates the mechanical framework of a Section 1983 lawsuit. With some exceptions, this basic sequential process is followed. A Section 1983 claim in corrections may originate in one of two possible ways. A prisoner may allege that a constitutional deprivation may be the result of an incident (i.e., a cell or personnel search, use of force, and so on) in which an officer acts, in performance of his or duties, under color of law. Depending on the situation, the act may or may not be within the scope of the officer's duties. Further, a prisoner may file a Section 1983 lawsuit challenging that a policy, rule, or regulation has violated his constitutional rights in addition to filing a complaint about an incident in which an officer violated his protected rights. As previously discussed, the plaintiff must follow the appropriate statute of limitations in filing the lawsuit. The plaintiff may file the lawsuit with legal counsel or *pro se* (without the aid of counsel).

The plaintiff will normally name individual officers that may have participated in the incident and will also work up the chain of command, naming supervisors, administrators, and the governmental entity. This procedure is frequently known as the "deep pocket" theory (del Carmen 1991). This theory encourages the plaintiff to name multiple defendants in the lawsuit in an effort to find culpability with as many in the agency as possible. The idea behind the theory is that the more defendants named within the hierarchy of the agency, the more likely the award will be higher should the plaintiff prevail. Officers may have only limited resources to pay, but the city or the county have greater access to insurance or taxes in paying awards.

If the prisoner secures counsel, his or her attorney will file the appropriate legal form with the court, outlining and describing the nature of the consti-

Figure 4.3   Mechanics of a Civil Lawsuit

Incidence Occurrence or Regulation/Right Contested
↓
Suit Filed (Summons on Civil Suit)
↓
Defendant's Motion to Dismiss
↙   ↘
Motion Granted=No Liability   Motion Denied
↙
Discovery
↙
Interrogatories
Requests for Production
Request for Admission
Deposition
Examination of Injuries
↘
Mediation or Arbitration

Settlement or Consent Decree (No Trial)
↓
Trial
↙   ↘
No Liability   Liability

Types of Relief

Compensatory, Punitive and Nominal
Damages, Attorney Fees,
Declaratory or Injunctive Relief

tutional rights that were allegedly violated on his behalf. All involved parties (defendants) will be named, and the complaint will describe each defendant's liability. Each defendant will receive a copy of the complaint. Legal representation of each defendant will also receive a copy of the complaint. Counsel will meet with the named defendants to discuss the alleged incident. Review of pertinent documents, such as officer's incident reports, appropriate policies or regulations, and any evidence, will be performed. After this discussion, the defense counsel will normally file a written response to the court, denying the allegations or claiming immunity from the lawsuit.

Shortly after receiving the complaint, the defense counsel may file a motion to dismiss the case. A motion to dismiss is filed by the defendant's counsel, which requests the court to throw out the plaintiffs' lawsuit since it is without merit, is not founded in law, or is insufficient to state a valid legal claim. The judge may indeed agree and dismiss the case, or he or she may allow the plaintiff to amend the complaint.

Should the prisoner's case survive the motion to dismiss, both parties enter into a period of time known as discovery. Discovery is a procedure by which one party gains information held by another party (Franklin 1993). It is a period of time established by the court to allow the plaintiff and defendant to explore each another's case. Discovery provides for full disclosure prior to trial. It also allows the parties to search for evidence which may be useful in their case that may not be obtained through other means or sources. All jurisdictions provide for discovery.

There are five basic tools allowed in discovery in which to obtain information:

1. interrogatories;
2. requests for production;
3. requests for admission;
4. depositions; and
5. examination of physical evidence.

Interrogatories are written questions intended to solicit written or verbal responses to the questions. Interrogatories are commonly used and inexpensive. Under the federal rules of civil procedure the number of questions are limited to thirty. Named parties in the lawsuit, with the aid of counsel and under oath, answer each question stated. Second, a document known as "a request for production" is filed. This tool allows the requesting party an opportunity to obtain, examine, and review physical evidence in the possession of the responding party. Documents may include departmental policies and procedures, incident reports, photos, audio and video recordings, drawings, personnel files, investigative reports, autopsy reports, medical reports, and numerous other documents.

A third type of discovery tool is a request for admission. This document is a statement of fact under law requesting the responding party to admit or deny. If the issue at question is admitted as true, it will be settled prior to trial. If the issue is contested, it must be determined at trial. Both parties may use request for admission, which can be helpful in settling issues prior to trial.

The fourth type of discovery tool is known as a deposition, which can be the most costly form of discovery. A deposition is an out-of-court transcribed testimony under oath. Both parties are allowed to take depositions of each other's clients. Although a deposition is an informal questioning process in which the deponent must answer verbally, rules of evidence still apply, and the responses are transcribed by a court reporter. Video and phone depositions may be performed and used in conjunction with the transcribed document at trial. Deposition responses may be researched as to their accuracy and read to the jury at trial. All responses therefore must be truthful. Although this tool is used infrequently, the defendant may be requested to submit a written affidavit describing his or her actions in the incident. This, too, is taken under oath.

Finally, defense counsel will have an opportunity to examine the physical and/or mental injuries claimed by the prisoner. This examination will be performed by a physician.

The discovery period is determined by the judge and may be extended at the court's discretion. At the conclusion of discovery, defense counsel may file a motion for summary judgement, requesting the court to decide the case based on all evidence obtained through discovery. The court has several options: It can deny the motion, accept portions of the motion requiring it to move to trial on those portions, and fully accept the complete motion. If the case involves both Section 1983 claims and state tort actions, the federal court may dismiss the constitutional claims and remand the case to state court to deal with the remaining state issues.

If the defense counsel filed the motion for summary judgment, the plaintiff has a right to respond. Many courts are reluctant to grant summary judgment, based on the idea that each side is entitled to their "day in court." Frequently the court may hold that the issue(s) is (are) a matter for the jury and the case will move to trial. If the court grants summary judgment, the losing party has a right to appeal.

Because of the burgeoning court dockets across the country, many parties are attempting to find alternatives to going to trial. The predominate alternative methods are known as mediation and arbitration. Mediation is the more common of the two and involves the parties and a third disinterested person coming together in order to settle the case. The mediator does not have the authority to order the parties to settle the case. The mediator facilitates discussion and keeps the talks going in an attempt to work toward a resolution.

Arbitration, however, takes a more powerful judicial role in the dispute. The arbitrator listens to all the arguments from each side, weighs the evidence, and based on the evidence makes a recommendation. With mediation and arbitration, both parties must agree to the alternative method in reaching the resolution.

If the case goes to trial, selection of a jury begins. The judge and attorneys interview prospective jurors from a jury pool to determine who is qualified to serve as a juror. Those individuals who cannot participate in an impartial manner will be excused from duty. Once the jury is impaneled, the trial begins. The trial starts with opening statements which provide an overview of the facts from the plaintiff and the defendant. Since the plaintiff filed the lawsuit, he or she presents his or her case first. Once the plaintiff presents his or her witnesses and evidence, the defense presents its case. When both parties are finished presenting their evidence and witnesses, they are allowed closing arguments to the jury. Both parties attempt to persuade the jury to find on behalf of their client.

After closing arguments, the judge will instruct the jury about the law and their deliberations. The jury will take a period of time to deliberate the outcome of the case. The standard used in civil court is preponderance of evidence. The losing party may appeal the verdict. Should the jury find in favor of the plaintiff, the judge could issue a directed verdict in favor of the defendant officers. The plaintiff may still appeal such a verdict. If the plaintiff should prevail, he or she would recover damages as discussed earlier and may be awarded attorney fees.

This brief description of the basic mechanics of a Section 1983 lawsuit is provided to illustrate the high points and normal path of a case. From the time of the initial incident to finalization can take years, depending on the complexity and legal issues of the case. The case may even take longer to be decided, should the verdict be appealed. Many of the original complaints and allegations may never make it to court, owing to rulings by the court and motions made by either party. Prolonging the case with extensions and motions are planned strategies in an effort for evidence to be lost, memories to fade, and witnesses to retire or die. No matter the case, civil litigation is costly and is highly stressful for those named in the lawsuit.

HABEAS CORPUS PETITIONS

As discussed in Chapter 1, habeas corpus actions filed by prisoners have increased since the passage of the Prison Litigation reform Act (1996). Historically, the provision of habeas corpus actions pre-date Section 1983 legal actions by centuries. These actions were the foundations of English liberty for prisoners challenging their prison confinement. Before the fourteenth century, habeas corpus was designed to simply compel the appearance of parties before a court and had little importance as a guarantee of liberty. A change in the use of habeas corpus actions occurred in the fourteenth century, when prisoners were now able to challenge the validity of their confinement in the King Chancery Court. This change benefitted prisoners by allowing them a forum for challenging their confinement. At the same time it diminished some of the authority of local authorities and expanded royal power. The use of habeas corpus actions increased from the seventh through the fifteenth centuries. It was soon observed that habeas corpus actions were used more often in the Common Law courts of Common Pleas and King's Bench to stop cases from proceeding in the rival Courts of Chancery, Admiralty, Request, and the ecclesiastical (church) Court of High Commission (Zalman and Siegel 1997). This increase resulted in legal battles between the courts over fines and fees associated with the costs of criminal proceedings and over claims concerning arbitrary imprisonment by executive officers and courts who did not use common law procedures.

With their history embedded in English law, habeas corpus actions are important to the liberty of individuals confined in either a jail or a prison. This importance was underscored by the framers of the Constitution of our country and is observed in the United States Constitution, as Article 1, Section 9, states: "The privilege of the Writ of Habeas Corpus shall not be suspended, unless when in Cases of Rebellion or invasion the public Safety may require it." A writ of habeas corpus is not an appeal but means to "produce the body." Habeas corpus actions are petitions filed, usually by prisoners, challenging the legitimacy and nature of their confinement. The document commands authorities to show cause why a prisoner should be confined in either a prison or a jail. It is a written order by the court to any person, including a law enforcement officer, directing that person to bring the named individual before the court so that it can determine if there is adequate cause for continued detention (Champion 1997). Habeas corpus petitions play the role of a check into potential governmental oppression involving arbitrary confinement.

The process of managing habeas corpus petitions has been addressed by the United States Supreme Court in *Ex parte v. Royall* (1886). The Court ruled that circuit courts of the United States have jurisdiction on habeas corpus to discharge from custody a person who is restrained of his liberty in violation of the Constitution of the United States. When a person is in custody, under process from state court of original jurisdiction, for an alleged offense against the laws of such state, and it is claimed that he is restrained of his liberty in violation of the Constitution of the United States, the circuit court of the United States has discretion whether it will discharge him in advance of his trial in the court in which he was indicted. After the conviction of the accused in the state court, the circuit court has still discretion whether he shall be put to his writ of error to the highest court of the state, or whether the circuit court will proceed by writ of habeas corpus summarily in order to determine whether he is restrained of his liberty in violation of the Constitution of the United States.

Habeas corpus petitions have been used by prisoners for a multitude of confinement issues as the following cases reveal. In *Gibson v. Puckett* (2000) a prisoner was granted habeas corpus relief when he challenged a transfer from correctional institution to another. The prisoner complained that the facility he was being transferred to did not have the same facilities to accommodate his disability. The district court ruled that the prisoner could use a habeas corpus petition to challenge the transfer. Frequently prisoners use habeas corpus actions to challenge the loss of earned good time (reduction in sentence for "good behavior") as a result of disciplinary action. In *Henson v. U.S. Bureau of Prisons* (2000) a federal prisoner petitioned for habeas corpus relief, challenging the loss of good-time credit as a result of incurring a disciplinary report. A search of the prisoner's cell found a pipe which tested positive for marijuana residue, but a urinalysis of his blood was negative. A disciplinary board found he had violated prison rules, and he lost fourteen days of good time, visits, and commissary and telephone privileges for thirty days. The district court denied the petition and the court of appeals affirmed. In *Piggie v. Hanks* (2000) a state prisoner petitioned the court with a writ of habeas corpus challenging a disciplinary committee's finding that he was guilty of a sexual assault which warranted confinement in a segregation unit and loss of good time. The district court granted the petition, finding that the prisoner was entitled to have the committee either consider a videotape that may have recorded the incident at issue or to have the board state on the record why it would not do so. The court noted that the videotape was available at the time the hearing was held and the prisoner had made a timely request for it to be viewed by the committee.

Prisoners have also used habeas corpus petitions to challenge issues surrounding a death penalty sentence. In *Young v. Hayes* (2000), a prisoner on death row in Missouri submitted a habeas corpus petition asserting that the actions of a district attorney, who had threatened to fire an attorney under her supervision if she provided information to the governor in connection with a clemency petition the prisoner wished to file, violated his due process rights. The district court granted summary judgment to the defendant, but the appeals court reversed and remanded, granting a stay of execution. The appeals court held that the Due Process clause does not require that a state have a clemency procedure but does require that if such a procedure is created the state's own officials must refrain from frustrating it by threatening the job of a witness. In *LaGrand v. Stewart* (1999), an Arizona death row prisoner challenged the use of lethal gas as a means of execution and filed a habeas corpus petition. The district court denied the petition and the appeals court reversed and remanded with instructions. The appeals court held that the prisoner's voluntary choice of lethal gas as method of execution did not waive his claim that the use of lethal gas was unconstitutional. The appeals court held that Arizona's method of using lethal gas to execute prisoners was unconstitutional.

SUMMARY

Title 42 U.S.C., Section 1983, also known as Section 1983 lawsuits, constitutes the most common types of litigation filed against corrections personnel. Students and practitioners alike should be aware of the potential liability of corrections personnel under the Title's provisions. Since the early 1960s the number of civil rights cases have inundated the courts. Section 1983 cannot be used by citizens or prisoners seeking to hold federal officials liable. It allows citizens, pretrial detainees, prisoners, and legal or illegal aliens to seek redress in federal court for alleged constitutional rights violations of officers acting under color of law. Commonly, acting under "color of law" is interpreted as meaning that the named officer has acted outside the scope of his or her sworn authority.

The chapter provided the basic mechanics of a Section 1983 claim and the process for working its way through the system. Understanding the stages of discovery is significant to the criminal justice officer named in the lawsuit. Discovery allows counsel of the plaintiff and the defendant to obtain information relevant to the pending litigation. Correctional personnel should be prepared to respond to various legal requests made by either party's counsel which will reveal their knowledge of or participation in the case. Named defendants should also be prepared for a potentially lengthy process which can be disruptive to personal and job-related activities. Prisoners using Section 1983 have been seeking to hold state and local correctional personnel liable for causing a constitutional injury and may be awarded compensation and punitive damages, as well as attorney's fees. However, just because a Section 1983 lawsuit has been filed does not necessarily mean that any defendant's conduct was improper.

REFERENCES

Branham, L. S. 1998. *The law of sentencing, corrections, and prisoners' rights*. St. Paul, MN: West Publishing, Co.

Champion, D. J. 1997. *The Roxbury dictionary of criminal justice*. Los Angeles: Roxbury Publishing Company.

Collins, M. G. 1997. *Section 1983 litigation*. Egan, MN: West Publishing.

del Carmen, R.V. 1991. *Civil liabilities in American policing: A text for law enforcement personnel.* Englewood Cliffs, NJ: Prentice-Hall.

Esienberg, T., and S. Schwab. 1987. The reality of constitutional tort liability. *Cornell Law Review* 72: 641–95.

Franklin, C. J. 1993. *The police officer's guide to civil liability.* Springfield, IL: Charles C. Thomas.

Gressman, E. 1992. The unhappy history of civil rights legislation. *Michigan Law Review* 50: 1323–58.

Kappeler, V. E. 1997. *Critical issues in police civil liability.* 2nd ed. Prospect Heights, IL: Waveland Press.

Vaughn, M. S., and L. F. Coomes. 1995. Police Civil liability under Section 1983: When do police officers act under color of law? *Journal of Criminal Justice* 23: 395–415.

Zalman, M., and L. J. Siegel. 1997. *Criminal procedure: Constitution and society.* Belmont, CA: Wadsworth Publishing.

Cases Cited

Anderson v. Creighton, 483 U.S. 635 (1987)

Alliance to End Repression v. City of Chicago, 561 F. Supp. 537 (N.D. Ill. 1982)

Alyeska Pipeline Service Co. v. Wilderness Society, 421 U.S. 240 (1975)

Berry v. Oswalt, 143 F. 3d 1127 (8th Cir. 1998)

Benton v. Maryland, 395 U.S. 784 (1969)

Bivens v. Six Unknown Federal Narcotics Agents, 403 U.S. 388 (1971)

Brandon v. Holt, 469 U.S. 464 (1985)

Brawner v. Irvin, 169 F. 694 (C.C.D. Ga.1909)

Bultema v. U.S., 195 F. Supp. 2d 1001 (N.D. Ohio 2002)

Carlson v. Green, 100 U.S. 1468 (1980)

Carey v. Piphus, 435 U.S. 247 (1978)

Chapman v. Houston Welfare Rights Organization, 441 U.S. 600 (1979)

City of Newport v. Fact Concerts, 453 U.S. 247 (1981)

Cleavinger v. Saxner, 474 U.S. 193 (1985)

Correctional Services Corp. v. Malesko, 534 U.S. 61 (2001)

Daniels v. Williams, 474 U.S. 327 (1986)

Ralston v. McGovern, 167 F. 3d 1160 (7th Cir. 1999)

Richardson v. McKnight, 117 S. Ct. 2100 (1997)

Robinson v. California, 370 U.S. 660 (1962)

Screws v. United States, 325 U.S. 91 (1945)

Smith v. Wade, 461 U. S. 30 (1983)

Spell v. McDaniel, 824 F.2d 1380 (4th Cir. 1987)

Tenney v. Brandhove, 341 U.S. 367 (1951)

United States v. Classic, 313 U.S. 299 (1941)

West v. Atkins, 108 U. S. 2250 (1988)

Will v. Michigan Department of State Police, 491 U.S. 58 (1989)

Wilson v. Garcia, 471 U.S. 261 (1985)

Wolf v. Colorado, 338 U.S. 25 (1949)

Young v. Hayes, 218 F. 3d 850 (8th Cir. 2000)

CHAPTER 5

DELIBERATE INDIFFERENCE AND MEDICAL CARE

Deliberate indifference to serious medical needs of a prisoner constitutes the "unnecessary and wanton infliction of pain."

Estelle v. Gamble 1976

An ongoing challenge for prison and detention personnel is providing health care services for the confined. Jails and prisons are plagued with an unhealthy and a destructive population. It is common for this population to enter a period of incarceration with such illnesses as tuberculosis, gonorrhea, syphilis, alcoholism, cancer, and skin disorders (Raba 1998). A significant number of prisoners are admitted with an active substance-abuse history and are more likely to suffer from withdrawal symptoms, liver and pancreas diseases, heart ailments, muscle disorders, and respiratory and immune deficiencies. This segment of the population is more likely to share needles and more likely to enter jail or prison as HIV positive or with AIDS. Many prisoners have a history of abusing tobacco products and are more prone to cardiovascular disease, lung disorders, cancers, immune deficiencies, and hypertension (May and Lambert 1998).

Maruschak and Beck (2001), of the Bureau of Justice Statistics, reported that at the time of prison admission, 30 percent of state and federal prisoners indicated having a physical or mental condition. The three most common medical problems included: a physical condition, a mental health condition, and a learning disability. Since admission to prison, almost 20 percent of these prisoners reported a medical condition requiring surgery for such conditions as a heart attack, circulatory problems, respiratory aliments, kidney/liver problems, cancer, and diabetes. Nearly 25 percent of the prisoners reported that they had sustained an injury while incarcerated, resulting from an accident or a fight with another prisoner.

Prisons and jails also confine a significant number of mentally impaired prisoners. The deinstitutionalization of the serious mentally ill population has forced jails and prisons to become the new "asylums." These prisoners may suffer from several mental disorders and can require more direct supervision. Generally these prisoners need antipsychotic medications to function properly, and in the correctional environment access to such medications can be problematic for the prisoner, other prisoners, officers, and health care providers.

Previous studies on the prevalence of severe mental illness among incarcerated populations estimate a range from 8 to 16 percent (Guy et al. 1985; Steadman et al., 1989; Teplin, 1990). Beck and Maruschak (2001) found that over 16 percent of jail prisoners were identified as mentally impaired. Approximately 30 percent of jail prisoners were confined for either a violent or property offense; 38 percent exhibited a history of alcohol dependence; and 60 percent reported that they were under the influence of alcohol or other substances at the time of the offense. Ditton (1999) also reported that state and federal mentally ill prisoners account for 14 percent of the total prison population. Mentally ill prisoners are highest among white, middle-aged prisoners, and over 40 percent are female. This population has reported at least three prior convictions and is more likely to serve a sentence for a violent offense; over 50 percent are taking medication during confinement.

Most correctional agency's budgets comprise a significant percentage of dollars allocated to providing health care services for prisoners. Camp and Camp (2002) reported that the annual average amount spent on providing medical services amounted to slightly over $74 million, or about 10 percent of a department's operational budget. They reported that 47 jurisdictions spent almost $4 million on medical services annually. California spent the largest dollar amount on medical services, $522 million, while North Dakota spent the least, $2.44 million. Nevada spent approximately 8 percent of its operational budget, while Louisiana spent 2 percent. Annually, the average daily medical costs per prisoner are slightly over $7 per day.

Responding to the health care needs of the prisoner population is an important component in corrections and liability issues. Ross (1997) found in his study of over 3,000 prisoner lawsuits that medical claims accounted for the most frequent claims filed by prisoner and jail detainees (12 percent). He also reported that medical care claims were second to failure-to-protect claims, with damages awarded to prevailing prisoners averaging over slightly $190,000 per award, including attorney's fees. Ross (2001) also found in a separate study of Michigan jails that medical claims were the second most frequent claims filed against jail personnel in claims filed from 1994 to 1999. He found that prisoners prevailed in about 18 percent of the claims and on average were awarded $115,000 per claim. Claims involving medical care issues have revolved around denial of medical care, delay in medical care, inadequate medical care, failure to have the necessary resources, equipment, or health care personnel accessible to ailing prisoners, failure to dispense medications, dispensing the wrong medication, defective policies and practices regarding medical care, malpractice of physicians, failure to train officers in signs and symptoms of medical or psychological emergencies. This chapter will discuss the frequent liability issues raised by prisoners under Section 1983 and examine the court's standard of review when determining a claim of failing to provide medical or psychological care for prisoners.

APPLICATION OF THE DELIBERATE INDIFFERENCE STANDARD

Arguably, one of the most common and far reaching standards applied to correctional litigation developed by the United States Supreme Court is that of "deliberate indifference." The genesis of this standard was established in the seminal case *Estelle v. Gamble* (1976). In this Texas prison case, the prisoner sustained a work assignment back injury and claimed he was repeatedly denied or delayed medical care, despite seventeen examinations by medical doctors, X rays, prescribed medication, and bed rest. The Supreme Court determined that the proper method for examining claims of denial of medical care under the Eighth Amendment is whether correctional officials were deliberately indifferent to the needs of the prisoner. The Court ruled that liability will attach when corrections personnel actions constitute cruel and unusual punishment contravening the Eighth Amendment. In *Estelle*, the Court found that the officials' response did not rise to a level of deliberate indifference.

Deliberate indifference is not easily definable and is problematic to apply. The Court distinguished deliberate indifference from "negligence." Since the creation of its distinction, the Court has held that deliberate indifference resides on a continuum between "mere negligence and something less than acts or omissions for the very purpose of causing harm" (*Farmer v. Brennan* 1994). "Deliberate" means that a particular course of action has been chosen from among various alternatives, and "indifferent" means that there has been some conscious disregard for a person's rights (Plitt 1997).

Officials must be deliberately indifferent to a "serious" medical need and officials must act with a culpable state of mind (*Wilson v. Seiter* 1991) before liability will attach. If a correctional official has knowledge of an excessive risk to a prisoner's health or safety and disregards that risk, liability will most likely attach. When the official is aware of facts from which an inference can be drawn that a substantial risk of serious harm exists, liability will most likely attach.

For example, in *Petricko v. Kurtz* (1999), an injured prisoner filed suit claiming officials knew of his shoulder injury but deliberately delayed providing proper medical care. The prisoner sustained a dislocated shoulder, requested to be transported to a hospital, but officers allegedly informed him they could not do so and instructed another prisoner to manually "pop" the shoulder back into position. The prisoner claimed he wrote the warden over the course of two weeks requesting medical care, and the warden ignored his requests. The court concluded that the prisoner stated a valid claim—that the warden had known of the prisoner's injuries for two weeks—and that, therefore, the warden deliberately failed to provide standard emergency treatment. However, the court failed to hold the supervisors liable for failing to train the officer.

Deliberate indifference requires certain criteria: (1) serious medical complaints, especially of a continuing nature, should not be ignored (whether correctional personnel regard them as false or exaggerated); (2) medically trained personnel should make medical judgments; (3) serious, chronic symptoms require attention; and (4) a blind eye or a deaf ear should not be tolerated regarding a prisoner's complaint, if with proper care, a corrections officer could have known about the complaint (Silver 2003). Under the deliberate indifference standard, there is a general expectation that "adequate" or "reasonable" care" will be provided to prisoners under the jurisdiction of correctional personnel. A system which provides adequate medical and mental health care to prisoners at intake and throughout incarceration must be in place. Most, if not all, detention and prison facilities have instituted health care services to prisoners, despite continued prisoner claims of inadequate medical care. Prisoners generally have no right to be treated by a private physician (*Hawley v. Evans* 1989).

Deliberate indifference can be manifested in a number of ways. The refusal of correctional or medical personnel to provide or delay in providing care may be actionable under deliberate indifference. A series of incidents which, if viewed in isolation appear to involve only negligence, may give rise to deliberate indifference. Problems stemming from understaffing, a lack of or deficient equipment, substandard facilities, and a lack of adequate procedures may be so egregious that the ensuing inability to render adequate medical care is so evident that the failure to redress these problems is tantamount to "deliberate indifference" (Krantz 2003).

A prisoner must allege in a medical care claim that a protected constitutional right was violated in order to prevail in such a claim. Actions emerging from a pretrial detainee's claims of being deprived of needed medical care are examined under the due process clauses of the Fifth and Fourteenth Amendments rather than the Eighth Amendment. The courts have agreed that the cruel and unusual clause of the Eighth Amendment does not apply to pretrial detainees; rather, the due process clause affords them protections like convicted prisoners.

Prisoners possess the right to be afforded adequate medical care for a serious medical need but are not guaranteed a flawless system or the right to be cured from an illness. Moreover, correction or detention officers are not absolute guarantors to a prisoner that he will be cured of a medical or psychiatric illness. In *Priest v. Cupp* (1976) the court concluded that medical care, such as treatment or diagnosis, be reasonably available during a prisoner's incarceration based on his or her medical condition. The main issue in medical care litigation focuses on the nature of so-called adequate or reasonable medical care (Palmer and Palmer 2004).

Deliberate Indifference to Adequate Medical Care

Providing health care services to pretrial detainees and state prisoners is a fundamental responsibility of correctional officials. Frequently claims asserting that correction officials or health care providers failed to provide adequate care for the prisoner when the provider or official knew that the prisoner suffered an ailment requiring care are filed. The degree of medical care depends on the need of the prisoner and is evaluated on a case-by-case basis.

The issue regarding inadequate medical care was examined in *Rosen v. Chang* (1993). The estate of a prisoner brought a Section 1983 action against the prison director, physician, and nurse, claiming they violated the prisoner's Eighth Amendment rights by failing to provide treatment for his acute appendicitis. Testimony in court claimed that the prisoner suffered from appendicitis for at least two weeks prior to his death and that the physician failed to detect the symptoms when he examined him six days before his death. The estate also claimed that the nurse failed to relay the seriousness of the chronic pain so that the treating physician could provide timely adequate care. The court found that the prison director and health care providers were entitled to qualified immunity. The court concluded that the prison director did not possess personal knowledge of the prisoner's condition or that there was a causal link between the procedure of having physicians available only one day a week and having nurses limit prisoners' access to physicians. The court determined that the health care providers did not act with deliberate indifference to the prisoner's medical needs but responded to the prisoner with informed medical judgment in providing adequate health care.

The court's decision in *Morales Feliciano v. Rossello Gonzalez* (1998) provides an instructive example of how deliberate indifference was applied to systematic deficiencies of providing medical care within a total prison system. Legal action was brought before the court citing numerous failures demonstrating that the correctional system was deliberately indifferent to the needs of medical and mental health care to prisoners. The court found that correctional officials' inactions contributed to the deaths of prisoners and to the infliction of pain and suffering. The court determined a systematic failure existed in a failure in staffing, facilities, procedures, and administration. The court further determined that the administration acted in a manner deliberately indifferent to the basic human and health needs of prisoners, thus violating their constitutional rights. Further, the court found that officials were aware of these deficiencies and failed to fully screen incoming prisoners for infectious diseases; failed to detect mental health problems; failed to provide a sick call system ensuring access to care; failed to respond to medical emergencies; failed to provide necessary medications to prisoners; failed to transport prisoners to scheduled health care appointments outside of the facility; failed to provide medical diets; failed to adequately train, supervise, or retain health care providers, resulting chronic understaffing; failed to provide mental health treatment for prisoners, allowing severely mentally disturbed prisoners to continue to cohabit with the general population without follow-up care or prescribed medication; failed to provide treatment for prisoners outside of the facility when a serious condition required it; and demonstrated "manifest ineptitude" in maintaining medical records. The court also held that budgetary limitations or inadequate resources can never be a valid justification for constitutional violations. The court found that the "entire" system of so-called health care was deliberately indifferent and defective in providing adequate medical care for prisoners.

In *Lawson v. Dallas County* (2002) a paraplegic prisoner submitted a Section 1983 action against the sheriff and the detention center's medical officer, alleging deliberate indifference to his medical needs. The appellate court affirmed a lower court's decision in awarding the prisoner $250,000 in damages, finding that detention officials violated his Eighth Amendment right to adequate medical care. The court determined that the detention center's medical staff, rather than the staff as a whole, acted with deliberate indifference since all of the nurses who primarily treated the prisoner had actual knowledge of the risks posed by the development and worsening of ulcers. The court found that the nurses responded by disobeying the doctor's orders, by not providing him with adequate mobility equipment, by not personally assisting him in turning himself, bathing, or moving, by not providing necessary dressing changes, and by not seeking an alternative placement for the prisoner.

The adequacy of providing medical care under contract with a private physician was the focus of the United States Supreme Court's decision in *West v. Atkins* (1988). The Court addressed the question of "whether a physician, under contract with the State to provide health care on a part-time basis acts under 'color of law,' within the meaning of Section 1983, when he treats a prisoner." While confined in a North Carolina prison, West injured his Achilles tendon playing volleyball. He was transported to the prison hospital in Raleigh, where Dr. Atkins, a private physician under contract with the state, treated him. West was not allowed to see a physician of his own choosing. Over several visits, Dr. Atkins placed West in a cast. West filed a Section 1983 action claiming that he had never received the corrective surgery which Dr. Atkins had stated he required and that such negligence was, therefore, cruel and unusual punishment in violation of his Eighth Amendment rights. West claimed Dr. Atkins was deliberately indifferent to his serious medical need by having failed to provide the necessary surgery. The lower court first granted summary judgment to the physician. West appealed, and the appellate court (4th Circuit) remanded to the lower court for a rehearing. The lower court dismissed the suit; West appealed a second time; the appellate court affirmed the lower court's decision; and West appealed to the Supreme Court.

Relying on past Section 1983 decisions, the Supreme reversed the lower court's decision and remanded, stating that it is the physician's function for the prison system, not the nature of his employment, which determines whether his actions are attributable to the state under Section 1983. The court noted that physicians are not removed from the purview of a Section 1983 action simply because they are professionals acting in accordance with professional discretion and judgment. Therefore, a physician, who under contract with a correctional entity to provide medical care at a state hospital on a full-time or part-time basis, acts under color of law, within the meaning of Section 1983, when he provides such treatment. The Court also held that contracting out prison medical care does not relieve the state, of its constitutional duty to provide adequate medical treatment to those in its custody and does not deprive the state's prisoners of a means of vindication of their Eighth Amendment rights under Section 1983.

In *Veloz v. New York* (1999) a prisoner brought a Section 1983 action against the prison physician for failing to perform surgery on his foot. The court dismissed the case, ruling that the prisoner failed to state a legitimate Section 1983 claim. The court found that the pain experienced by the prisoner in his foot did not constitute a serious medical need and that the prisoner's claim that he needed a wheel chair or crutches was merely a difference of opinion as to the correct course of treatment.

In *Tucker v. Randall* (1993) a pretrial detainee alleged inadequate medical care by detention officers. The appeals court affirmed the lower court's holding that the officers did not act with deliberate indifference to the medical needs of the detainee, even when they failed to treat him with ice and aspirin as instructed by a doctor or delayed the treatment for over two months before having the injuries viewed again. A reasonable person would not have viewed the detainee's injuries as life threatening or serious. The detainee had been transported to a hospital prior to booking, and the hospital doctor did not treat the injuries as serious or life threatening. Further, the detainee did not complain of injuries to the booking officer upon arrival.

In *Reed v. McBride* (1999) an appellate court found in favor of a prisoner's Eighth Amendment claim of withholding food and life-sustaining medication from him while incarcerated. The court found that the prisoner's medical condition progressively worsened, making it serious, and supported his claim of deliberate indifference. The court stated that depriving a prisoner of food may be so objectively serious as to support a claim of cruel and unusual punishment under the Eighth Amendment, when the amount and duration of the deprivation is considered. The prisoner suffered from a variety of ailments, including paralysis, heart disease, Hunt's syndrome, high blood pressure, rheumatoid arthritis, and other crippling diseases of the legs, ankles, feet, hands, and spine.

Claims for Delaying Medical Care

The duty to provide medical care is a continuing one, and delay of such care either at the onset or continuation of serious medical symptoms may be actionable. While not entirely quantifiable, claims of delay in providing medical care to prisoners are reviewed in accordance with deliberate indifference.

A sheriff and several of his detention officers were found to be deliberately indifferent to serious medical needs of an alcoholic pretrial detainee who had died from seizures brought on by withdrawal symptoms, in *Lancaster v. Monroe County, Alabama* (1997). The detainee was lodged in jail for driving under the influence of alcohol and placed on a top bunk in a holding cell, since lower bunks were occupied. Detention officers were notified twice by the detainee's wife that he was alcoholic and suffered from delirium tremens. The officers acknowledged the condition and promised to watch him. The detainee's father notified the sheriff of his condition, and the sheriff informed the father that the detainee would be taken to the hospital should he suffer a seizure. During the night, several prisoners stated that the detainee suffered from the "shakes" and a headache. During midmorning, the detainee sat up in his bunk, began shaking, and fell out of bed, landing on his head. He was transported to the hospital, where he died three days later because of the head injuries. The pathologist determined that the detainee was having a seizure when he fell out of his bed. The detainee's wife filed a Section 1983 action for wrongful death and deliberate indifference to the deceased's serious medical condition. The court found in favor of the plaintiff and determined his inebriated condition progressed into seizures, constituting a serious medical condition. The evidence showed that the condition would worsen with delay and that the sheriff had failed to plan for medical care until after the detainee had a seizure. The officers had known the deceased's condition was serious yet allowed him to remain in the top bunk and failed to plan to obtain medical attention until after the seizure.

In *Gutierrez v. Peters* (1997), however, the appellant court affirmed judgment in favor of prison officials when a prisoner claimed that he received inadequate medical treatment for an infected cyst on his eye. The court did acknowledge that the cyst was a serious medical condition but failed to find the officials acted with deliberate indifference despite isolated delays in treatment. The court found that a six-day wait to see the physician was not an unreasonably long delay for the condition since the physician had seen the prisoner one week earlier, had concluded the cyst was not infected, and had promptly prescribed a course of treatment.

County commissioners of a detention facility settled out of court for $2.1 million when an intoxicated detainee died in an observation cell from the medical conditions associated with his delirium tremens in *Estate of Taft v. County of Isabella* (2002). Taft was brought into the detention center highly intoxicated and placed in an observation cell. Later in the morning, Taft was seen by a physician's assistant for a respiratory problem, a fever of 100 degrees, a dry hacking cough, and he was prescribed medication. Taft refused to take the medication later that evening, but he did eat his meal. Later that night he began to suffer the effects of alcohol withdrawal. He became agitated, disoriented, unsteady in his balance, and fell down several times; his hands and fingers began shaking, and he exhibited hallucinatory behaviors by picking imaginary bugs off the glass of the cell door. Officers observed these behaviors and instead of obtaining medical assistance, videotaped Taft's actions in the cell. The officer stated in his deposition that he began taping the detainee so that he could show the tape to a DARE class later that week.

Taft's delirium tremens worsened, resulting in severe shaking. Approximately one hour later an officer observed Taft on the floor of the cell, unresponsive. He entered the cell and found that Taft was not breathing and summoned an ambulance. Paramedics responded, were unsuccessful in revival efforts, and Taft was pronounced dead at the hospital. His body temperature at the hospital was 105 degrees. Taft's family filed a Section 1983 lawsuit claiming that the officers knew that he was intoxicated, had refused his medication, made no effort to call the physician informing him of the prisoner's condition and refusal, failed to recognize the symptoms of delirium tremens, knew he was suffering from a deteriorating medical condition, and delayed/denied summoning medical care. Despite this knowledge, they videotaped the incident rather than providing medical care, an action which constituted deliberate indifference. The family also claimed that the sheriff was deliberately indifferent in providing training to the officers and supervisors about the signs of the D.T.'s and how to respond to a serious medical condition/emergency and that he patently tolerated policies and practices of indifference to the medical needs of detainees, knowingly and recklessly failing to instruct, supervise, and discipline the officers' conduct, actions which amounted to the deliberate indifference of Taft's constitutional rights. Based on the nature of the incident and the video tape, the retained attorney for the county, the risk manager, and the county commissioners decided that the best course of action was to settle the case.

In *Bridges v. Rhodes* (2002) a prisoner died from heat stroke and his family filed a Section 1983 lawsuit alleging deliberate indifference to his serious medical needs. The prisoner had been assigned to work on the hoe-squad, clearing weeds, and collapsed in the hot sun. The district court granted summary judgment and the appellate court affirmed the decision. The appellate court found that the twenty-minute delay in getting the prisoner to the hospital after the heat-related collapse was not unreasonable. The court held that the affidavit of the physician who reviewed the medical records of the prisoner, in which he listed the heat-related symptoms that the correction officer should have recognized while supervising the prisoner, was insufficient to establish liability against the officer.

Deliberate Indifference and Psychological Care

Another important component of providing medical care in correctional facilities involves providing treatment for the mentally impaired. With more frequency, prisons and jails are increasingly confining mentally impaired prisoners. These prisoners commonly require closer supervision, medical care, and medications to control their illness (Stein and Alaimo 1998). In some situations prisoners have refused to be treated with medications, resulting in uncontrollable behaviors which cause a risk of harm for the prisoner, other prisoners, officers, and mental health providers. In providing treatment for the mentally ill prisoner, correctional officers and mental health personnel often face the need to involuntarily medicate a prisoner. This issue was addressed by the United States Supreme Court in *Washington v. Harper* (1990).

Harper was a prisoner confined in a prison in Washington and suffered from bipolar disorder. In compliance with operational policies, Harper was diagnosed by two prison psychiatrists as being "gravely disabled" and a danger to others and medicated him without his consent. He filed a Section 1983 lawsuit challenging the decision of being medicated without his voluntary consent.

Rejecting Harper's position that he should be able to refuse the medication, the Court stated that the state has a clear legitimate interest in prison security and thus in medicating a prisoner for treatment concerns to assist him in bona fide self-protection and to ensure the safety of others. The Supreme Court held that involuntarily medicating a prisoner implies a due process component and must therefore be examined in accordance with the Fourteenth Amendment. Prior to involuntarily medicating a prisoner, a hearing must be provided. Citing its decision in *Turner v. Safely* (1987), the Court held that the state of Washington Department of Correction's policy was related to legitimate penological objectives and provided for a hearing, protecting the prisoner's due process rights under the Fourteenth Amendment. The Court emphasized its concern that without a hearing officials may hasten to medicate prisoners merely to control their behaviors for purposes less than therapeutic ones and without concerning the legitimate interests of the prisoner. The Court held that given the requirements of the prison environment, the Due Process Clause permits the state to treat a prisoner who has a serious mental illness with antipsychotic drugs against his will, if the prisoner is dangerous to himself or others and the treatment is in the prisoner's medical interest.

Since the *Harper* decision, lower courts have applied the holding on several occasions. In *Breads v. Moehrie* (1991) the district court found in favor of a prisoner challenging the policy to medicate him without his consent. The court found that the prisoner did not suffer from a serious mental illness and questioned the legitimacy of the policy: if it truly had the best interest of the prisoner in mind. The court questioned whether drugs were administered more for the benefit of the department, as opposed for the true need for the prisoner. In *Wilson v. Chang* (1997) a prison doctor injected a prisoner with a sedative after he became disruptive, and the prisoner filed a lawsuit claiming the doctor violated his constitutional rights. The jury ruled in favor of the physician and the court ruled against the prisoner's motion. The court ruled that the doctor could inject the prisoner with medication to deal with an emergency situation and supported the jury's verdict. The prisoner became enraged when the doctor refused to provide him with an extra blanket in his cell. The prisoner repeatedly ran his head and body into the cell, striking the wall and cell fixtures. The prisoner refused to calm down, and the physician. knowing the prisoner's past violent history of mental instability, injected him with the sedative.

In a case that caught national attention, *U.S. v. Weston* (2001), the appellate court ruled that the Federal Bureau of Prisons could involuntarily medicate a prisoner. In 1998, Weston, a schizophrenic, entered the hallways of the Capitol in Washington, D.C., looking for aliens, and shot and killed two Capitol police officers. Prison psychiatrists determined that Weston needed to be medicated, but he refused. His attorney filed a legal action requesting that officials be prohibited from medicating him without his consent. The appellant court upheld the lower court's decision to medicate Weston without his consent. The court held that the government should be permitted to medicate Weston involuntarily because the action was essential in order to render the prisoner nondangerous, based on medical/safety concerns. Further, in *Fuller v. Dillon* (2001) the appellate court affirmed summary judgment for prison and medical personnel's decision to medicate a prisoner without his consent. The court found that the treating psychiatrist's decision complied with the state's requirement for involuntary administration of medication.

Since the *Harper* decision, the United States Supreme Court has examined whether the Constitution permits the government to administer medication against the will of a criminal defendant in order to render the mentally impaired defendant competent to stand trial. This issue was addressed in *Sell v. U.S.* (2003). A federal criminal defendant with a long history of mental illness was initially found competent to stand trial for a criminal charge of fraud. He was released on bail but bail was later denied since his condition worsened. His counsel requested a reconsideration of his competence. After an examination at a medical center for federal prisoners, the defendant was found incompetent to stand trial and was hospitalized to determine whether he would attain the mental capacity to allow his trial to proceed. The defendant refused to take his antipsychotic medication, and after a hearing a psychiatrist authorized that he be medicated involuntarily. A U.S. magistrate judge issued an order forcing the administration of drugs. The district court found no evidence that the defendant was dangerous but upheld the order, finding that involuntary medication was the only viable hope of rendering the defendant competent to stand trial necessary to obtain an adjudication of his guilt or innocence.

The appellate court affirmed and the Supreme Court ruled that the Constitution allows the government to administer psychiatric drugs even against the defendant's will, in limited circumstances.

The Court held that in order to administer such medication against the will of the accused defendant for trial purposes, the following four criteria must be met: (1) There are important governmental interests at stake, such as a timely prosecution, bringing the defendant to trial, assuring the trial is fair, and the court's evaluation of the facts of each case; (2) involuntary medication will significantly further such governmental interests that the administration of drugs will likely render the defendant competent to stand trial; (3) involuntary medication is necessary to further such interests and any alternative and less intrusive treatments are unlikely to produce the same results; and (4) the administration of drugs is medically appropriate—that is, in the defendant's best medical interest in light of the defendant's medical condition.

Claims of failing to diagnose symptoms of psychological disorders and of failing to provide adequate treatment of the mentally impaired have been frequently filed. In *Arnold v. Lewis* (1992) a prisoner filed a Section 1983 claim against correctional officials for being deliberately indifferent to his mental health care needs. The district court ruled in favor of the prisoner, finding that the officials' actions constituted deliberate indifference to serious medical needs in violation of the Eighth Amendment. The officials had placed the prisoner in lock-down as punishment for symptoms of her paranoid schizophrenia rather than providing mental health care. The officials knew that the mental health program at the facility was deficient and were aware that the prisoner's mental condition had deteriorated when she was locked down in a small cell without treatment, but they failed to correct the grossly inadequate psychiatric care. Prison officials' actions warranted injunctive relief, ensuring that she would receive the appropriate treatment.

Occasionally prisoners have filed actions claiming that the entire prison system provided inadequate mental health treatment. This action was the focus in *Coleman v. Wilson* (1995). Prisoners claimed that the inadequacies of the mental health treatment provided by the Department of Corrections represented cruel and unusual punishment in violation of their Eighth Amendment rights. The district court concurred with the prisoners, awarded injunctive relief, and appointed a special master to monitor the progress by the department to correct the deficiencies.

The court found that the evidence supported findings of deficiencies in the following six areas: (1) failing to institute a systematic program for screening and evaluating prisoners to identify those in need of mental health care; (2) failing to provide a treatment program that involved more than just segregating mentally ill prisoners; (3) failing to hire a sufficient number of mental health professionals; (4) failing to maintain accurate and confidential treatment records of prisoners; (5) failing to administer psychotropic medication with appropriate supervision and periodic evaluation; and (6) failing to provide a basic program to identify, treat, and supervise prisoners at risk of suicide.

Additionally, the court found that the evidence supported that correctional officers were inadequately trained in signs and symptoms of mental illness and that disciplinary and behavior control measures were inappropriately used against mentally impaired prisoners. The three-hour training course received by all new officers and the in-service training conducted at the institutional level were not sufficient to prevent some officers from using punitive measures to control behaviors without regard to the cause of the behavior.

In a similar case, *Madrid v. Gomez* (1995), prisoners incarcerated at the Pelican Bay Prison in California brought a class action suit challenging the conditions of confinement, including allegations of excessive force and deficiencies in providing medical and mental health services. The court ruled in favor of the prisoners finding evidence that grossly excessive force was used on a frequent basis and that such a practice posed a substantial risk of harm to the prisoners. The court also found deficiencies in the delivery of mental and medical health services, supporting claims of deliberate indifference to the prisoners' Eighth Amendment rights. The court held that staffing levels of health care providers were insufficient, that training and supervision of medical personnel was almost nonexistent, and that screening for communicable diseases was poorly implemented. Frequently prisoners experienced serious delays in receiving medications and treatment; there were no protocols or training programs which addressed responding to emergencies or trauma; there were no procedures addressing the management of chronic illnesses; and there was no program of significance to ensure the quality of services provided.

A lower district court granted summary judgment to correctional officials in a Section 1983 action brought by a female prisoner in *Giron v. Corrections Corp. of America* (1998). After being raped by a corrections officer, the plaintiff alleged that correction officials deliberately disregarded a substantial risk of harm to her and denied her psychological care. The court concluded that the officials' awareness of two prior incidents of sexual misconduct by other officers was insufficient to establish that the officials must have drawn the inference that a substantial risk of harm existed. The court held she was not deprived of necessary medical care after the sexual assault. The plaintiff was seen by a psychiatrist 18 times and a by psychologist at least 100 times during a six month period.

Booking and Intake in Detention Facilities

One of the most critical moments in a detention center occurs at the time of admitting a prisoner, a procedure called "booking." Intake screening of newly admitted prisoners is an important component to ensuring the safety and welfare of the prisoner throughout his or her period of confinement. Components of the intake process are determining the prisoner's immediate criminal charge, the nature of the arrest, the prior criminal history, fingerprinting, the functioning level of the detainee, taking the detainee's photo, and deciding a housing classification. When feasible, medical and psychological screenings should also occur within a reasonable period of time after intake. Frequently a prisoner may be admitted who is too violent, mentally disoriented, or under the influence of a chemical substance to be medically screened. Once the prisoner sobers up, efforts should be made to determine the medical and/or psychological needs/history of the prisoner.

These intake components are useful in determining the housing and security needs of the prisoner population. Further, information solicited from the intake process is also helpful in providing medical and psychological care for the prisoner during confinement. Issues surrounding intake screening have emerged in a number of lawsuits alleging that the prisoner's constitutional right to proper medical care was violated by detention or by medical personnel for failing to properly screen the prisoner.

In *Turner v. Knight* (2002) a female detainee brought a Section 1983 action for claiming that the booking officers at the jail were deliberately indifferent to her serious medical needs. The detainee was admitted into the jail and the officers removed a neck brace and seized her medication. She complained that the officers never gave her medication, despite her repeated requests, and that she was in acute pain owing to muscle spasms throughout her six-hour confinement. The court granted qualified immunity to the officers, ruling that there was no evidence that the officers actually knew of, and ignored, a serious need for medical care. The court also found that the officers were not deliberately indifferent by failing to dispense medication in response of the detainee's complaints of pain, since the officers were not allowed to dispense medication and they had notified the facility's medical personnel.

The family of an intoxicated detainee who died in the hospital after a short confinement in jail filed a Section 1983 claim against the sheriff in *Butler v. Tp. Police Department* (2000). An intoxicated detainee refused to submit to sobriety tests and was placed in a cell after completing intake and booking procedures. The detainee experienced an alcohol withdrawal seizure seventeen hours after admission, fell in his cell, and sustained a head injury. He was immediately transported to the hospital and died three days later. The court held that the detainee's slurred speech and appearance of intoxication did not make the potential for an alcohol seizure so obvious as to draw an inference that officers acted with deliberate indifference to his medical needs. The court noted that the detainee never complained of physical distress, that he signed a medical form stating that he suffered no medical ailment other than bad knees, and that he noted that he typically suffered no ill effects when he ceased drinking.

Detainees housed in a detention facility filed a legal action to find correctional officials in contempt of a consent decree in *Carty v. Farrelly* (1997). The detainees asserted that officials failed to house prisoners based on a classification system at the time of intake and that intake health evaluations were also inadequate. These deficiencies resulted in mentally impaired prisoners being housed with general population prisoners, resulting in fights and assaults. The prisoners also claimed that sick call was handled by officers rather than medical personnel, that the officers failed to respond promptly to medical needs of prisoners, that they taunted mentally impaired prisoners, and that they excessively placed these prisoners in restraints without justification. The court found that the consent decree comported with the principles of the PLRA and that the officers were in contempt of the decree as structured. The court held that such actions and failures constituted a deliberate indifference to the detainees' safety, care, and security. Further, the court held that officials failed to maintain an objective classification system with which to house detainees and that they could only place detainees in restraints under special circumstances.

In *Estate of Hocker by Hocker v. Walsh* (1994) a detainee committed suicide in a detention facility, and the estate filed suit claiming that an intake policy of admitting intoxicated and unconscious detainees violated the detainee's constitutional rights. The detainee was admitted into the jail intoxicated, placed in a cell, and later hanged himself. The appeals court affirmed the lower court's finding of summary judgment for the sheriff and his officers, holding that they were not deliberately indifferent to the serious medical needs of the detainee. The appeals court did not find any evidence that officers admitted an unconscious detainee or any evidence that the detainee was observed as unconscious after he was admitted. The court concluded that the admitting officers had no reason to suspect that the detainee, who was intoxicated or under the influence of drugs, posed a risk of suicide to support a claim of deliberate indifference.

Deliberate Indifference and Environmental Hazards

It is highly common for prisoners to smoke in prison. Not only do prisoners smoke, but "squares" (cigarettes) serve as part of the prisoner economy system. Debts and favors are frequently paid with cigarettes. The United States Supreme Court has taken the opportunity to further apply the "deliberate indifference" standard to issues of environmental hazards behind prison and jail walls. The Supreme Court in *Helling v. McKinney* (1993) concurred with a prisoner who brought a Section 1983 action claiming his constitutional rights were violated since he was exposed to secondhand smoke. The prisoner was double-celled with a chain-smoking prisoner and claimed that the smoke created harm to his health. Justice Byron White emphasized that when prisoners are exposed to dangerous or unhealthy conditions, they need not wait until they suffer from a serious or life-threatening illness before asserting claims about improper conditions. The Court held that *Helling* did show that the corrections officials' actions under the Eighth Amendment supported a deliberate indifference claim, since Helling was exposed to high levels of environmental tobacco smoke (ETS) that posed an unreasonable risk of serious danger to his future health (Figure 5.1).

Since the *Helling* decision, numerous correctional officials have enacted a ban on smoking within prison living units, and lower courts have frequently rejected prisoner claims of ETS. In three separate cases (*Weaver v. Clarke* 1997; *Scott v. District of Columbia* 1998; *Caldwell v. Hammonds* 1999), prisoners all claimed that corrections officials were "deliberately indifferent" to their medical needs since they were exposed to ETS. In *Caldwell*, the appellate court affirmed a prisoner's claim that he indeed was exposed to ETS. Prison officials had instituted a policy banning smoking within the prison. Cigarettes were still sold in the prisoner canteen and officers permitted smoking in cell blocks. The court found that pervasive unsanitary and unhealthy conditions in the prisoners' cell block were obvious to any observer. The director of corrections was aware of these conditions and was, therefore, deliberately indifferent to them, giving support to the prisoner's claim. In *Weaver* and *Scott*, prison officials were not deliberately indifferent as they had instituted reasonable measures to ensure that prisoners observed the no-smoking policy and had improved ventilation.

Physicians and correction executives of the Michigan Department of Corrections were denied summary judgment for failing to maintain a smoke-free environment in *Reilly v. Grayson* (2001). Physicians determined that the prisoner be placed in a smoke-free environment, but the nonsmoking regulations in the prisoner's cell block were consistently violated and correctional officials were aware of the violations. After receiving notice that the regulations were not followed, neither the warden nor the deputy warden of the prison did anything to remedy the situation. The court determined that the officials were reckless and were deliberately indifferent to the medical needs of the prisoner's Eighth Amendment rights, and it awarded the prisoner $18,250 in punitive damages and $36,500 in compensatory damages for the five years of inaction by the wardens. The court concluded that the officials ignored their supervisory obligations and as a consequence awarded punitive damages.

Figure 5.1   *Helling v. McKinney* (1993)

Nevada state prisoner McKinney filed a Section 1983 action claiming he was exposed to environmental tobacco smoke (ETS) from his cellmate who smoked five packs of cigarettes a day. He asserted that being subjected to the smoke caused health problems in violation of his Eighth Amendment right to be free from cruel and unusual punishment. The lower court found no medical evidence to support his claim; he did not have a constitutional right to a smoke-free environment, and correctional officials were not deliberately indifferent to his rights.

The prisoner appealed, the lower court reversed, and correctional officials appealed to the United States Supreme Court.

The Court assessed the issue of whether involuntary exposure to ETS and its potential of a health risk supported a Section 1983 lawsuit in accordance with the Eighth Amendment. The Court held that a sufficiently high risk of future harm stemming from a prisoner's conditions of confinement could give rise to an Eighth Amendment claim. In such claims the prisoner must prove he was exposed to high levels of ETS. The Court further held that a prisoner seeking damages must convince a court that being exposed to such a risk violates contemporary standards of decency. The Court also determined that deliberate indifference was the proper standard with which to evaluate such claims.

This case is significant in that prisoner challenges to such claims need not cause a current health problem for the condition to be actionable. The Court agreed that being exposed to second-hand smoke can create a health concern for prisoners and that smoking may be prohibited. This decision grants authority to officials to develop policies which prohibit smoking within prisons and detention facilities. Counterclaims filed by prisoners requesting the right to smoke during confinement are unlikely to prevail.

Other claims have been brought against correctional officials in this environmental category beyond issues of secondary smoke. Several claims have been lodged for exposure to asbestos. A prisoner brought a *pro se* action to recover for exposure to asbestos in *Johnson v. DuBois* (1998). The district court ruled that while the prisoner could recover for exposure to asbestos without actually suffering from asbestosis, cancer, or other physical ailments, the prisoner failed to establish that he was exposed to asbestos. Based on news articles, the prisoner alleged that almost all buildings erected prior to 1970 used asbestos as fireproofing material, which the court found to be insufficient evidence. The prisoner contended that he was exposed to asbestos while working on several corrections department work crews during his confinement and that he was not provided with protective clothing or devices. Contrast the decision in *LaBounty v. Coughlin* (1998) when a prisoner brought a Section 1983 claim for exposure to asbestos in prison. The appellate court overturned summary judgment granted by the lower court, finding that the prisoner stated an Eighth Amendment deliberate indifference claim based on allegations that he was exposed to asbestos while incarcerated and that prison officials knowingly failed to protect him from such exposure.

The Americans With Disabilities Act and Prisoners

The Americans With Disabilities Act (ADA) was enacted in 1990 to protect qualified people with disabilities. The act not only applies to free citizens but also to prisoners in state prisons and other correctional facilities (*Pennsylvania Dept. of Corrections v. Yeskey* 1998). In *Yeskey*, a prisoner who had been denied admission to a prison boot camp program because of his history of hypertension sued correctional officials under the ADA. The United States Supreme Court held that Title II of the ADA, prohibiting a "public entity" from discriminating against a "qualified individual with a disability," applied to prisoners in state prisons. As applied in the correctional environment, the ADA was instituted to protect disabled prisoners from discrimination under the Fourteenth Amendment and has been primarily applied to health care issues.

A district court let stand a jury verdict and monetary damages in the amount of $150,000 in a Section 1983 action stemming from an ADA claim in *Beckford v. Irvin* (1999). The plaintiff prisoner had been confined to a wheelchair since 1984. In 1994 he was transferred from a psychiatric center to another correctional facility, where he was assigned to a Mental Health Observation Unit (MHOU). He was placed in the MHOU so his wheelchair could fit within the cell. Shortly after the transfer, officials took away the wheelchair and denied him access to it for the majority of his time at the facility, despite his repeated requests. The jury concluded that the prisoner's rights had been violated because he was unable to participate in outdoor exercise or to take a shower since he was denied the use of his wheelchair. The jury awarded damages against two supervisory officials for being deliberately indifferent to the prisoner's serious medical needs.

In *Hanson v. Sangamore County Sheriff's Dep't.* (1998), failure to provide a known deaf arrestee with an interpreter or physical means to make a telephone call was actionable under the ADA. A Section 1983 claim based on violation of the ADA was not defensible by qualified immunity. The district court rejected summary judgment of county officials in *Roe v. County of Com'n of Monongalia*

County (1996) when a mental health patient brought action under the ADA. The plaintiff was picked up on a mental health warrant and held in a padded cell, was handcuffed and shackled, was not given proper treatment or a hearing, and was not allowed to use a bathroom, change clothes, or eat without handcuffs. The court found that the prisoner stated a valid claim since he was unable to communicate with his family, was unable to attend to his personal hygiene, and was isolated in a manner that the ADA was designed to prevent.

Diabetic prisoners brought a class action Section 1983 action against state correctional officials, alleging Eighth Amendment violations and the ADA in *Rouse v. Plantier* (1998). The court denied summary judgment for the defendants on the issue of whether the prisoners' diabetes was a disability under the ADA. The court ruled that the prisoners might be substantially limited in the foods they could eat, in the exercise regime in which they could engage, and by the numerous special complications of diabetes. If the prisoners' condition was considered without mitigating measures such as medicines or assistive or prosthetic devices, the court found it was clear that they could be considered disabled.

In two similar cases, with differing judgments, *Schmidt v. Odell* (1999) and *Hallett v. New York State Department of Correctional Services* (2000), prisoners filed ADA legal actions asserting they each had been denied wheel chairs while confined. In *Schmidt*, the court granted summary judgment to detention officials who denied the prisoner the use of a wheel chair during his confinement. The court noted that there were legitimate concerns about the prisoner using the wheelchair while in the general population. The court also held that the prisoner could move through the jail, that he could use the toilet, the shower, and other services, and that he could access other areas without restriction. In *Hallett*, the court determined that the prisoner stated a legitimate claim, noting that prison officials failed to provide him with an adequate wheelchair for five months despite receiving notification that the prisoner was in severe back pain.

Deliberate Indifference and AIDS

Since the 1980s, more prisoners entering correctional facilities have been diagnosed with HIV/AIDS. Between 1991 and 1995 (Maruschak 1997) the number of HIV-positive prisoners grew at about the same rate (38 percent) as the overall prison population (36 percent). At the end of 1995, 4 percent of all female state prisoners were HIV positive, compared to 2.3 percent of male state prisoners. Maruschak (2001) reported a slight decline in the estimates of prisoners with HIV. At the end of 1999 about 3 percent of female prisoners were positive for HIV compared to 2 percent for male prisoners. In state prisons, 27 percent of HIV-positive prisoners were confirmed AIDS cases and accounted for 37 percent in Federal prisons. New York held more than a quarter of all prisoners (7,000) known to be HIV positive. AIDS-related deaths in prison make up the second most common cause of death, behind natural causes.

Detention facilities have also seen a steady increase in prisoners being admitted with AIDS or known to be HIV positive. Among jail prisoners, the HIV infection rate has been highest in the largest jail jurisdictions. In 43 of the 50 largest jurisdictions, 2.3 percent were HIV positive, compared to 1.1. percent in jurisdictions with fewer than 100 prisoners. From July 1, 1998 to June 30, 1999, 1 in 12 deaths among jail prisoners were due to AIDS-related complications.

Prisoners with HIV/AIDS entering a period of confinement have posed a significant problem for correctional officials in terms of classification, housing, medical care, and privacy. Liability issues under the Eighth Amendment have also emerged for correctional officials.

Testing prisoners for HIV/AIDS has resulted in litigation based on the notion that testing is unconstitutional or, conversely, that failure to test is impermissible. In *Harris v. Thigpen* (1991), the court held that testing prisoners for HIV/AIDS and segregation of HIV-positive and AIDS prisoners violated neither the Eighth nor Fourteenth Amendments. Providing medical care to HIV-positive and AIDS prisoners was not deliberately indifferent. Assisting a prisoner terminally ill with AIDS was seen as therapeutic, and isolation involved no deprivation of any constitutional right to privacy because institutional concerns outweighed any prisoners' rights. Conversely, failure to mandatorily test all prisoners for HIV infection and to segregate carriers was not deliberately indifferent where extensive educational programs and some testing were in place (*Meyers v. Maryland Div. of Corrections* 1992).

Expanding the disabilities associated with the Americans With Disabilities Act, the United States Supreme Court ruled in *Bragdon v. Abbott* (1999) that HIV infection is a "disability" under the ADA, even when the infection has not yet progressed to the so-called symptomatic phase, and therefore is a physical impairment which substantially limits the major life activity of reproduction. A patient infected with HIV brought an action under the ADA against a dentist who refused to treat her at his office. The court held that when assessing the risk associated with treating or accommodating a disabled person under the ADA, the risk assessment must be based on medical or other objective evidence and not simply on a person's good faith belief that a significant risk existed.

In *Polanco v. Dworzack* (1998) an AIDS-infected prisoner brought an action against prison medical personnel alleging deliberate indifference to his serious medical needs. The district court granted summary judgment to the defendants, holding that the medical personnel's failure to provide the prisoner with a specific, name-brand dietary supplement which he had requested was deliberately indifferent to his serious medical needs. The court further noted that a prisoner does not have the right to the medical treatment of his choice and that, therefore, a mere disagreement with a doctor's professional judgment is not a constitutional violation. The prisoner had been maintaining steady weight and was given daily supplementary snacks, and medical personnel met with him whenever he requested sick call.

The district court in *McNally v. Prison Health Care Services, Inc.* (1998) found that a pretrial detainee stated a valid claim that his constitutional rights were violated when he was denied his medication for HIV. The court found that the jail's failure to provide him the medication was deliberately indifferent to his medical needs, causing the detainee to suffer significant harm. The detainee was arrested by police and injured by arresting officers. The police took him to a hospital for treatment of cuts on his nose and a blackened eye prior to transporting him to the jail. Once at the jail, the detainee informed booking personnel that he had been diagnosed with HIV, was on a strict regimen of medication, and needed his medication since he had missed a dosage earlier in the day. The detainee's physician confirmed this, but the detainee was denied his medication during his three-day confinement. Upon release from the jail, he was hospitalized for several days as a result of having been deprived of his medication.

Compare, however, the court's ruling in *Evans v. Bonner* (2002). A prisoner confined in a county correctional center brought a Section 1983 claim against the nurses, claiming they failed to provide him with his medication for his HIV condition in a timely manner. The district court granted summary judgment, holding that even the aches and pains and joint problems suffered by the prisoner were caused by the nurses' negligence and that the symptoms did constitute a condition of urgency or one that might produce death, degeneration, or extreme pain.

Summary

It should be evident from this discussion that prisoners possess a fundamental right to adequate medical and mental health care for their serious medical needs. The standard of review for examining a claim of inadequate medical care during confinement is deliberate indifference. This standard is applied to detention and prison facilities. Deliberate indifference means officers or officials acted with a culpable state of mind and with a conscious disregard for a prisoner's right.

Whether in a detention center or in a prison, correctional officials must have a system whereby prisoners have access to medical and psychiatric care. Such a system starts at the time of admission and continues until the prisoner is released. Policies, procedures, and training should be in place for such a system and should direct officers and medical personnel in their responsibilities of responding to the needs of prisoners.

Correctional administrators are encouraged to take a proactive risk management approach to delivering health services to prisoners within their custody. A team approach is recommended, which involves supervisors, health care providers, and officers who periodically review the services within the facility. This review should address the following: admission policies; medical/psychiatric screening; medical examinations; the summoning of health care providers; sick call and referral systems; the use of observation cells; identifying, responding to, and monitoring "special needs prisoners"; intervention protocols such as the use of force and restraints for medical purposes; dispensing and documenting medications; housing classification of prisoners; chemical substance withdrawal procedures; providing contractual health care services and access to local health care services; and documenting health care services. Conducting a periodic risk assessment, as well as implementing changes as necessary, is a proactive management responsibility which can improve security and health care services and simultaneously protect prisoners' rights. Such an assessment also enhances the ability to predict future incidents which can be addressed by the agency to reduce the risk of incurring liability.

Administrators should be familiar with their state standards for delivery of health care services for prisoners. They are also encouraged to review health care standards and recommendations published by the American Correctional Association, the American Jail Association, the National Commission on Correctional Health Care, and other agencies when developing or revising their own procedures.

While the court does not require correction officers to be make a clinical diagnosis of the medical and mental health of prisoners, they are the first line of defense to claims asserting that a prisoner was delayed or denied adequate medical care. Officers must adequately perform their duties within the legal parameters of the law, their department's policies, and their training. When intervening with prisoners needing medical care, officers should carefully document their actions. Therefore, officers should know about their agencies' health care policies and how to refer a prisoner to a health care provider. Train-

ing in health care services commensurate to their job functions should be provided on a regular basis. Such training and a commitment to performing their
custodial job tasks will assure that adequate health care services will be provided to all prisoners. Such endeavors will be useful in defending a legal claim
of an inadequate response to providing health care to a prisoner.

References

Alexander, E. 1996. Inmate advocate raises questions about PLRA's constitutionality. *Correctional Law Reporter* 8: 19, 26.

Beck, A. J., and L. M. Maruschak. 2001. Mental health treatment in state
prisons, 2000. *Bureau of Justice Statistics.* Washington, DC: U.S. Department of Justice.

Camp, G., and G. Camp. 2002. *The 2001 corrections yearbook.* Middletown,
CT: Criminal Justice Institute, Inc.

Ditton, O. M. 1999. Mental health and treatment of inmates and probationers. *Bureau of Justice Statistics.* Washington, DC: Department of Justice.

Guy, E., J. Platt, I. Zwerling, and S. Bullock. 1985. Mental health status of
prisoners in an urban jail. *Criminal Justice and Behavior* 1: 29–53.

Krantz, S. 2003. *The law of sentencing, corrections, and prisoners rights.* 6th
ed. St. Paul, MN: West Publishing.

Maahs, J. R., and R. V. del Carmen. 1995. Curtailing frivolous section
1983 inmate litigation: Laws, practices, and proposals. *Federal Probation*
59: 53–61.

Maruschak, L. M., and A. J. Beck. 2001. Medical problems of inmates,
1997. *Bureau of Justice Statistics.* Washington, DC: Department of Justice.

Maruschak, L. M., and A. J. Beck. 2001. HIV in prisons and jails: 1999. *Bureau of Justice Statistics.* Washington, DC: Department of Justice.

Maruschak, L. 1997. HIV in prisons and jails, 1995. *Bureau of Justice Statistics Bulletin.* Washington, DC: U.S. Department of Justice.

May, J. P., and W. E. Lambert. 1998. Preventive health issues for individuals
in jails and prisons. In *Clinical Practice in Correctional Medicine,* edited
by M. Puisi, 259–74. St. Louis, MO: Mosby, Inc.

Palmer, J. W., and S. E. Palmer. 2004. *Constitutional rights of prisoners.* 7th
ed. Cincinnati, OH: Anderson Publishing Co.

Plitt, E. A. 1997. *Police civil liability and the defense of citizen misconduct complaints manual.* Chicago: Americans for Effective Law Enforcement, Inc.

Raba, J. 1998. Mortality in prisons and jails. In *Clinical Practice in Correctional Medicine*, edited by M. Puisi, 301–13. St. Louis, MO: Mosby, Inc.

Ross, D. L. 1997. Emerging trends in correctional civil liability cases: A content analysis of federal court decisions of Title 42 United States Code Section 1983: 1970-1994. *Journal of Criminal Justice* 25: 501–15.

_____. 2001. *A risk analysis of the claims, losses, and liabilities of Michigan jails: 1994–1999*. Unpublished technical report for the Michigan Municipal Risk Management Authority, Livonia, MI.

Silver, I. 2003. *Police civil liability*. Newark, NJ: Matthew Bender.

Steadman, H., S. Fabisiak, J. Dvoskin, and E. Holohean. 1989. A survey of mental disability among state prison inmates. *Hospital and Community Psychiatry* 10: 1086–89.

Stein, L., and C. Alaimo. 1998. Psychiatric intake screening. In *Clinical Practice in Correctional Medicine*, edited by M. Puisi, 209–20. St. Louis, MO: Mosby, Inc.

Teplin, L. A. 1990. The prevalence of severe mental disorder among male urban jail detainees: Comparison with the epidemiologic catchment area program. *American Journal of Public Health* 6: 663–69.

Cases Cited

Abdul-Wadood v. Nathan, 91 F.3d 1023 (7th Cir. 1996)

Anderson v. County of Kern, 45 F. 3d 1310 (9th Cir. 1995)

Antonelli v. Sheahan, 81 F. 3d 1422-1428, 1431-1432 (7th Cir. 1996)

Arnold v. Lewis, 803 F. Supp. 246 (D. Ariz. 1992)

Beckford v. Irvin, 49 F. Supp. 2d 170 (W.D.N.Y. 1999)

Beverati v. Smith, 120 F. 3d 500 (4th Cir. 1997)

Bragdon v. Abbott, 526 U.S. 1131 (1999)

Breads v. Moehrie, 781 F. Supp. 953 (W.D.N.Y. 1991)

Bridges v. Rhodes, 41 Fed. Appx. 902 (8th Cir. 2002)

Butler v. Tp. Police Department, 93 F. Supp. 2d 862 (N.D. Ohio 2000)

Caldwell v. Hammonds, 53 F. Supp. 2d 1 (D.D.C. 1999)

Carty v. Farrelly, 957 F. Supp. 727 (D. Virgin Islands 1997)

City of Canton, Ohio v. Harris, 489 U.S. 378 (1989)

Coleman v. Wilson, 912 F. Supp. 1282 (E.D. Cal. 1995)

Davis v. Scott, 157 F. 3d 1003 (5th Cir. 1998)

DeShaney v. Winnebago County Department of Social Services, 489 U.S. 189 (1989)

Dixon v. Godinez, 114 F.3d 640 (7th Cir. 1997)

Dowling v. Hannigan, 995 F. Supp. 1188 (D.Kan. 1998)

Estate of Hocker by Hocker v. Walsh, 22 F.3d 995 (10th Cir. 1994)

Estate of Taft v. County of Isabella, No. 98-CV-10436-BC (E.D. Mich. 2002) [unpublished]

Estelle v. Gamble, 429 U.S. 97 (1976)

Evans v. Bonner, 196 F. Supp.2d 252 (E.D.N.Y 2002)

Farmer v. Brennan, 511 U.S. 825 (1994)

Freeman v. Godinez, 996 F. Supp. 822 (N.D. Ill. 1998)

Fuller v. Dillon, 236 F. 3d 876 (7th Cir. 2001)

Geder v. Godinez, 875 F. Supp. 1334 (N.D. Ill. 1995)

Giron v. Corrections Corp. of America, 14 F. Supp. 2d 1252 (D.N.M. 1998)

Greer v. Shoop, 141 F.3d 824 (8th Cir. 1998)

Gutierrez v. Peters, 111 F.3d 1364 (7th Cir. 1997)

Hallett v. New York State Department of Correctional Services, 109 F. Supp. 190 (S.D.N.Y. 2000)

Hamilton v. Lyons, 74 F. 3d 99, 104-106 (5th Cir. 1995)

Hampton v. Hobbs, 106 F.3d 1281 (6th Cir. 1997)

Hanson v. Sangamore Co. Sheriff's Dep't., 991 F. Supp. 1059, 1062-1065 (C.D. Ill. 1998)

Harris v. Thigpen, 941 F. 2d 1495, 1511, 1516 (11th Cir. 1991)

Hawley v. Evans, 716 F. Supp. 601, 603-04 (N.D. Ga. 1989)

Helling v. McKinney, 509 U.S. 25 (1993)

Holt v. Sarver, 309 F. Supp. 362 (E.D. Ark.1970)

Ingalls v. Floyd, 968 F. Supp. 193, 197-202 (D. N.J. 1997)

Johnson v. DuBois, 20 F. Supp. 2d 138 (D. Mass. 1998)

LaBounty v. Coughlin, 137 F.3d 68 (2nd Cir. 1998)

Lancaster v. Monroe County, Alabama, 116 F. 3d 1419 (11th Cir. 1997)

Lawson v. Dallas County, 286 F.3d 257 (5th Cir. 2002)

Lopez v. Le Master, 172 F. 3d 756 (10th Cir. 1999)

Lopez v. Smith, 160 F. 3d 567 (9th Cir. 1998)

Luong v. Hatt, 979 F. Supp. 481 (N.D. Tex. 1997)

Lyon v. Vande Krol, 940 F. Supp. 1433 (S.D. Iowa 1996)

Madrid v. Gomez, 889 F. Supp. 1146 (N.D. Cal. 1995)

Malek v. Haun, 26 F.3d 1013 (10 Cir. 1994)

Martinez v. State of California, 444 U.S. 277 (1980)

Matthews v. Armitage, 36 F. Supp. 2d 121 (N.D.N.Y. 1999)

McCarthy v. Madigan, 503 U.S. 140 (1992)

McNally v. Prison Health Care Services, Inc., 28 F. Supp. 2d 671 (D.Me. 1998)

Meyers v. Maryland Div. of Corrections, 782 F. Supp. 1095 (D. Md.1992)

Montero v. Travis, 171 F. 3d 757 (2nd Cir. 1999)

Morales Feliciano v. Rossello Gonzalez, 13 F. Supp. 2d 151 (D. Puerto Rico 1998)

Morgan v. Arizona Dept. of Corrections, 976 F. Supp. 892 (D. Ariz. 1997)

Newkirk v. Sheers, 834 F. Supp. 772 (E.D. Pa. 1993)

Olds v. Hogg, 774 F. Supp. 1202 (E.D. Mo. 1991)

Patsy v. Florida Board of Regents, 457 U.S. 496 (1982)

Pennsylvania Dept. of Corrections v. Yeskey, 524 U.S. 206 (1998)

Perkins v. Grimes, 161 F. 3d 1127 (8th Cir. 1998)

Petrichko v. Kurtz, 52 F. Supp. 2d 503 (E.D.Pa. 1999)

Polanco v. Dworzack, 25 F. Supp. 2d 148 (W. D. N.Y. 1998)

Priest v. Cupp, 545 P.2d 917 (Org. Ct. App. 1976)

Reed v. McBride, 178 F 3d. 849 (7th Cir. 1999)

Reilly v. Grayson, 157 F. Supp.2d 762 (E.D. Mich. 2001)

Rhodes v. Chapman, 452 U.S. 337 (1981)

Robeson v. Squadrito, 57 F. Supp. 2d 642, 646-648 (N.D. Ind. 1999)

Roe v. County of Com'n of Monongalia County, 926 F. Supp. 74 (N.D. W. Va. 1996)

Roller v. Gunn, 107 F.3d 227 (4th Cir. 1997)

Rosen v. Chang, 811 F. Supp. 754 (D. R.I. 1993)

Rouse v. Plantier, 997 F. Supp. 575 (D. N. J. 1998)

Schmidt v. Odell, 64 F. Supp. 2d 1014 (D. Kan. 1999)

Scott v. District of Columbia, 39 F. 3d 940 (D.C. Cir. 1998)

Sell v. U.S., 123 U.S. 2174 (2003)

Sellars v. Procunier, 641 F. 2d 1295 (9th Cir. 1981)

Simpson v. Horn, 25 F. Supp. 563 (E.D. Pa. 1998)

Tucker v. Randall, 840 F. Supp. 1237 (N.D. Ill. 1993)

Turner v. Knight, 192 F. supp. 2d 391 (D. Md. 2002)

Turner v. Safley, 482 U.S. 78 (1987)

U.S. v. Weston, 134 F. Supp. 2d 115 (D.D.C. 2001)

Washington v. Harper, 494 U.S. 201 (1990)

Weaver v. Clarke, 120 F. 3d 852 (6th Cir. 1997)

West v. Atkins, 487 U.S. 42 (1988)

Wilson v. Chang, 955 F. Supp. 18 (D. R.I. 1997)

Wilson v. Seiter, 501 U.S. 294 (1991)

Wolff v. McDonnell, 418 U.S. 539 (1974)

Veloz v. New York, 35 F. Supp. 305 (S.D.N.Y 1999)

CHAPTER 6

CIVIL LIABILITY
AND THE USE OF FORCE

*Not every push or shove, even if it may later seem unnecessary in the
peace of a judge's chambers, violates a prisoner's constitutional rights.*

Johnson v. Glick (1973)

Working inside the contemporary prison or detention facility is not only a
stressful job but is also a dangerous task for correctional employees. In assessing five of seven studies on stressors of the job, five identify danger as a
primary stressor for correction officers. In 1996 the Bureau of Justice Statistics ranked the job of corrections officers as the fourth most dangerous occu-
pation per 1,000 workers (117/1,000), behind police officers (306/1,000), private security personnel (218/1,000), and taxi drivers (184/1,000). The close
proximity to prisoners in performing the tasks of the officer makes him or her
vulnerable to physical assault. Even routine interactions between officers and
prisoners in the coercive environment can produce structured conflict (Griffin 1999). With some regularity these confrontations require the officer to use
a level of force to preserve order and instill discipline (del Carmen 1992).

Correctional personnel possess legal authority to use force in the performance of their duties and may legitimately use force in self-defense and defense
of another, in breaking up prisoner fights, in protecting a prisoner from self-
injury, in enforcement of facility rules and regulations, in prevention of an escape, and in prevention of crime (Palmer and Palmer 2004). When using
force, officers must justify the type and degree of force used in any situation
and are required to use force within a framework of legally prescribed guidelines. Using force outside these legal guidelines can give rise to civil liability
whereby a prisoner asserts that the officer violated his constitutionally protected right of unreasonable use of force. Force can never be used for purposes
of punishment (*Jackson v. Bishop* 1968).

Use of force by correctional officers is one of the most controversial aspects
of the legal authority granted to them. Frequently, in incidents when force is

used, claims of excessive force arise and numerous questions emerge, such as the following: What constitutes excessive force? What is reasonable force? Was the amount or type of force used by the officer appropriate and needed? Was the degree or type of force used as punishment? What is the appropriate standard with which to evaluate the use of force? Did the officer violate the constitutional rights of the prisoner plaintiff? These and many more questions will be raised by the plaintiff who seeks to win monetary damages. This chapter examines the liability issues surrounding claims of excessive force in correctional work. This issue is of critical importance to officers since they must be aware of the courts' standards with which to evaluate liability claims. Moreover, supervisory personnel must also understand the importance of their role in training officers in proper force decision making and force procedures, developing guidelines for agency personnel and investigating claims of excessive force. Specifically, this chapter will address allegations of excessive force and brutality and will present legal precedents.

RESEARCH ON USE OF FORCE IN CORRECTIONS

Physical encounters between prisoners and correctional personnel are intrinsic to the institutional environment, and deciding to use force is an extremely critical issue. Deciding to use force in corrections has spawned riots, disturbances, human death and injury, property damage, and, of course, civil liability.

Statistics regarding prisoner assaults against prison and detention officers reveal that assaults on officers have increased over 28 percent in prisons and 15 percent in detention facilities from 1995 to 2001 (Bureau of Justice Statistics [BJS] 2003, 8-9; Camp and Camp 2002, 12-13). During this period, prisoner assaults on prison officers averaged 13,000 annually, while prisoner assaults on detention officers averaged 4,000 annually. Deaths of prison officers from prisoner assaults averaged 3 per year (N=20). Prison disturbances involving over 5 prisoners averaged 500 annually. An annual average of 200 officers sustained injuries in these disturbances, and injuries to prisoners occurred at the rate of 680 per year. Prisons averaged 9,500 escapes annually and 6,200 these prisoners were captured. Prisoner-on-prisoner assaults averaged 27,000 annually, resulting in an annual average of 60 prisoner deaths. Research studies analyzing force used by correctional officers are virtually nonexistent, while a small number of studies have examined prisoner assaults on correctional officers (Bowker 1980; Kratcoski 1987; Light 1991; Ross 1996a; Rowan 1996). Prior studies reveal that a majority of prisoner assaults occur while the officer is performing routine tasks such as enforcing facility rules, breaking up fights, and supervising prisoners. These studies suggest that prisoner assaults on officers are often unprovoked and spontaneous and that prisoners lose control, lashing out against officers as the nearest symbols of authority. Bowker (1980) found that most prisoner attacks on correction officers occurred unexpectedly, primarily in a random manner, when the officers were performing basic correctional functions. Examining officer incident reports in New York, Light (1991) found that a majority (50 percent) of prisoner assaults on officers occurred in a general housing unit, that the assaults normally did not involve a weapon (75 percent), and that the assaulting prisoners tended to be younger than the nonassaulting prisoners.

In a national study of prisoner assaults on correction officers in 53 prisons, Ross (1996) revealed that the veteran housing unit officer was more likely to be assaulted spontaneously by one prisoner without the use of a weapon. The most common injury sustained by an officer was a back injury requiring limited medical treatment. Prisoners tended to be ten to fifteen years younger than the assaulted officer, and most of them were serving a sentence for robbery/armed robbery, murder, and aggravated assault. Rowan (1996) analyzed prisoner assaults on female correction officers. He found that female officers were less likely to be assaulted and that male officers were approximately four times more likely to be assaulted.

Other studies suggest that the environment of the facility may increase the potential of violence against officers (Ekland-Olsen, Barrich, and Cohen 1983; Marquart 1986; Griffin 1999). Consequently, when correction officers are attacked, they may use force in self-defense. Marquart (1986) suggested that the use of force, particularly excessive force, by correction officers working in prisons may be a result of a subculture of violence by some officers which supports "institutional force" as a method for controlling prisoners. Griffin (1999) found that the perceptions of detention officers regarding the interactions and relationships with prisoners and supervisory personnel have a direct influence on the officers' readiness to use force. More specifically, the youth of the officer, the officer's perception of his or her role, and the quality of supervision significantly influenced the officer's readiness to use force.

Use-of-force polices in corrections have previously been studied. Ross (1990) conducted a national examination of the status of use-of-force policies in state and federal adult institutions (facilities in 41 states and the Federal Bureau of Prisons). He reported that 90 percent of the respondents had a use-of-force policy which had been written within three years of the survey. Hemmens and Atherton (1999) conducted a study on the use of force in corrections for the American Correctional Association. They surveyed officials in state adult correctional institutions (facilities in 46 states, 2 military prisons, and the Federal Bureau of Prisons), in jails (n=30), in institutions in Canada (n=8 departments), and in juvenile institutions (n=39). They reported that the U.S. and Canadian prison systems have written policies on the use of force and that 97 percent of jails and juvenile institutions have written policies. All respondents are less likely (45 percent) to have policies covering specialized applications of force (special response teams and use of specialized equipment and restraint techniques). Over 80 percent of the agencies allow officers to use chemical agents on prisoners in various situations, and less than 45 percent allow the use of stun guns. Firearms usage is authorized in over two-thirds of the U.S. correctional institutions and jails, in only 17 percent of the Canadian institutions, and in 11 percent of the juvenile departments. Forty-six percent of the respondents revealed that they had not experienced an "excessive force" incident in 1997. Approximately 51 percent, however, indicated that they had experienced between 1 and 25 incidents of "excessive force," and 94 percent reported that they had disciplined the officer.

This review of the limited literature concerning correctional use of force reveals that the issue is paramount for the public and for correctional officers. In response, the United States Supreme Court has established guidelines for determining the components of excessive force and has established standards of review when considering allegations of excessive force (*Whitley v. Albers* 1986; *Hudson v. McMillian* 1992). While not easily definable, these standards indicate how claims of "excessive" force in corrections are determined. The United States Supreme Court has developed different standards for determining the appropriate use of force, and the appropriate standard is based on the status of the individual. First, the remaining discussion will explain how the courts specifically apply use-of-force standards in examining lethal or non-lethal force in detention and prison facilities; second, it will present and explore case examples.

STANDARDS OF REVIEW CONCERNING THE USE OF FORCE IN CORRECTIONS

Claims alleging the use of excessive force by correctional personnel which violate the constitutional rights of a prisoner may be filed in state court using state tort laws or in federal court using Section 1983. The major distinction between the uses of the two court systems lies in the kind of constitutional violation. To be successful in a federal action, the plaintiff must prove that the officer's actions caused the deprivation of a constitutionally protected right

(Kappeler 2001). Excessive-force lawsuits are filed in state court as torts for assault and battery or for wrongful death. Existing tort law or statutes will govern the examination of such claims. Because most claims of excessive force in prisons and detention facilities are filed in federal court under provisions of Section 1983, case discussion will focus on these claims.

As previously indicated, there are five legitimate rationale for permitting a correction officer to use a level of force. These rationale provide a framework for justifying the use of force or force equipment in the correctional context. Within this framework are two court standards used to determine whether an officer used force appropriately, and these standards are based on three court decisions. When examining an excessive force prisoner claim, it is important to keep in mind the status of the prisoner to determine which standard of review a particular court will use (see Figure 6.1). First, if the plaintiff is a pretrial detainee (in jail awaiting arraignment or trial), generally courts will apply the "shocks the conscience" standard, consistent with the Fourteenth Amendment's and Fifth Amendment's due process clauses. Because jail detainees are not convicted, the Eighth Amendment's clause of cruel and unusual punishment does not apply, although some courts will infrequently apply the Eighth-Amendment standard in use-of-force cases in jails. The leading case for use-of-force claims emerging from detention facilities with pretrial detainees is *Johnson v. Glick* (1973).

Second, case analysis of claims alleging excessive force in the prison context stem from the Eighth Amendment's clause of cruel and unusual punishment. Cruel and unusual punishment has been defined as "the unnecessary and wanton infliction of pain." This definition is not always easy to interpret, and application of the standard can therefore be problematic. For example, can using a "pain compliance wristlock" by a correctional officer to control a disruptive prisoner fit within the cruel-and-unusual-punishment definition? The answer is generally no, since using force control techniques would require administering "pain" to control the prisoner. Should the officer, however, use the tactic in a "wanton" fashion, with the intention of causing injury or harm to the prisoner, the officer may be held liable in accordance with the Eighth Amendment.

The United States Supreme Court has established a standard of review when examining use of excessive force claims emerging from the prison context. Circumstances stemming from the use of nonlethal or less-than-lethal force are scrutinized under the Eighth Amendment in accordance with the decisions *Whitley v. Albers* (1986) and *Hudson v. McMillian* (1992). The courts use the "malicious and sadistic for causing harm" standard under the Eighth Amendment when examining all cases of excessive force applied against con-

Figure 6.1   Use of Force Case Law and Standards

Pretrial Detainee	Convicted Offender
(14th Amendment)	(8th Amendment)
↓	↓
Johnson v. Glick (1973)	*Whitley v. Albers* (1986)
"Shocks the conscience"	"Obduracy and wanton infliction of pain"
↓	↓
1. Need to use force	*Hudson v. McMillan* (1992)
2. Relationship between need and amount used	"Force used maliciously and sadistically to cause harm" and serious injury not a factor
3. Extent of injury	
4. Force used in good faith or maliciously and sadistically to cause harm	

victed and sentenced prisoners. Each case and the applicable standard will be discussed in detail.

Pre-Trial Detainees and Shocks the Conscience Test

Prior to the United States Supreme Court's decisions on the use of force, the lower courts had authorized police and correctional officers to use reasonable and necessary force in the following circumstances (*Skinner v. Brooks* 1944; *Stein v. State* 1976; *Fobbs v. City of Los Angeles* 1957; *Hostin v. United States* 1983): to effect an arrest and overcome unlawful resistance, in self-defense, in defense of a third party, and to prevent an individual from harming himself. Prior to the United States Supreme Court decisions regarding appropriate use of force, there was considerable controversy among the lower federal courts over which standard should be used in determining excessive force claims. A majority of the courts held that excessive-force claims should be viewed as deprivations of liberty without due process of law. This approach was premised upon the notion that individuals have a substantive due process right, under the Fourteenth Amendment, to be free from an unreasonable and unwarranted violation of their physical integrity by police officers, even in the course of an otherwise valid arrest (*Screws v. U.S.* 1945; *Brazier v. Cherry* 1961; *Monroe v. Pape* 1961; *Johnson v. Glick* 1973; *Shillingford v. Holmes* 1981). For many years a majority of the courts used the decision in *Johnson v. Glick* (1973), employing the "shocks the conscience" test. This test originated in *Rochin v. California* (1952), when Justice Felix Frankfurter stated that due process prohibits governmental actions that "shock the conscience." Under that formulation, the due process standard has generally been construed to incorporate subjective factors, such as the intent or motivation of the government actor. In use-of-force cases, the question usually turns on whether the type of and the degree of force were designed to "punish" an individual rather than to accomplish some legitimate law enforcement goal, such as maintaining or restoring control.

Johnson involved a claim by a pretrial detainee alleging that he had been subjected to excessive force by an officer who struck him in the head with an object the officer held in his closed fist. The officer struck Johnson for failing to follow orders. Johnson did not physically resist, attack, or threaten the officer. Johnson sustained a slight bump on his head and ringing in his ear. Medical treatment was not administered until several hours later. The detainee filed a Section 1983 action claiming police brutality.

Using Justice Frankfurter's "shock the conscience" test, the Court of Appeals for the Second Circuit stated that not every push and shove by a prison guard violates a prisoner's constitutional rights. The court established four factors for evaluating the actions of the officer: (1) the need for the use of force, (2) the relationship between the amount of force needed and the amount that was used, (3) the severity of the injuries sustained by the plaintiff, and (4) whether force was applied in good faith or maliciously and sadistically for the purpose of causing harm. The court ruled in favor of the officer.

The court's decision was based upon the premise that constitutional protection against brutality is not limited to conduct violating the specific commands of the Eighth or the Fourth Amendment. Use of force would violate due process under the Fourteenth Amendment if the force was used for punishment or was unrelated to a legitimate nonpunitive governmental objective, in which case an intent to punish may be inferred. The assessment of use-of-force claims depends on the state of mind of the actor.

The four-factor test requires the officer to justify the need for using force. One test or a combination of these tests must exist to justify the need to use force. Second, the force must be proportionate to the need. For example, in order for an officer to use lethal force, a situation must exist where severe injury or death are likely to occur to the officer before he or she may use a firearm. Third, in light of the need of the use of force, the court will examine the severity of the injury sustained by the prisoner, if any. Fourth, the need for the officer's use of force and the extent of the injury sustained by the prisoner must be examined by assessing the officer's state of mind. If the evidence indicates that the officer used force for malicious purposes, liability will attach regardless of the severity of injury.

An officer's decision to use force is also controlled by additional considerations. When determining a level of force to use in a given situation, correctional officers must also consider the type and degree of resistance demonstrated by a prisoner, the prisoner's possession of and/or access to a weapon, the reasonable perception of danger or threat of danger the officer is facing, and the means of force available to the officer.

Although the *Glick* standard originated from a use-of-force incident in a detention facility, it was applied by many courts to police and correctional force situations until 1985 (i.e., *Tennessee v. Garner*). Uniform application of the "shock the conscience" test was not universally accepted by the courts. The test created judicial disagreement over what actions actually constitute significant bodily injury before the plaintiff could prevail in a Section 1983 action. Some courts held that only "serious" or "severe" injuries were actionable under Section 1983 (*Raley v. Fraser* 1984; *Owens v. City of Atlanta* 1985; *Gumz v. Morrissette* 1985). These courts strictly applied the test, concluding that not every tort committed by a police officer violates a person's rights guaranteed by the Fourteenth Amendment. In *Owens*, an arrestee died from positional asphyxia as a result of having been placed in a "stretch" hold position known as the "mosses crosses" in a jail cell. The court concluded that the method of restraint did not violate the decedent's constitutional rights. If it can be shown by the plaintiff that force used by the officer was not needed, inflicted an injury, and was performed for sadistic and malicious purposes rather than to restore order, liability will most likely attach. Application of the "shocks the conscience" standard is applied on a case-by-case basis.

For example, in *McClanahan v. City of Moberly* (1998), a pretrial detainee alleged that she was the victim of excessive force in connection with her transfer from a police department to a county jail. The district court granted summary judgment for the defendants, finding that the detainee's allegations of being slapped three times, without evidence of any resulting injury, was at most a *de minimis* (trifle) injury that did not violate the due process clause of the Fourteenth Amendment.

In *Santiago v. C.O. Campisi Shield #4592* (2000), a pretrial detainee submitted a Section 1983 claim alleging that an officer assaulted him in his cell.

According to the prisoner, the officer slapped him in the face with an open hand after an altercation. The court granted summary judgment for the officer, holding that the slap was *de minimis*, since the prisoner did not suffer any physical injury. The court held that the slap was not sufficiently repugnant to the conscience of mankind to amount to a due-process violation.

Claims of detainee brutality by officers frequently fall within the context of excessive force. One particularly egregious example is illustrated in *Mathie v. Fries* (1996). While confined as a pretrial detainee, Mathie claimed that the facility's Director of Security sexually abused him. The district court entered summary judgment for the detainee, finding sufficient evidence to support claims that the director repeatedly sodomized the detainee while he was handcuffed to pipes in the security office. Finding that these acts violated the detainee's due process rights, the court rejected a petition for qualified immunity and awarded the detainee $250,000 in compensation and $500,000 in punitive damages. The court called the director's action an outrageous abuse of power and authority.

The estate in *Brothers v. Klevenhagen* (1994) brought a Section 1983 claim alleging excessive force by the county and the sheriff. The deceased, an unarmed pretrial detainee, attempted to escape during transport from one holding cell to another. The deputies fired at the detainee to prevent an escape, but only as a last resort, since the detainee would have escaped if the deputies had not used lethal force. The appeals court affirmed the lower court's summary judgment for the county. The court found that the Due Process Clause of the Fourteenth Amendment, rather than the Fourth Amendment, provided the appropriate constitutional standard for evaluating the deputies' use of force. The sheriff"s department policy allowed deadly force only when immediately necessary to prevent escape, and it was designed in a good-faith effort to maintain or restore discipline and not to maliciously and sadistically cause harm.

Correctional Use-of-Force Standards Established by the Supreme Court

Johnson was the controlling use-of-force decision in corrections from 1973 until 1985, when the United States Supreme Court established a standard of review in lethal-force situations in prison. Lethal force is generally defined as that force which is reasonably likely to cause death (*Cruz v. Escondido* 1997). Lethal force normally involves the use of firearms and may include impact weapon strikes to certain areas of the body. Generally, correction officers may use lethal force when faced with the following circumstances: prisoner escape, protecting property in cases of arson, an act likely to cause serious injury or death, a prisoner's possession of a weapon or intention to obtain a weapon by force and to cause death of another, an officer's observation of a prisoner or another whom the officer has seen kill or seriously injure another, quelling a riot or disturbance, and self-defense. When possible, an officer should give a verbal warning prior to using lethal force. In reviewing a case of lethal force, the courts do not generally consider the result of a particular incident, but whether the force used had a reasonable probability of causing death.

Whitley v. Albers (1986)

Following on the heels of the *Tennessee v. Garner* (1985) decision, which established guidelines for using lethal force in police incidents (Fourth Amendment), the Supreme Court, in *Whitley v. Albers* (1986), reviewed a deadly-force incident which occurred during a prison riot. The Court established how the Eighth Amendment applies to protect against cruel and unusual punishment, including allegations of excessive force asserted by prisoners. In *Whitley*, Oregon prison officials were confronted with a disturbance by prisoners who had killed one prisoner and had taken a correction officer hostage. Threats to kill the hostage and other prisoners were made by prisoners, should force be used by officials. Officials ultimately decided to use force to free the hostage and retake the cellblock. The prison response team, armed with shotguns, entered the housing unit and issued several warnings to release the hostage. After verbal commands failed and after two warning shots had been ignored, prisoner Albers was shot in the left knee, sustaining severe physical injury as well as emotional and mental distress. He filed a Section 1983 lawsuit against prison officials. claiming that his Eighth and Fourteenth Amendments' rights had been violated.

The Supreme Court reversed the appeals court's decision which had found in favor of Albers. The Court ruled that the infliction of pain in the course of a prison security measure is only an Eighth Amendment violation if it is inflicted "unnecessarily and wantonly." The standard of deliberate indifference was rejected by the Court as not sufficiently broad enough to be used in analyzing deadly force claims associated with prison riots. The Court held that the force measure taken inflicted unnecessary and wanton pain and suffering ultimately turns on whether the use of force was applied in a good-faith effort to maintain or restore discipline or whether it was applied maliciously and sadistically for the purpose of causing harm. This language is taken from the fourth component indicated in the *Glick* (1973) decision. Other relevant considerations noted by the Court were: (1) the need for the application of force,

(2) the relationship between the need and the amount of force used, (3) the extent of injury inflicted, (4) the extent of threat to the safety of officers and prisoners, and (5) any efforts to temper the severity of a forceful response.

The Court noted that when correction officials are confronted with a prison disturbance, they must balance the threat that prisoners' actions pose to correctional staff, prisoners, and others against the harm prisoners may incur if officers use force. Realizing that officers must make decisions to use force under pressure, speedily, and without the luxury of a second chance, the Court held that liability would attach in deadly-force situations if the prisoner could show such force manifested "obduracy and wantonness." *Obdurate* can be defined as "having hardened feelings" or "being without remorse." *Wanton* can be defined as "malicious," "without regard," "inhumane," or "merciless." In applying this standard to the officers' actions, the Court held that the officers did not violate the Eighth Amendment and that they were entitled to a directed verdict. The Court ruled that the officers' actions failed to rise to the level of "wantonness" since prison security was breached by the prisoners, a hostage's life was at stake, and prisoners had threatened to kill the hostage.

For example, in *Kinney v. Indiana Youth Center* (1991), the court found that an officer did not act with obduracy and wantonness when he shot a prisoner attempting to escape from the facility. The court of appeals affirmed the lower court's summary judgment for the officer and found that the prisoner had been notified that the correction officer would shoot him when he ventured to climb the outer fence to make his escape and that therefore the officer did not use excessive force. The court also noted that the officer acted in good faith in shooting the escaping prisoner.

Hudson v. McMillian (1992)

The United States Supreme Court sought to examine what standard of review should be applied in prisoner excessive use-of-force claims and whether the extent of the injury should apply to such allegations in *Hudson v. McMillian* (1992). The explicit language of the Eighth Amendment prohibits the imposition of "cruel and unusual punishments." According to the Court, this language was designed to protect those convicted of crimes. The Court noted in *Ingraham v. Wright* (1977) that the clause applies after the state has complied with constitutional guarantees associated with criminal prosecution. Therefore, applying the Eighth Amendment standard to convicted persons should not be problematic.

Using the *Whitley* standard, courts have ruled in favor of prison officials when the use of deadly force is warranted. However, the question emerges:

Does the *Whitley* standard apply to all use-of-force situations or to cases involving only deadly force? For a time the courts were divided on this question. The Supreme Court's decision in *Hudson* resolved this controversy and held that all excessive-force claims must show malice, sadism, and intent to cause harm (Figure 6.2). In establishing this standard of excessive-force review in corrections, the Court underscored their earlier standard of review in the *Whitley* decision: whether force was applied in good faith, in an effort to maintain or restore discipline, or maliciously and sadistically for the purpose of causing harm.

The *Hudson* case arose out of an incident in the Angola, Louisiana, prison where two correctional officers beat a compliant and handcuffed prisoner during an escort to another cell. As the officer punched Hudson, a supervisor observed the beating and merely cautioned the officers "not to have too much fun." Hudson sustained minor bruises and swelling of his face, lip, and mouth. A punch to the face also cracked his dentures and loosened his teeth. He filed a civil action claiming excessive force. A federal district court found in favor of Hudson and awarded him $800.00, but an appellate court reversed. The U. S. Supreme Court granted certiorari to answer the question of whether or not the use of excessive physical force by correction officers against a prisoner constituted cruel and unusual punishment. The Court responded "yes," holding that an injury to a prisoner does not have to be "serious" or "significant" to constitute cruel and unusual punishment in violation of the Eighth Amendment. The Court held that the officers' actions did indeed violate Hudson's constitutional rights, despite the fact that he sustained only minor injuries.

In deciding *Hudson,* the Supreme Court held that in use-of-force cases the extent of injuries sustained is irrelevant and rejected the third component from the *Glick* decision (extent of injury sustained). The Court emphasized that when prison officials "maliciously and sadistically use force to cause harm," contemporary standards of decency are violated, regardless of whether or not significant injury is evident (del Carmen 1992). This clause becomes the standard assessing all excessive-force claims and not just in prison disturbances or riots. *Hudson* states that in order to establish a valid claim of excessive force under the Eighth Amendment, it must be shown that the defendant used force in a "malicious and sadistic manner for the purpose of causing harm."

The Court noted that not every push or shove or every injury leads to civil liability. It noted that the Eighth Amendment excludes from constitutional review *de minimis* (trifle) uses of physical force, provided that such force is not "repugnant to the conscience of mankind." A definitive meaning of this phrase

Figure 6.2   *Hudson v. McMillian* (1992)

After an earlier argument, two correction officers at the state prison at Angola, Louisiana, handcuffed prisoner Hudson, and removed him from his cell. While escorting Hudson to an administrative segregation cell area, the officers punched and kicked him, although he was compliant. The supervisor on duty observed the officers striking Hudson but merely told the officers "not to have too much fun." The blows were strong enough to dislodge Hudson's dental plate, which broke as it hit the floor. Hudson also sustained minor bruises and swelling of his face, mouth, and lip. Hudson filed a Section 1983 lawsuit claiming excessive force in violation of his Eighth Amendment constitutional rights to be free of cruel and unusual punishment. He prevailed in the lower court, winning $800.00. On appeal the Fifth Circuit of Appeals reversed. Hudson appealed to the United States Supreme Court.

The Court examined the issue of whether the use of force against a prisoner constituted cruel and unusual punishment even if the prisoner has not sustained a serious injury. The Court held, in a 7-2 vote, that a prisoner does not have to sustain a serious injury to prevail in a civil action. A prisoner will prevail on a claim of excessive force when he can show that the officer used force "maliciously and sadistically" to cause harm. The severity of injury is not at issue. The Court established that the standard for the use of less-than-lethal force for correction officers is whether the officer used force in a good-faith effort to maintain or restore order, or maliciously or sadistically for the purpose of causing harm. The court concluded that the officers used force in a malicious and sadistic fashion, thereby violating Hudson's constitutional right to be free from cruel and unusual punishment. Hudson did not possess a weapon, was not threatening the officers, was secured in handcuffs, and was compliant with the officers.

The questions to be addressed in the correctional use of excessive claims are: What was the need for the use of force? Was the force used repugnant to the sensibilities? The standard established by the Court makes it easier for prisoners to prevail in civil actions asserting excessive-force allegations.

remains unclear. Generally, the intent of the officer is examined, along with the legitimate objective and basis for the application of force. The standard is applied on a case-by-case basis, depending on the circumstances of the incident.

For example, in *Samuels v. Hawkins* (1998), the court found that throwing a cup of water at a cuffed and shackled prisoner who had thrown a cup of urine at the corrections officer was not malicious and sadistic. Compare, however, *Madrid v. Gomez* (1995), where the court found evidence of sadistic and malicious conduct of corrections officers who beat mentally impaired prisoners. Prisoners of the Pelican Bay State Prison in California brought a class action lawsuit citing numerous constitutional violations, including excessive-force allegations. The court held that prisoners established that prison officials had used unnecessary and grossly excessive force against prisoners on a frequent basis and that these practices had posed a substantial risk of harm to prisoners. The court found that officials had an affirmative management strategy to permit the use of excessive force for the purpose of punishment and deterrence. Such practices and actions of officers constituted wantonness and malicious conduct in violation of the Eighth Amendment.

While the *Hudson* decision was in favor of the prisoner and created a standard of review in correctional-force encounters, it is less clear if "all and every" injury sustained by a prisoner in a force situation will create civil liability. The Court did emphasize that not every "malevolent" touch by an officer constitutes a federal cause of action. The Court examines the state of mind of the officer at the time force was used. Hence, when prisoner control efforts by an officer have gone outside the boundaries of the five legitimate bases justifying the use of force, or when force has been used for retaliatory purposes, the constitutional line for using legitimate force has been crossed. When correctional personnel take it upon themselves to supplement a prisoner's punishment by beating him or to create a situation where harm is likely to occur, a case of cruel and unusual punishment will most likely be determined. Contemporary standards of decency are always violated when prison officials maliciously and sadistically use force to cause harm.

Application of the Court Standards

For ten years the lower courts have applied the *Hudson* standard to prison excessive-force claims. Ross (2004) conducted a ten year content analysis, from 1992 to 2002, of 1,025 published lower court decisions in order to examine the trends of how these courts were applying the standard. He reported that in five common excessive-force claim categories (see Figure 6.3) that prison officials prevailed in 79 percent of the claims. This reveals almost a 30 percent increase in the likelihood that officials would prevail in excessive-force claims than reported in an earlier study (Ross 1997).

In the detention and prison context there are numerous situations in which these standards may be applied. The following Section 1983 case decisions illustrate how the lower federal courts have applied the Fourteenth and Eighth Amendments to various prisoner claims of excessive force.

Figure 6.3   Trends in Excessive Force Claims by Category Type: 1992–2002

Category Type	Number Studied	Percent Studied	Prisoner % Prevailed (n)	Correction Official % Prevailed (n)
Physical force	455	44	20 (90)	80 (365)
Restraints	355	35	19 (77)	78 (278)
Aerosols	110	11	26 (26)	76 (84)
Force devices	100	9	22 (22)	78 (78)
Lethal force	5	1	0	100 (5)
Total number	1,025	100	21 (215)	79 (810)

LETHAL FORCE

While the use of lethal force is an uncommon occurrence in corrections, correctional officers are granted more deference in using it than police officers (Walker 1996). This philosophy was underscored in an early decision, *U.S. v. Nix* (1974), where the appellate court for the Seventh Circuit noted that an escaped prisoner is dangerous and may kidnap a hostage, kill a guard, steal an automobile, or rob a store to facilitate his escape. The court's reasoning concerning the danger level of escaped prisoners was illustrated in December 2000, when six prisoners escaped a Texas prison and later shot and killed a police officer in Dallas, Texas, as they were exiting a sporting goods store. The escaped prisoners had broken into the store to steal firearms and ammunition when they were discovered by the officer.

Because of the danger potential of escaped prisoners, the courts have generally upheld the use of lethal force by correction officers. In *Clark v. Evans* (1988) the estate of a deceased prisoner brought a Section 1983 lawsuit against the Commissioner of the State Department of Corrections (GA), the warden, the officer that shot and killed the prisoner, and other officers on the yard at the time of the attempted escape. Summary judgment was denied for the defendants by the lower court but the appellate court reversed. The court determined that in examining the officer's use of lethal force against an escaping prisoner, it is not whether the officer should have used an alternative means of force, but whether a reasonable officer with information available to the guard who shot the prisoner could believe that lesser means were not reasonably available. The court also disagreed with plaintiff's counsel who argued that the shooting was an execution of an insane prisoner in violation of the Eighth Amendment's cruel and unusual clause. The court noted that the officer shot only in an effort to prevent the escape.

In *Ryan Robles v. Otero de Ramos* (1989), the father of a deceased prisoner brought a Section 1983 action against the shooting officer, his supervisor, and the warden of the prison. The prisoner was attempting to escape and held a homemade spear. The officer instructed him to stop, but he ignored the warning and a warning shot. The officer fired a second shot when the prisoner entered the street, running. The court granted summary judgment, noting that the use of lethal force was not unnecessary, was not wanton infliction of pain, and therefore did not violate the Eighth Amendment. The father was unable to establish a valid Section 1983 claim for failure to train and failure to supervise.

An officer was granted summary judgment in *Henry v. Perry* (1989) when he used lethal force and only wounded an escaping prisoner. During the return to the prison from a track meet, the plaintiff, believing the two transporting officers unarmed, attempted to escape. One officer shot five or six times and did not order the prisoner to stop. The prisoner escaped but was recaptured. The appellate court reversed the lower court's denial of summary judgment and found that the officer was entitled to qualified immunity. The appeals court held that the officer's use of deadly force was necessary to prevent a crime from occurring.

The court in *Gravely v. Madden* (1998) found that a correction officer who shot and killed an escaping prisoner did not act with obduracy and wantonness in violation of the Eighth Amendment. An appeals court reversed a lower court's decision against the officer since the court determined that he had acted within the scope of his authority and that the force had been reasonable and therefore granted him qualified immunity. The prisoner had escaped from a minimum security facility and was staying at a friend's residence. When the officer entered the house, the prisoner was twice instructed to stop and give up. The prisoner leaped off a porch and the officer fired one round, killing him.

As indicated in the *Whitley* decision, the court stated that lethal force is permissible in a disturbance or riot situation. The court in *McCullough v. Cady* (1986) ruled against a correction officer when he shot and killed a prisoner during a disturbance. A prison officer at the State Prison of Southern Michigan (Jackson) attempted to break up a fight between prisoners. The officer fired one warning shot and then shot a second round which killed a bystander not involved in the fight. The court determined that the officer deliberately and wantonly inflicted pain upon the prisoner in violation of the Eighth

Amendment. The court held that the overwhelming weight of the evidence showed that the officer intentionally shot the prisoner who had not posed a threat to the safety of anyone.

Use of Physical Tactics

With more frequency, correction officers may encounter situations where they are required to use tactics of physical force. Such situations may require self-defense, the defense of another, or the prevention of the commission of a crime. Physical force tactics may include wristlocks, control/compliance holds, takedown techniques, pressure points, hand and leg strikes, and neck restraints. Having emerged from these tactics, prisoners may make allegations of brutality and assault and battery claims, besides general claims of excessive force. The standard developed by the United States Supreme Court in *Hudson* governs physical force used in these situations. In the jail context, the *Johnson* standard generally prevails, although some courts have applied the *Hudson* standard.

In *Giroux v. Sherman* (1992) a prisoner prevailed in an excessive-force claim, asserting that eight officers on four separate occasions beat and tormented him without provocation. For one beating from a corrections officer, the prisoner was awarded $10,000. This beating was so severe that the prisoner was hospitalized, having sustained internal injuries. While in the hospital, other officers punched his kidneys, further complicating his first surgery. He was awarded additional compensation amounting to $10,000 and punitive damages of $10,000. The prisoner was awarded further damages resulting from two other attacks in which one correctional officer punched him in the throat and head without provocation and another officer wantonly and without cause beat the prisoner in the kidneys, causing further injury and surgery. The prisoner was awarded over $38,000 in damages. Similarly, in *Stanley v. Hejiria* (1998), a videotaped cell extraction of a riot ringleader did not demonstrate sadistic or malicious conduct on the part of the response team and liability did not attach. Minor injuries were not constitutionally severe enough to be characterized as significant when force was reasonably necessary.

In *Shanton v. Detrick* (1993) the court found that using a "takedown technique" to control a combative prisoner in a dayroom was reasonable and necessary. During a security check of the detention center's dayroom, officers opened the door and the prisoner attempted to push past them and flee. The prisoner was shouting, swinging his arms wildly, and running around. The officers physically controlled him and forced him to the floor with a takedown tactic, in order for him to be restrained with handcuffs. The prisoner sued, claiming excessive force and denial of medical care. The court found the force reasonable since the officers had prevented the prisoner from entering another secure area within the facility.

A prisoner filed a Section 1983 lawsuit alleging that his Eighth Amendment right to be free of cruel and unusual punishment was violated by correction officers in *Sheldon v. C/O Pezley* (1995). The appeals court for the Eighth Circuit upheld the dismissal of the case, holding that the use of a "pain compliance" hold (arm bar/wristlock) on the prisoner was justified to maintain order in the facility and to maintain the safety of prison personnel and other prisoners during a strip search. The prisoner had refused a direct order to return to his cell from the shower area. Therefore, the use of force did not constitute an infliction of cruel and unusual punishment.

Using the *Hudson* standard under the Eight Amendment, the court awarded a jail prisoner $25,000 in compensatory damages and $27,000 in attorney fees when he complained of excessive force in *Valencia v. Wiggins* (1993). Ruling it was impractical to draw a line between convicted prisoners and pretrial detainees for the purpose of maintaining security in the facility, the court determined that an officer used excessive force disproportionate to the need when he applied a "chokehold" to and struck a handcuffed and compliant prisoner after a disturbance. The chokehold was not authorized by policy, and the court determined it was used maliciously and sadistically to cause harm.

In *Wilson v. Groaning* (1994) a prisoner appealed a lower court's ruling against him in an excessive-force claim. The appellate court affirming the decision found that the evidence in which the prisoner spat on the officer immediately before the officer allegedly punched the prisoner was relevant and admissible to support the officer's claim that he felt threatened at the time he used force. Just before the prisoner spat on the officer, he sprayed another officer with urine and fecal matter. The appellate court found that the lower court did not abuse its discretion in admitting evidence of three of the prisoner's six convictions to impeach his testimony.

In *Parkus v. Delo* (1998) the court entered judgment in favor of correction officers who were forced to use physical-control holds to subdue a violent prisoner. After contact with a female prison psychiatrist, the prisoner attacked, choked, sexually assaulted and injured her, and then the prisoner fought with correction officers. They subdued and controlled him. One officer was dismissed from duty for using excessive force against the prisoner. The appellate court affirmed the decision, stating that the lower court did not abuse its discretion when it defined "sadistically" in its instructions to the jury as "extreme or excessive cruelty or delighting in cruelty." The court also found that although one officer was dismissed for using "excessive force," this action did not unambiguously decide the issue of whether the officer used excessive force in violation of the Constitution.

Use of Restraints

The use of restraints in corrections is a frequent job-related task performed by correction and detention officers since such tasks are used for prisoner transports, medical intervention, controlling combative prisoners, protecting a prisoner and correctional personnel, and preventing escapes. Restraint devices commonly used include mechanical handcuffs, leg shackles, belly chains, restraint straps for ankles, soft restraints, strait jackets, padded helmets, padded gloves, four-point or restraint boards, and restraint chairs. The use of restraint equipment and/or restraint devices in corrections has a long and somewhat sordid history. Lawsuits alleging that correction officers have abused or injured prisoners with restraint equipment have emerged.

For example, in *Austin v. Hopper* (1998), an onerous and barbaric "security" measure was condemned when it was determined that there was no immediate threat to security nor was an attempt to restore order present. A practice of compelling prisoners to stand for hours shackled to a "hitching post," spread-eagled, without the ability to stretch or move in direct sunlight caused great pain, heat exhaustion, dehydration, and injury, for nondangerous rule infractions. This practice clearly violated the Eighth Amendment and exemplified the Court's meaning of obduracy and wantonness.

The United States Supreme Court in *Hope v. Pelzer* (2002) determined that handcuffing prisoners to a "hitching post" for an extended period of time failed to comport with a legitimate penological objective, that it constituted the unnecessary and wanton infliction of pain forbidden by the Eighth Amendment's cruel and unusual punishment clause, and that it was consistent with their former decision in *Whitley*. The Court noted that there were no safety concerns existing in this case which caused an emergency situation. Prisoner Hope refused to work on a prison work squad and the Arkansas prison regulation authorized the use of a hitching post when a prisoner refused to work or was otherwise disruptive to the work crew. Hope's hands were handcuffed and his arms extended above his head and secured to the post. The Court ruled that the officers had knowingly subjected him to a substantial risk of physical harm, unnecessary pain, and unnecessary exposure to the sun, and that they had prolonged his thirst and deprived him of bathroom breaks, creating a risk of particular discomfort and humiliation.

The Court concluded that a reasonable officer would have known that using a hitching post as Hope alleged was unlawful and violated the basic concept

Figure 6.4   *Hope v. Pelzer* (2002)

Larry Hope, an Alabama prisoner in 1995, was twice handcuffed to a hitching post for disruptive conduct by a correction officer while working on a prison work crew. Hope's handcuffed arms were extended above his head and secured to the post. When he attempted to move, the handcuffs cut into his wrists, causing pain and circulatory problems. He was secured to the post for seven hours in the sun, without his shirt, and he was granted one or two water breaks but no bathroom breaks. One officer taunted him regarding his thirst. Hope filed a Section 1983 lawsuit against three officers. The District Court awarded summary judgment for the officers and the Eleventh Circuit affirmed. However, the appellate court ruled that the use of the hitching post for punitive purposes violated the Eighth Amendment. In finding that the officers were entitled to summary judgment, the appellate court found that Hope could not show, as required by Circuit precedent, that the officer's conduct violated federal law established by the facts in prior cases similar to his. Hope appealed the decision, and the United States Supreme Court granted certiorari to review the qualified immunity holding.

The Court examined whether it was clearly established in 1995 that handcuffing a prisoner to a restraining bar violated the Eighth Amendment. In a 7-2 vote, the Court reversed the appellate court's decision, finding that it had erred in granting summary judgment. The Court held that despite the clear lack of an emergency, officers knowingly subjected Hope to a substantial risk of physical harm, unnecessary pain, unnecessary exposure to the sun, prolonged thirst and taunting, and a deprivation of bathroom breaks that created a risk of particular discomfort and humiliation. The Court concluded that a reasonable officer would have known that using a hitching post as evidenced in this case was unlawful. Further, the Court agreed with Court of Appeals, ruling that the policy and practice of cuffing a prisoner to a hitching post or similar stationary object for a period of time which surpasses that necessary to quell a threat or restore order is a violation of the Eighth Amendment and therefore is cruel and unusual punishment.

underlying the Eighth Amendment, which is nothing less than the dignity of man. The Court ruled that this practice would end, stating that Hope was treated in a way antithetical to human dignity and that the wanton treatment was done not out of necessity but as punishment for prior conduct.

The district court in *Spicer v. Collins* (1998) dismissed the case against correction officers since a state prisoner had failed to state a valid claim. The prisoner had alleged that the officers verbally threatened him, harassed him, and placed him in handcuffs. The court ruled that the prisoner failed to suffer "some injury," as required for a Section 1983 claim, when he claimed that he had sustained pain only in his neck, arms, and hands as the result of having been handcuffed; furthermore, he claimed no physical injury as the result of having been grabbed by the arm. Therefore there was no evidence that the force used by the officers was repugnant to the conscience of mankind. Conversely, in *Davidson v. Flynn* (1994), the Second Circuit Court of Appeals reversed a lower court's ruling, finding that correction officers misused handcuffs. Although the prisoner was an escape risk and the use of restraints were necessary, the prisoner stated a valid claim for cruel and unusual punishment by alleging that the handcuffs were placed too tightly, leading to serious and permanent physical injury, and that excessive force was applied wantonly and maliciously in retaliation for being litigious.

Periodically, correction officials are forced to protect a prisoner from self-destructive behaviors and may utilize a four-point restraint system. This procedure involves the prisoner's placement in the supine position on a bed or board with his ankles and wrists restrained independent of each another for immobilization purposes (DeLand 2000). This restraint system has generated legal actions claiming cruel and unusual punishment.

For example, in *Williams v. Burton* (1991), the court determined that placing a prisoner in four-point restraints for 28 hours did not violate his constitutional rights. The prisoner had caused a disturbance in the living unit and was seeking other prisoners to join him. Correction officers moved in, controlled him without injury, and placed him in an adjustment cell. In the cell he continued to kick and scream, and the officers placed him in the supine position on the bed and restrained him in a "4-point" position and placed gauze and tape over his mouth to prevent him from yelling at other prisoners. The court found that this response by officers was prudent and proper and did not violate the prisoner's Eighth or Fourteenth Amendment rights. The prisoner failed to prove a medical-care claim since he had been monitored by officers and medical staff, allowed to use the toilet, and allowed periodic exercise. Compare, however, *Jones v. Thompson* (1993), where the officers placed a detainee in a "3-point" restraint position. The court found that continuing use of this restraint procedure, without medical intervention or treatment; denying the prisoner the use of the toilet; and failing to provide the prisoner with any personal hygiene violated the prisoner's constitutional rights. The court awarded the prisoner $5,000 in compensatory damages and $2,000 in punitive damages against the jail administrator.

In *Williams v. Vidor* (1994), a prisoner brought a Section 1983 action against a correction officer and warden, alleging that he was subjected to cruel and unusual punishment when he was shackled to his bed for 73 hours. The appellate court granted summary judgment for the officer but denied summary judgment for the warden since he had been responsible for condoning the practice for an extended period of time. Further, in *Williams v. Benjamin* (1996), a prisoner filed a civil action claiming that his rights were violated when officers sprayed him with pepper spray, restrained him in a "4-point" position on a bare metal bed for eight hours, refused to wash off the spray, and denied him medical care or the use of the toilet. The court found that it was proper to use the pepper spray since the prisoner had been involved in a prison disturbance and that using the 4-point restraint system was justified in response to the prisoner's throwing water on the officers. The court, however, ruled that the officers had crossed over the line of controlling the prisoner by punishing him when they denied him medical care and failed to wash the spray from his face.

Use of the Restraint Chair

The use of the restraint chair as a viable and humane method of restraint for violent prisoners has increased within prisons and detention facilities. The chair has been useful in decreasing injuries to officers when controlling prisoners, in restoring order by immobilizing the agitated prisoner, in allowing the prisoner time to calm down, and in prohibiting the agitated prisoner from agitating other prisoners.

The prisoner is secured in the chair in a seated position. The chair is metal, set on rollers, and comprised of nylon straps and soft cuffs which immobilize the wrists/arms, ankles, and chest of the prisoner. The restraint chair is commonly used to control combative and self-destructive prisoners. Like the uses of other forms of restraints, the use of the restraint chair has generated civil lawsuits filed by prisoners who claim that it is a form of cruel and unusual punishment.

In *Fuentes v. Wagner* (2000) a prisoner awaiting sentencing filed a Section 1983 action claiming that his constitutional rights were violated since officers had used excessive force. The prisoner was placed in a restraint chair for eight hours to stop his disruptive behavior and to maintain order in the facility. The lower court ruled in favor of the defendant officers and the appeals court affirmed. The court determined that the prisoner was not kept in the chair for a longer duration than authorized by policy. The prisoner was checked every fifteen minutes and he was released every two hours for stretching and to use of the toilet. He was examined by a nurse at the end of the eight-hour period. The court stated that a prisoner awaiting sentencing had the same status under the Constitution as a pretrial detainee and that the Due Process Clause of the Fourteenth Amendment protected him from the use of excessive force amounting to punishment.

A former pretrial detainee in *Moore v. Hosier* (1998) filed a civil action against the sheriff's department alleging excessive force, denial of medical care, and assault and battery under state law in Indiana. The detainee admitted that he was intoxicated upon arrest and booking and that he was combative with detention officers at intake. Detention officers controlled the detainee and placed him in the restraint chair for a period of time. While the prisoner was in the chair, a canister of pepper spray malfunctioned and spray contacted the prisoner's face. The officers decontaminated the detainee by washing his face with water. The detainee alleged that he was beaten about his head and face while strapped in the chair. The court granted summary judgment for the officers, stating that even if the allegations were true, they did not amount to a constitutional violation.

Forced Cell Extractions

With some frequency, correction officers are required to respond to a violent or mentally impaired prisoner who may be tearing up his cell and/or attempting to injure himself seriously. These tactical response operations are among the most high-profile and potentially dangerous tasks performed by correctional personnel. Since prisoner behaviors are highly unpredictable, decisions must be carefully weighed prior to specific courses of action. In response, many correctional agencies have developed a tactical team known as a Correctional Emergency Response Team (CERT) to handle these situations. CERT members generally consist of four or five officers who have been trained as a team in physical control techniques, restraints, weaponry, and aerosols, in order to forcibly enter a cell or other area and extract violent prisoners (Ross 1996b).

In some circumstances the team may be mobilized to assist in physically controlling a prisoner for health care intervention. Because of their "high profile" nature, these response operations have initiated claims of excessive force against CERT, and the courts have used the *Hudson* decision in making their rulings.

In *Campbell v. Sikes* (1999) an appellate court affirmed summary judgment for corrections officers and a doctor on a claim that the officers used excessive force by restraining a mentally impaired prisoner. The prisoner became a threat to himself and the housing unit when he began tearing up his cell. Earlier, a prison psychiatrist had misdiagnosed him as suffering from abuses of many substances rather than from a bipolar disorder. A "movement team" entered the cell and attempted to place him in other restraints, but they were ineffective. On advice of the psychiatrist, the officers placed the prisoner in a straitjacket. The court found that using a straitjacket to restrain the prisoner failed to constitute excessive force, since evidence was lacking that the force was applied maliciously and sadistically. The court noted that the prisoner posed a serious threat to herself and others, that lesser restraints were ineffective, that the restraints caused no physical injury, and that the prisoner's physical condition was carefully monitored.

In *Dennis v. Thurman* (1997) a prisoner brought a Section 1983 claim alleging that 36 officers withheld water from him for 36 hours after a forced cell extraction. The prisoner had to be forcibly extracted from his cell in order to search it because officers had learned that he was planning to kill a corrections officer. Officers had to use a block gun, which shot rubber blocks at high velocity. The court held that the officers did not use excessive force against the prisoner in removing him from his cell. The court found that no officer acted maliciously or sadistically for the purpose of causing pain to the prisoner. Shutting off the water to his cell for an extended time did not violate his Eighth Amendment rights, since he had previously used water to flood his cell, creating a dangerous condition for himself, other prisoners, and officers.

In *Estate of Davis by Ostenfeld v. Delo* (1997), a court held that officers, a supervisor, and the prison superintendent were liable in using excessive force when they forcibly removed a prisoner from his cell. The court found evidence to support the claim that the prisoner was struck in the face and head 20 to 25 times by several officers while other officers held him down, after he had complied with an order to lie face down. The prisoner sustained numerous injuries, and the court found that the officers used force maliciously and sadistically for the purpose of causing harm. After an investigation ordered by the superintendent, he failed to take corrective action against an officer who had failed to submit a mandatory force report, who had been found to have sustained numerous complaints of excessive force in the past, and for whose termination recommendations had been submitted. The superintendent was held liable, and the prisoner was awarded $70,000 in compensation and $40,000 in punitive damages.

The Use of Pepper Spray and Other Less-Than-Lethal Equipment

Additional equipment designed to incapacitate or control combative prisoners has been on the market for years and is used in corrections and detention facilities. These products include oleoresin capsicum (OC, i.e., pepper spray), impact weapons (batons), stun guns, tasers, stun belts, electric capture shields, sting-ball grenades, and various chemical agents. Not all of the products are used in all correctional facilities, but their use has assisted in lowering officer injuries and in enhancing the humane methods for controlling violent prisoners when verbal intervention or other attempts of control have failed. Claims of excessive force and cruel and unusual punishment have surfaced, as with other uses of force.

The California Supreme Court (Associated Press 2002) ruled that the use of an electric-shock stun belt could impair a criminal defendant's ability to participate in his/her trial and that courtroom personnel should instead use handcuffs and leg restraints. The court's decision reversed the conviction of a man who had been forced to wear a stun belt, which is wrapped around the waist and can deliver an 8-second, 50,000-volt of electricity when activated by a remote transmitter. Even if the belt was concealed, the court concluded, it could impair the defendant's capacity to concentrate on the events of the trial, could interfere with the defendant's ability to assist his/her own counsel, and could adversely affect his/her own demeanor in the presence of the jury.

A prisoner in *Collins v. Kahelski* (1993) brought a civil action against corrections officials claiming that his Eighth Amendment rights were violated when they deployed tear gas to disperse and control prisoners during a prison disturbance. During the uprising, a prisoner attempted to enter the recreational area where the disturbance was occurring. He was instructed to leave but continued to attempt to gain access. Officers discharged tear gas in the vicinity and the prisoner was exposed to it. The court concluded that the use of tear gas to quell a prison disturbance was clearly reasonable and failed to exhibit malicious and sadistic actions amounting to cruel and unusual punishment. There was apparent danger posed by the disturbance, the amount of tear gas used was not excessive, and use of the tear gas was not intended to inflict emotional distress.

The appellate court in *Jasper v. Thalacker* (1993) affirmed the lower court's decision to grant summary judgment to officers who used a stun gun on a violent prisoner. The court found that the prisoner had threatened an officer with physical harm. The officer responded in self-defense, by subduing the prisoner with a stun gun. The court concluded that the use of the stun gun did not violate the Eighth Amendment since it was not used sadistically or maliciously. In *Collins v. Scott* (1997) a Muslim prisoner filed suit claiming that his religious rights were violated arising from a strip search in which a female officer was present. He failed to submit to the search based on his religious rights regarding his disrobing in front of a female. Officers shocked him with an electric capture shield and controlled him with restraints. The court dismissed the case, holding that the strip search did not substantially burden his religious rights and that the officers did not use excessive force in conducting the search.

In *Jones v. Shields* (2000) a prisoner brought a Section 1983 action against a correction officer claiming that excessive force was used when he was allegedly unjustly sprayed with pepper spray. The district court ruled in favor of the prisoner, but the appellate court reversed the judgment. The appellate court found that the officer's use of pepper spray did not violate the prisoner's Eighth Amendment rights because the spray resulted in a *de minimis* injury and the officer did not use the spray in a sadistic or malicious manner. The prisoner admitted that the effects of the spray diminished within 45 minutes, that he was taken to the prison infirmary and treated with water during that period, and that a medical examination the following day revealed no ill effects.

Compare, however, *Harris v. Morales* (1999), where the court ruled in favor of a prisoner sprayed with pepper spray. The district court found that the prisoner was unnecessarily subjected to pepper spray and was then denied medical attention. The court found that the officer used excessive force when he spayed the prisoner and was deliberately indifferent to his medical needs by denying him medical care.

In *Baldwin v. Stadler* (1998) the appellate court reversed the district court's holding that officers used excessive force by discharging pepper spray on two successive days on the same prisoner. A prisoner alleged that he was forced to be exposed to pepper spray during a prison disturbance on one day and during a disturbance on the transport bus on the next day—two incidents which violated his Eighth Amendment rights. The appeals court held that using pepper spray to quell a disturbance and work stoppage was proper and legitimate. Moreover, the officer used pepper spray the second time during a prisoner transport on the bus since the prisoners had begun fighting—a potentially dangerous situation. The officer did not allow the prisoners to leave the bus to wash off the spray because there was a high potential of escape.

Using CN gas twice on a martial artist was not excessive according to the court in *Norris v. Detrick* (1996). The prisoner sued the officer under Section 1983, claiming cruel and unusual punishment and excessive force. A state corrections officer ordered the prisoner numerous times to return to his cell; he refused and the officer sprayed him, having known he was skilled in the martial arts. The prisoner then charged the officer, and he sprayed him a second time. The court concluded that whether or not the use of gas is unconstitutional depends on all of the circumstances, including provocation, the amount of gas used, and the purposes for which the gas was used.

Summary

The use of force by corrections officers is of fundamental importance in civil liability. One must understand how the courts examine claims of excessive force. Legitimate force used by officers must be within the framework of the standards established by the United States Supreme Court. Officers can never justify their use of force for punishment or revenge. Case analysis reveals that courts are inclined to rule favorably for a prisoner when they have determined that the officer used force indiscriminately, in retaliation, or as a form of punishment and/or that the officer knowingly subjected the prisoner to a substantial risk of harm with a penological objective. A correction officer's decision to use force should be based on a reasonable justification and should be made in response to the prisoner's actions. Factors to for the officer to consider include the need to use force, the perceived threat to the officer or others at the time, the prisoner's possession of or access to a weapon, and the officer's reaction time during which to make the decision.

Second, as an arrestee's status changes to that of a pretrial detainee, the courts utilize the "shocks the conscience" standard of review as articulated in the *Glick* decision. Examining allegations of excessive force in this category appears to create the most confusion: Does the Fourteenth Amendment apply? Or does the Eighth Amendment apply? Generally, the due process clause under the Fourteenth Amendment applies to pretrial detainees, although from time to time courts have been known to apply the Eighth Amendment.

Third, the *Hudson* ruling underscores that excessive-force claims arising out of the prison context will be evaluated in accordance with the Eighth Amendment. The applicable standard of using force in good faith, and not maliciously or sadistically for causing harm, corresponds to the cruel and unusual punishment clause of the Eighth Amendment. Severe or significant injury need not occur for a valid excessive claim. While the general trend of rulings by the contemporary Supreme Court has been to limit substantively a plaintiff's ability to prevail in civil rights actions, the *Hudson* decision seemingly has opened the door for increased Section 1983 litigation concerning use-of-force issues.

However, since the passage of the Prison Litigation Reform Act (PLRA) in 1996, this is not the case. One of the requirements of the PLRA is that prisoners must first exhaust administrative remedies at the institutional level prior to filing a lawsuit. This requirement was challenged in an excessive-force claim, in *Porter v. Nussle* (2002). The United States Supreme Court ruled that Congress did not intend to exclude use-of-force cases from the provision and concluded that such cases fall within the requirement of the PLRA and that the exhaustion requirement applies to "all prisoner lawsuits."

Finally, prevailing on summary judgment is a clear trend in these cases. Although such cases are still being litigated in court, correction officers are prevailing more frequently in civil actions claiming excessive force. Corrections officers are receiving better training and more precise guidance by department policy, and they appear to be making better decisions in the field regarding the use of force. They also have more equipment options at their disposal than in former years, which give officers viable ranges of force to utilize when they encounter resistance.

Administrators and trainers should continue to review court decisions in their jurisdictions, as well as across the nation, in order to design more effective guidelines that provide officers with a range of options with which to make decisions regarding the appropriate level of force in a given situation. Further, training in the use of all force equipment, including training within the classroom and through scenario practical applications, should be regularly and continually provided. Supervisors should receive ongoing training in methods of evaluating officers' incident reports on force and should enforce departmental guidelines when unreasonable force is discovered. Supervisors play a significant role in determining if reasonable force was employed in a confrontation. Officers' reports should be reviewed by supervisory personnel, and an investigation should be performed concerning those situations where force may have been used outside the department's policies, concerning outside training, and concerning cases involving a custodial death. A continual commitment by administrators, trainers, and officers assists in developing a balance between the rights of prisoners to be free of cruel and unusual punishment and the interests of society in maintaining legitimate correctional control while protecting the officers who must perform that duty.

In light of past case decisions and the current philosophy of the courts examining claims of excessive force, officers should continue to adhere to court guidelines and their department's policy when deciding to use a physical-control tactic, force equipment, or a firearm. Civil liability will most assuredly attach in cases where an officer has used force as a form of punishment, as retaliation, and/or for revenge. Officers need a comprehensive knowledge of their department's policy and must exhibit competency in employing physical-control tactics, force equipment, restraints, and firearms. Figure 6.5 outlines suggested components of a use-of-force policy in corrections. When using aerosols and other force equipment, officers should follow the manufacturer's guidelines. After the use of an aerosol, the prisoner should be monitored and decontamination procedures should be employed as warranted. After a use-of-force incident, prisoners should receive medical attention/examination as the need arises. A use-of-force report should also be submitted, documenting all officers' participation in using force. Following departmental training and these recommendations will assist in defending the next claim of excessive force.

References

Associated Press. 2002. California court dislikes stun belts, 8 August, 2B, 5.

Bowker, L. 1980. *Prison victimization.* New York: Elsevier.

Figure 6.5   Use of Force Policy Considerations in Corrections

- Policy Statement
- Procedural Guidelines
- Definitions
    Control
    Prisoner behaviors
    Less-than-lethal force and lethal force
- Authority to use force (state and federal guidelines and force circumstances)
- Types of prisoners behaviors/resistance (psychological intimidation; verbal, passive, defensive, and active aggression; and aggravated active aggression)
- Levels of force
    Officer(s) on location
    Verbal commands used
    Empty-Hand control (control-holds, wrist-locks, come-along holds, take-down tactics, pressure points, hand/leg strikes, stuns, and neck restraints)
    Aerosols (pepper spray or various chemical agents)
    Impact weapons and other equipment (batons, tasers, stun-guns, sting-ball grenades, and so forth)
    Use of water hoses
    Lethal force guidelines
- Escalation/deescalation of force
- Description of authorized equipment and restraints (handcuffs, leg restraints, restraint chair, kick strap, straitjacket, and so forth)
- Medical attention considerations
- Force and restraint of "special needs" prisoner
- Reporting use of force
- Investigation of force incidents

Bureau of Justice Statistics. 2003. *Census of state and federal correctional facilities in 2000.* Washington, DC: Department of Justice.

Camp, C., and G. Camp. 2002. Prisoner assaults on correction officers. *Corrections Yearbook.* Middletown CT: Criminal Justice Institute, Inc.

del Carmen, R. V. 1992. *The Supreme Court and prison excessive force cases: Does one test fit all?* Federal Probation 77: 44–47.

DeLand, G. W. 2000. Restraint chairs, Part I: Reasonable control aid or the "Devil's Chair"? *Corrections Manager's Report* 3: 36–37, 43–45.

Ekland-Olson, S., C. Barrich, and L. Cohen. 1983. Prison overcrowding and disciplinary problems: An analysis of the Texas prison system. *Journal of Applied Behavioral Science* 19: 163–76.

Griffin, M. L. 1999. The influence of organizational climate on detention officers' readiness to use force in a county jail. *Criminal Justice Review* 24: 1–26.

Hemmens, C., and E. Atherton. 1999. *Use of force: Current practice and policy.* Lanham, MD: American Correctional Association.

Kappeler, V. E. 2001. *Critical issues in police civil liability.* 3rd ed. Prospect Heights, IL: Waveland Press, Inc.

Kratcoski, P. 1987. The implications of research explaining prison violence and disruption. *Federal Probation* 52: 27–32.

Light, S. 1991. Assaults on prison officers: Interactional themes. *Justice Quarterly* 8: 243–61.

Marquart, J. 1986. Prison guards and the use of physical coercion as a mechanism of prisoner control. *Criminology* 24: 347–66.

Palmer, J. W., and S. E. Palmer. 2004. *Constitutional rights of prisoners.* 7th ed. Cincinnati, OH: Anderson Publishing Co.

Ross, D. L. 1990. Study examines non-deadly physical force policies. *Corrections Today,* July, 64–66.

_____. 1996a. A national assessment of prisoner assaults on correction officers. *Corrections Compendium* 25: 1–8.

_____. 1996b. Examining the administrative liability issues of correctional tactical teams. *American Jails,* November/December, 9–19.

_____. 1997. Emerging trends in correctional civil liability cases: A Content analysis of federal court decisions of Title 42 United States Code Section 1983: 1970-1994. *Journal of Criminal Justice* 25: 501–15.

_____. 2004. An analysis of *Hudson v. McMillian*: Ten years later. *Criminal Law Bulletin* 6: 15–48.

Rowan, J. R. 1996. Who is safer in male maximum prisons? *Corrections Today* 58: 2–4.

Walker, J. 1996. Police and correctional use of force: Legal and policy standards and implications. *Crime and Delinquency* 41: 144–56.

Cases Cited

Austin v. Hopper, 15 F. Supp. 2d 1210 (M.D. Ala. 1998)

Baldwin v. Stadler, 137 F. 3d 836 (5th Cir. 1998)

Brazier v. Cherry, 293 F. 2d 401 (5th Cir. 1961)

Brothers v. Klevenhagen, 28 F. 3d 345 (5th Cir. 1994)

Campbell v. Sikes, 169 F.3d 1353 (11th Cir. 1999)

Chimel v. California, 395, U.S. 752 (1969)

Clark v. Evans, 840 F. 2d 876 (11th Cir. 1988)

Collins v. Kahelski, 828 F. Supp. 614 (E.D. Wis. 1993)

Collins v. Scott, 961 F. Supp. 1009 (E.D. Tex. 1997)

Cruz v. Escondido, 126 F. 3d 1214 (10th Cir.1997)

Davidson v. Flynn, 32 F. 3d 27 (2nd Cir. 1994)

Dennis v. Thurman, 959 F. Supp. 1253 (C.D. Cal. 1997)

Estate of Davis by Ostenfeld v. Delo, 115 F. 3d 1388 (8th Cir. 1997)

Fobbs v. City of Los Angeles, 316 P.2d 668 (Cal. Ct. App.1957)

Fuentes v. Wagner, 206 F. 3d 335 (3rd Cir. 2000)

Gilmere v. City of Atlanta, 774 F. 2d 1495 (11th Cir. 1985)

Giroux v. Sherman, 807 F. Supp. 1182 (E.D. Pa. 1992)

Graham v. Connor, 490 U.S. 386 (1989)

Gravely v. Madden, 142 F.3d 345 (6th Cir. 1998)

Gumz v. Morrissette, 772 F. 2d 1395, 1400 (7th Cir. 1985)

Harris v. Morales, 69 F. Supp. 1319 (D. Colo. 1999)

Henry v. Perry, 866 F. 2d 657 (3rd Cir. 1989)

Hope v. Pelzer, 534 U. S. 1073 (2002)

Hostin v. United States, 566 F. Supp. 1125 (D.D.C. 1983)

Hudson v. McMillian, 503 U.S. 1 (1992)

Ingraham v. Wright, 430 U.S. 651 (1977)

Jackson v. Bishop, 404 F. 2d 571 (8th Cir. 1968)

Jasper v. Thalacker, 999 F. 2d 353 (8th Cir. 1993)

Johnson v. Glick, 481 F. 2d 1028 (2nd Cir.1973)

Jones v. Shields, 207 F. 3d 491 (8th Cir. 2000)

Jones v. Thompson, 818 F. Supp. 1263 (S.D. Ind. 1993)

Kinney v. Indiana Youth Center, 950 F.2d 462 (7th Cir. 1991)

Madrid v. Gomez, 889 F. Supp. 1146 (N.D. Cal. 1995)

Mathie v. Fries, 935 F. Supp. 1284 (E.D. N.Y. 1996)

McClanahan v. City of Moberly, 35 F. Supp. 2d 744 (E.D. Mo. 1998)

McCullough v. Cady, 640 F. Supp. 1012 (E.D. Mich. 1986)

Monroe v. Pape, 365 U.S. 167 (1961)

Moore v. Hosier, 43 F. Supp. 2d 978 (N.D. Ind. 1998)

Norris v. Detrick, 918 F. Supp. 977 (N.D.W. Va. 1996)

Owens v. City of Atlanta, 780 F. 2d 1564 (11th Cir. 1985)

Parkus v. Delo, 135 F. 3d 1232 (8th Cir. 1998)

Porter v. Nussle, 534 U.S. 516 (2002)

Raley v. Fraser, 747 F. 2d 287 (5th Cir. 1984)

Rochin v. California, 342 U.S. 165 (1952)

Ryan Robles v. Otero de Ramus, 729 F. Supp. 920 (D. Puerto Rico 1989)

Samuels v. Hawkins, 157 F. 3d 557, 558-560 (8th Cir. 1998)

Santiago v. C.O. Capisi Shield #4592, 91 F. Supp. 2d 665 (S. D. N.Y. 2000)

Screws v. U.S., 325 U.S. 91 (1945)

Shanton v. Detrick, 826 F. Supp. 979 (N.D. W. Va. 1993)

Sheldon v. C/O Pezley, 49 F. 3d 1312 (8th Cir. 1995)

Shillingford v. Holmes, 634 F. 2d 363, 265 (5th Cir. 1981)

Skinner v. Brooks, 288 58 N.E. 2d 697 (Oh. Ct. App.1944)

Spicer v. Collins, 9 F. Supp. 2d 673 (E.D. Tex. 1998)

Stanley v. Hejiria, 134 F. 3d 629, 634-638 (4th Cir. 1998)

Stein v. State, 385 S.2d 874 (N.Y. S. Ct.1976)

Tennessee v. Garner, 471 U.S. 1 (1985)

U.S. v. Nix, 501 F. 2d 516 (7th Cir. 1974)

Valencia v. Wiggins, 981 F.2d 1440, 1446 (5th Cir. 1993)

Whitley v. Albers, 475 U.S. 312 (1986)

Williams v. Benjamin, 77 F. 3d 756 (4th Cir. 1996)

Williams v. Burton, 943 F. 2d 1572 (11th Cir. 1991)

Williams v. Vidor, 17 F. 3d 857 (6th Cir. 1994)

Wilson v. Groaning, 25 F. 3d 581 (7th Cir. 1994)

Chapter 7

Civil Liability for Claims of Failure to Protect and for Prison/Jail Conditions

The Eighth Amendment does not outlaw cruel and unusual "conditions,"
it outlaws cruel and unusual punishments.

Wilson v. Seiter (1991)

Prisons and jails confine a diverse population. Many prisoners are mentally impaired, violent, depressed, chemically addicted, and assaultive. Within this population a variety of confinement behaviors are common, such as violence through physical and sexual assaults, intimidation, extortion, homosexuality, gang-related assaults and killings, and uncontrolled emotional outbursts.

Correction officials must be prepared to proactively respond to prisoners requiring protective custody through adequate classification systems, security intelligence, searches of the facilities, case management, the mail system, and prisoners requesting protective placement. Because this group is diverse, correctional personnel must be prepared to respond to a variety of human behaviors within the correctional context. Frequently legal actions for failure to protect are filed against correctional personnel through Section 1983 procedures. Liability concerns emerge from allegations of failure to protect stemming from several potential situations: prisoner-on-prisoner physical assaults, self-inflicted injuries, and prisoner-on-prisoner sexual attacks. Failure-to-protect claims have also emerged from female prisoners who have alleged sexual misconduct by a correction officer.

Prisoners have also filed lawsuits alleging that the conditions in which they are confined have violated their Eighth Amendment rights. Such actions have addressed the size of cells, the overcrowding of jails and prisons, sanitary conditions, the architecture of the facility, security measures, heating, plumbing, and the double-bunking of prisoners. An example of these issues was illustrated in the classic case *Holt v. Sarver* (1970), which was depicted in the 1981 movie *Brubaker*. In this case a class action claim was filed by Arkansas prisoners complaining of vermin-infested facilities, rampant sexual assaults by other prisoners, abuse of the trustee system, absence of meaningful rehabilitative programs, conditions of isolation cells, overcrowded living conditions, defective plumbing facilities, prisoner sexual assaults, excessive use of corporal punishment by correctional officials, and corruption between officers and prisoners. When a lower federal court examined these issues, it ruled that in the "totality of the circumstances"(cumulative impact) the Arkansas prison system, through its deplorable conditions, violated the Eighth and Fourteenth Amendment rights of prisoners.

This chapter examines the United States Supreme Court and lower court decisions which address various issues stemming from failure-to-protect claims and from lawsuits filed asserting that the inadequate conditions of the detention center or prison violated the prisoners' constitutional rights under the purview of the Eighth or Fourteenth Amendment. The chapter also addresses lawsuits filed by female prisoners claiming sexual misconduct of correction officers.

CLAIMS ALLEGING FAILURE TO PROTECT

Protective Custody

Protective custody is a special segregated housing unit used for different types of prisoners, including those who have testified against other prisoners, those who have failed to pay off gambling debts, those who have been pressured to engage in homosexual activities, those who have gang rival enemies, homosexual prisoners considered at risk for assault, those who are physically weak, facility informants, former officers of the criminal justice system, those who have been assaulted by other prisoners in the past, and high-profile celebrity status prisoners. Correctional systems are using protective custody with some regularity owing to the increased number of violent offenders entering the system and the increased number and activities of special-threat groups (gangs) within a facility. Classification systems and security measures must be in place in order for correctional officials to provide the security and care required for this protective-custody population.

Over the years, prisoners in protective custody have accounted for a significant percentage of the prisoner population. Henderson (1990) found in a survey of correctional institutions that 5.6 percent of the United States prisoner population were in protective custody. While the prison and jail populations have increased over the past ten years, the number of prisoners housed in protective custody has decreased from 1996 to 2001 (Camp and Camp 2002). The authors reported that in 1996, 1.7 percent of the total prisoner population in state adult prisons were in protective segregation. By 2001, the percentage fell to 1.2 percent of the total prisoner population. Although the percentages vary and appear to be decreasing, prisoners requiring protective custody can be costly to an agency's operational budget, can pose significant management responses and strategies within the prisoner population for correctional officials, and can expose the liability of the department for allegations of failing to protect the prisoner.

Standard of Review

Since the 1970s, several cases have addressed assertions that correction officials failed to protect prisoners. In *Landman v. Royster* (1971) the court required the Virginia Department of Corrections to create procedures to ensure prisoner protection. In *Woodhouse v. Virginia* (1973) the Fourth Circuit Court of Appeals held that in order for a prisoner to prevail in a lawsuit, he or she must prove a pervasive risk of harm from other prisoners to which officials failed to reasonably respond.

The landmark case where the United States Supreme Court addressed the issue of failing to protect comes from a case unrelated to corrections. In *DeShaney v. Winnebago Department of Social Services* (1989) the Court held that there is no constitutional right to protection under the due process clause of the Fourteenth Amendment. The case involved a young boy, who after his parents' divorce, was placed in the custody of his father. The Department of Social Services received information that the boy was being abused by his father but took little action to protect the boy and did not remove him from the home. The boy was beaten by his father to the extent that he sustained permanent brain injuries, leaving him mentally retarded.

The Court examined the issue of whether the state has a duty to protect an individual not in its custody from harm by a private person. The Court ruled that the Fourteenth Amendment does not require a state to protect a person not in its custody from harm by a private person. Although the Fourteenth Amendment does protect citizens from the actions and power of the state, it does not impose any requirement on the state to protect its citizens' life, liberty, and property. The Court determined that a state's failure to protect an individual from private violence does not constitute a violation of the due process clause.

This decision is important and carries implications for correctional officials. A Section 1983 claim can not successfully proceed when the harm comes from the hands of a third person. Correctional officials, however, can be sued for failing to protect a prisoner, since custodial care of the confined is an important function of the incarcerating facility.

In *Farmer v. Brennan* (1994) the United States Supreme Court specifically examined a failure-to-protect claim in corrections and expanded the Eighth Amendment's standard of deliberate indifference to these types of claims. In a unanimous decision, the Court held that prisoners may prevail in suits against correctional officials for prisoner-on-prisoner assaults if they can show that officials knew of substantial risk of harm and recklessly disregarded that risk. Plaintiff Farmer was serving a lengthy federal prison sentence for multiple crimes. Farmer entered prison as a preoperative transsexual and possessed feminine traits. He was classified as a "biological male" and housed in a male correctional institution. His "condition" posed problems for a housing assignment by the Federal Bureau of Prisons. Prior to his assault, Farmer was housed in protective custody away from the general population. After a disciplinary transfer to the U.S. Penitentiary in Terre Haute, Indiana, Farmer was placed in administrative segregation. He was later released to the general population. Approximately one week later he was raped and beaten in his cell after he rejected sexual advances of another prisoner (Figure 7.1).

With its decision, the Court expanded the scope of "deliberate indifference" in claims for failure to protect by holding that deliberate indifference can mean "reckless" behavior (on the part of correctional officials) "only when a person disregards a risk of harm of which he is aware" (at pp. 1978–79). This means that correctional officials were aware of facts from which they should have inferred that a substantial risk of serious harm existed. To prevail in a lawsuit asserting failure to protect, a prisoner must show that officials "consciously" and "recklessly disregarded" a "substantial risk" of harm to the prisoner.

In order to prove that correctional officials knew of a substantial risk of harm, a plaintiff can use "circumstantial evidence" to show that the risk was "obvious." The Court noted three situations in which a plaintiff may prevail: (1) if the assaults were pervasive, long-standing, well-documented, and expressly noted by correctional officials; (2) if officials refused to verify the underlying facts of such assaults; and (3) if prison officials declined to confirm inferences of risk that they strongly suspected to exist (at p. 182). Prison officials may be held liable if they know of a substantial risk of physical harm to a general class of prisoners but no harm has yet occurred. Prisoners do not have to be assaulted first before protective action is taken by correctional personnel. Moreover, correctional officials cannot be held liable when they can show that they responded reasonably to known risks (Vaughn and del Carmen 1995; Vaughn 1996).

Figure 7.1   *Farmer v. Brennan* (1994)

Prisoner Farmer, confined in a Federal prison, brought a *Bivens* action under the Eighth Amendment claiming correction officials were deliberately indifferent to his constitutional rights to be safe during his incarceration. Farmer acknowledged that he was a transvestite and suffered from a slight psychotic disorder. Prior to his confinement Farmer submitted to an unsuccessful "black market" testicle removal surgery. Farmer's appearance resembled a female's since he had undergone hormonal therapy. Because of his "condition" proper security placement of Farmer was difficult for officials. He was placed in segregation for disciplinary reasons and later released to the general population without objection. Within two weeks Farmer alleged he had been beaten and raped by other prisoners. He filed suit, and the lower court and appellate court found in favor of the correction officials. He appealed to the United States Supreme Court.

The Court examined the issue of whether prison officials may be held liable under the Eighth Amendment for unsafe conditions in prison when they are knowledgeable that prisoners face risks of harm and fail to take measures which would reduce or eliminate such risks. The Court held that the Constitution does not mandate "comfortable prisons" but that prison officials have a duty to protect prisoners from violence at the hands of other prisoners. The Court ruled that a prison official cannot be found liable under the Eighth Amendment unless the official knows of and disregards an excessive risk to the prisoner's health and safety. The Court stated that if the official knew that a prisoner faced substantive risk of serious harm and disregarded that risk by failing to take reasonable measures to alleviate or abate it, a violation under the Eighth Amendment would exist.

This case is significant since the Court applied the deliberate-indifference standard to claims of failing to protect prisoners from attacks of other prisoners. The standard is a high standard for the prisoner to overcome because he must prove that officials "knowingly disregarded an excessive risk of harm." To win such cases a prisoner must show evidence that prison officials knew that a substantial risk of harm existed through long-standing, pervasive, and well-documented assaults but that they failed to recognize such risks and to take steps to alleviate such conduct.

For example, in *Miller v. Shelby County* (2000) a detainee in jail brought a Section 1983 claim against the county alleging injuries sustained from an attack by other prisoners, which were the result of the jail's practice of allowing prisoners of different security levels to take recreation together. The district court found in favor of the prisoner, concluding that the jail's policy posed a substantial risk of harm and that officials acted with deliberate indifference to the risk posed by the policy. Jail officials argued that the "policy" was not an "official" policy, but the court determined that it was pervasive enough to be considered a "de facto" policy. The practice of the jail allowed prisoners of varying security levels to come together during recreation periods, including prisoners housed in protective custody. Miller had been attacked by gang members, and the court found that jail officials had general and specific knowledge of threats against the prisoner by members of the gang yet took no action to protect the prisoner, including prohibiting prisoners of various security levels from taking recreation together. Miller suffered permanent impairment to his shoulder and the court awarded him $40,000.

Prisoner-on-Prisoner Physical Assaults

There are two levels of deliberate indifference (Silver 2003). The first involves a failure to protect a prisoner from a pervasive risk at an institution. For example, in *Iwanski v. Ray* (2002), an appellate court upheld a jury verdict in favor of correction officials for allegedly failing to prevent an assault of the plaintiff prisoner who later died as a result of the attack. The plaintiff had been attacked by an intoxicated prisoner who beat him with a steel bunk bed stacking post. The family asserted that correction officials had violated their son's Eighth Amendment rights by failing to protect him from an assault, even having known of a history of assaults within the prison. The jury found that officials had not failed to protect the deceased prisoner, even though the attacking prisoner had had a history of assaultive behavior and alcohol abuse, and had engaged in two fights on the day of the attack. The court concluded that the officials had not known about the assaultive history of the attacking prisoner, that bed-posts had not been used as weapons before in the facility, that the officers had been unaware of any preassault fights, and that the officers had regularly patrolled the institution.

In *Matthews v. Armitage* (1999) the widow of a prisoner who had been stabbed by another prisoner brought a civil rights action against prison officials, alleging Eighth Amendment violations. The district court granted summary judgment, holding that the officials did not act with deliberate indifference to the prisoner's health and safety and were entitled to qualified immunity. The court noted that the two prisoners had been in each other's presence in the general population at least fifty times without incident and that there had never been a previous stabbing in the protective custody unit. In *Lopez v. Smith* (1998) a state prisoner filed a Section 1983 action against correctional officials, alleging that they had violated his civil rights by placing him in a cell with a dangerous cellmate, providing inadequate medical care, and placing him in a security unit. An appellate court affirmed a lower court's dismissal of the case, finding that the prisoner's fifteen-day confinement in the security unit while he awaited transfer did not violate his constitutional rights. The court held that officials were not deliberately indifferent for failure to provide the prisoner with a blanket and pillow, since the prisoner failed to produce any evidence that he had been denied adequate warmth or heating or that he had suffered from the cold. The court further found that the prisoner failed to state a claim regarding his alleged placement in a cell with a dangerous prisoner who subsequently broke his jaw.

In *Lopez v. Le Master* (1999) a pretrial detainee brought a Section 1983 claim against the sheriff, asserting that he had been beaten by fellow prisoners. The appellate court reversed summary judgment by the lower court. The detainee had been placed in a general-population cell and later threatened by a prisoner. The detainee notified a correction officer regarding the threat, and the officer interviewed him in an office. The detainee filed a written statement regarding the threat and the officer placed him back in the cell. Later the plaintiff was attacked and beaten by several prisoners. He was taken to the hospital for treatment of his injuries, brought back to the jail, and released the next day. Upon his release, he again went to the hospital and was diagnosed with postconcussion syndrome and severe strains of the cervical, thoracic, and lumbosacral spine. The appellate court found that material issues of fact precluded summary judgment in that the sheriff had been deliberately indifferent by failing to monitor prisoners, failing to protect prisoners, maintaining a policy of understaffing the jail, and failing to respond to the detainee's medical needs.

Enemies Within the System

The second level of deliberate indifference involves a failure to protect a prisoner after a specific reported threat, irrespective of the dangerous nature of the prison. Special-threat groups (gangs) and prisoners who become enemies of other prisoners for testifying against another prisoner or for informing ("snitching") on another prisoner can create security problems for correctional officials. Correctional officials were denied summary judgment in *Dowling v. Hannigan* (1998) when a state prisoner brought a claim of failure to protect from another prisoner's assaults. The district court found that correction officials had abdicated their responsibility to protect prisoners from other prisoners' attacks. A correctional officer had received a note stating that one prisoner was going to attempt to kill or injure the plaintiff because he had informed authorities about a drug transaction. Prison officials failed to inform the plaintiff about the threat, and he was attacked with an edged weapon (a razor blade melted in a toothbrush). The court found that there were fact issues regarding the adequacy of the officials' response—issues which precluded summary judgment. Likewise, in *Freeman v. Godinez* (1998) the court rejected summary judgment for correctional officials, finding that the prisoner had stated a valid claim arising from a physical attack by other prisoners. The court held that the prisoner had not needed to exhaust administrative remedies prior to filing a Section 1983 claim. The prisoner claimed that prison officials knew he was on a "hit list" and interrogated him about gang activities—an interrogation which may have put him in danger. He requested and was denied protection twice. He was later attacked by three prisoners. He was stabbed in the back, chest, and face, and he was beaten with pipes.

In *Benner v. Mc Adory* (2001) a warden was granted summary judgment in a claim of a failure to protect a prisoner from an assault by gang members in the prison. The prisoner asserted that he had informed correctional officials that certain members of a gang within the same housing unit had threatened to kill him and that he was denied a request to be moved out. The prisoner was later assaulted with scalding water as he approached a gang member prisoner's cell to retrieve legal papers. He then filed a Section 1983 action. The court concluded that, at the most, the failure to move the prisoner out of the housing unit was negligence and not deliberate indifference. The court found that the prisoner's choice of approaching the gang member prisoner's cell precluded recovery because the prisoner was the proximate cause of his own assault.

In *Benefield v. McDowell* (2001), a prisoner housed within the Federal Bureau of Prisons brought a *Bivens* action against correctional officials, claiming he was at significant risk of harm from other prisoners since the administrative personnel of the prison had labeled him a "snitch." Correctional officials moved for summary judgment. The court denied the motion and the officials appealed the decision. The appellate court affirmed the lower court's decision, finding that it had been clearly established at the time of the incident that identifying a prisoner as an informant to other prisoners clearly violated his Eighth Amendment rights. The court noted that even though the prisoner had not been assaulted, he suffered psychological injury owing to the fear of harm to which the officials had exposed him.

During a mass movement of prisoners to school and various prison assignments, a prisoner, who was the "enforcer" of a special-threat group, was beaten to death by two rival gang members in *Underwood v. Wackenhut Cor-*

rections Corporation (2003). The two attacking prisoners had learned that the rival gang had contracted to kill one of them and decided to kill the "enforcer" before he could fulfill the contract. The two attacking prisoners found the "enforcer" on a walkway outside, leading to the prison gymnasium. Both of the prisoners shoved him against a wall and began beating and kicking him. The enforcer fell into a metal firebox, striking his head. They continued to beat his head into the metal firebox until officers responded. The two prisoners were subdued, and the assaulted prisoner was transported to a nearby hospital where he died three days later.

The estate filed a Section 1983 claim against the officers and the warden for failing to protect the prisoner from "known" gang members, for failing to isolate known threat-group members from the general population, and for failing to allegedly remedy a history of assaults within the institution. The institution was six years old at the time of the assault and had been accredited and reaccredited by the American Correctional Association prior to the incident. Detailed records of prisoner fights and assaults in the prison were statistically analyzed by the officials' correctional expert. He found that the number of past prisoner-on-prisoner assaults, when compared with the prison population, was well below the national and state average of prisoner assaults in security prisons of similar size and that any prisoner in this institution had a 2 percent likelihood of being physically assaulted. The jury returned a verdict in favor of the correctional officials, concluding that a pervasive pattern of assaults did not exist. They further found that the officials were not aware that a substantial risk of harm existed for the prisoner and that they had taken more than reasonable preventative measures through training, policies, and security precautions to reduce the risk of an assault.

Failing-to-protect claims have emerged from riots and disturbances. Frequently prisoners allege that correctional officials abdicate their responsibility of custodial care and security while rioting prisoners ravage the institution and sexually and physically assault other prisoners before officials restore security. Such was the case in *Mayoral v. Sheehan* (2001). During a jail riot, a pretrial detainee was severely injured and brought a legal claim against the sheriff and detention officers for being deliberately indifferent to his safety and failing to segregate known gang members. The district court granted summary judgment for the officials and the appellate court affirmed, holding that failing to segregate prisoners by gang affiliation was not a constitutional violation, given the high number of gang members confined in the jail and the undue burden that such a policy would create for the jail. The appellate court denied summary judgment, however, finding that officials had denied a request that the prisoner be placed in protective custody and had delayed coming to the aid of the prisoner when the riot broke out.

Prisoner-on-Prisoner Sexual Assaults

Many of the failure-to-protect claims filed by prisoners have asserted that, as in the *Farmer* case, the prisoner was a victim of a sexual assault by another prisoner. Prison officials must be deliberately indifferent to the serious risk of harm to the prisoner in order for liability to attach.

In *Kemner v. Hemphill* (2002) a state prisoner brought a Section 1983 action against the prison administrator, alleging that he had been sexually assaulted by another prisoner. He claimed that he was forced to perform oral sex on the other prisoner, that he was sexually assaulted for two hours, and that he suffered cuts and bruises. The prisoner claimed that he suffered mental anguish, fright and shock, humiliation, and mortification, in addition to permanent psychological injuries. The court agreed with the prisoner that being forced to perform oral sex upon another male prisoner was analogous to a body cavity search performed by correction officers. The court concluded that Congress had intended, in their passage of the Prison Litigation Reform Act, to include the concept of physical injury to cover such repugnant use of physical force. The prisoner stated that he had informed the correction officials that he was being threatened by other prisoners and that they had refused to move him.

An Eighth Circuit Court of Appeals affirmed a lower court's granting of summary judgment for the detention officers and the sheriff in *Perkins v. Grimes* (1998). The plaintiff had filed a Section 1983 claim, alleging he had been raped by another prisoner. The appellate court ruled that neither the jailers nor the sheriff were deliberately indifferent to the detainee's safety when they housed him with a prisoner who later raped him. The court noted that although officers were on notice that the prisoner was easily provoked, they also knew that the detainee and the prisoner had previously been housed together without incident. The court also noted that the officers neither knew, nor had reason to know, that the prisoner was a violent sexual aggressor. The plaintiff had been confined in a holding cell for public intoxication. Another prisoner, who was larger and heavier and confined for the same charge, was subsequently raped. The detainee alleged that a detention officer was aware of the assault and failed to intervene.

In *Webb v. Lawrence County* (1998) a detainee in a detention center brought an action against the county and detention officers, claiming he had been raped by a cellmate. Granting summary judgment for county officials, the appellate court affirmed the lower court's ruling. The court concluded that the detainee had failed to establish that the officials knew of substantial risk of harm to him by his cellmate. While the court agreed that officials knew generally of the risk of prisoner rape and assault against young, physically slight prisoners such as the detainee, the court found that there was no evidence that the rape was common in this facility. Further, there was no evidence that the cellmate, a sexual offender, had assaulted other prisoners or caused any other problems while confined. In addition, the detainee had requested placement in the cell with the attacking prisoner.

In *Jones v. Bank* (1995) a prisoner brought a Section 1983 claim alleging that he was sexually assaulted by another prisoner and that correction officials failed to prevent the assault from occurring. The prisoner presented evidence to the court that he was well known in the institution as a homosexual and a self-proclaimed "drag queen" and that he was often in danger of being sexually attacked by prisoners desiring to have sex with him. The court granted a verdict in favor of the prisoner, finding sufficient evidence that the prisoner was in serious risk of danger and that officials were aware of it yet failed to take precautionary measures to minimize the risk of harm.

Officer-on-Prisoner Assaults

Prisoners have also brought Section 1983 actions claiming that they were assaulted by correction officers. These assertions may emerge from an incident of an alleged use of excessive force or, in some cases, from an incident involving officer retaliation. In those cases where liability attached, correction officers crossed the line of their official duties by misusing their power and authority over prisoners (Souryal 1999).

Prisoners have filed lawsuits claiming a failure to protect and an assault stemming from an officer's use of force. These claims generally assert that the officers used excessive force outside the scope of their authority. Frequently these claims assert assault and battery, brutality, and conspiracy to deprive the prisoner of his constitutional rights. For example, in *U.S. v. Daniels* (2002) a prisoner filed suit claiming three officers beat him without provocation. The appellate court affirmed a lower court's decision, finding in favor of the prisoner. The court found sufficient evidence that two of the officers beat the prisoner for no reason and that the third officer stood by and made no attempt to stop the beating.

In *Skritch v. Thorton* (2002) a prisoner filed a Section 1983 lawsuit claiming his Eighth Amendment right to be free from excessive force was violated. After repeated attempts to compel the prisoner to voluntarily remove himself from his cell for a search, correction officers forcibly removed him. They used an electronic shield to shock and subdue him and allegedly punched, kicked, and beat him to the point that he had to be airlifted to a hospital for treatment. The court noted that the prisoner admitted that some force was necessary in light of his past history of disciplinary problems and his refusal to cooperate with the search. The court, however, found in favor of the prisoner, claiming that the officers used excessive force when they punched, kicked, and beat him, thereby supporting the plaintiff's claim of an Eighth Amendment violation.

In *Townsend v. Moya* (2002) a state prisoner claimed that a correction officer had cut him with a knife, and the plaintiff sought damages. As a trusty, the prisoner had been caring for the officer's tracking dogs and claimed that the officer had approached him from behind and had told him "he would get him" and stabbed him in the buttocks with a pocketknife. The district court granted summary judgment for the officer, and the appeals court affirmed the decision. The court concluded that the officer's action with the knife was not taken under "color of law" for the purpose of a Section 1983 claim. The court ruled that if a prison officer takes personal actions without using or misusing the power granted to him by the state, then he is not acting under the color of law. Criminal charges were dropped for insufficient evidence and the officer was terminated.

In *White v. Fauver* (1998) a claim of a failure to protect was initiated by prisoners asserting that correction officers were retaliating against them for the murder of a correction officer. In their class action lawsuit, the prisoners alleged that officers and supervisors had engaged in a pattern of physical abuse and threats and had subjected them to a series of unconstitutional living conditions. The court held that the prisoners were not required by the PLRA to first exhaust the administrative remedies available to them at the institution, since the PLRA does not cover intentional physical attacks, conspiracy to use excessive force to intimidate prisoners, threats of further physical violence to conceal prior acts, filing false disciplinary reports, and retaliation for filing lawsuits. The court held, however, that mere allegations of threats do not constitute a civil rights claim and granted correctional officials qualified immunity with respect to the allegations of unconstitutional prison conditions.

A prisoner stated a claim of failure to protect and of retaliation in *Sprau v. Coughlin* (1998). The prisoner filed a Section 1983 lawsuit claiming that he had been denied his right to freedom of speech and to petition the government for redress of grievances. The prisoner had threatened to file a grievance against a correction officer, and the officer had grabbed the prisoner from behind the neck and hit him several times. The court found in favor of the prisoner, stating that the officer had abused his official capacity as a governmental employee and had violated the rights of the prisoner.

Failure to Protect and Sexual Misconduct of Correction Officers

While not new, a vexing administrative problem has emerged as litigation alleging sexual misconduct on the part of officers has gained national attention. Female prisoners make up about 6 percent of the prison population and about 10 percent of the jail population, and about 66 percent of the female population are serving sentences for violent or drug-related charges (Harrison and Beck 2003). Female prisoners bring into a confinement setting a range of various issues different from those of male prisoners. Generally, female prisoners leave their community with one to three children for which child care must be provided. A number of them were abused as children and poorly educated. A large majority were unemployed at the time they were arrested (Collins and Collins 1996).

As more women have been incarcerated in jails and prisons, more female correction officers have been hired to work in these facilities. Title VII of the Civil Rights Act of 1964 requires gender-neutral hiring. Hence, more women are being hired and are working in male prisons. Still, the majority of correctional facilities are operated by male correctional officers and supervisors. Male officers also work in female prisons, and male officers have routine contact with female prisoners in detention centers. Prisoners have filed lawsuits addressing issues of cross-gender supervision, privacy of prisoners, and the employee's right to an equal opportunity to work in the opposite gender's institution (Collins and Collins 1996; Moss 1999; Ingram 2000). In cross-gender supervision, an officer of one gender supervises prisoners of the opposite gender. Because correctional administrators do not a make a distinction between a male and a female officer, a gender-neutral practice exists when an assignment is made within a facility. Thus prisoners that were once supervised by officers of the same gender are now often being supervised by officers of the opposite gender. As a result, two liability issues emerge. The first issue concerns whether the prisoner's expectation of privacy during confinement is violated when the prisoner is supervised in the housing unit by an officer of the opposite gender while he or she performs searches, supervises prisoner showers, and observes the prisoner during stages of undress. The question arises: Does the officer's right to equal opportunity for employment outweigh the prisoner's expectation of privacy?

The second issue pertains to sexual misconduct, generally when a male officer forces a female prisoner to engage in some form of sexual contact with him, although some incidents have involved same-gender sexual misconduct. Most states have instituted criminal laws prohibiting sexual contact, including sexual abuse, sexual harassment, sexual obscenity, sexual invasion of privacy, and conversations or correspondence of an sexual nature between an officer and a prisoner. Further, most correctional departments have designed policies prohibiting sexual misconduct and procedures addressing cross-gender supervision. When sexual-misconduct actions arise, most correctional departments have conducted an investigation of the incident, criminally prosecuted the offending officer, and/or disciplined the officer as warranted, terminating the officer if necessary.

Sexual misconduct of correction staff in prisons has been studied by researchers of the General Accounting Office (GAO) (1999). In a survey of four correctional jurisdictions (Texas, California, the District of Columbia, and the Bureau of Federal Prisons), researchers found that from 1998 to 1999, female prisoners filed 506 allegations of staff sexual misconduct, of which 92 (18 percent) were sustained. Most of the sustained allegations resulted in employee resignations or terminations. There were only two criminal prosecutions for the misconduct, and each jurisdiction incurred at least two civil lawsuits related to the misconduct. Researchers found that common allegations were verbal harassment, improper visual surveillance, improper touching, and/or consensual sex. Claims of rape and other claims of forced sex were rare. The departments did not have a systematic method of collecting data regarding this subject.

These two issues have generated a number of civil lawsuits filed primarily by female prisoners. Generally, the legal action cites several claims on two levels and may be filed in either state court or in federal court through a Section 1983 action alleging a violation of the Eighth or Fourteenth Amendment. The first level of claims is directed at the offending officer for an invasion of privacy, a violation of the Violence Against Women Act, rape, sexual assault, a failure to protect, an illegal search, or cross-gender supervision as a violation of the prisoner's constitutional rights. The second level of claims is directed against the department administrator, asserting that there exists an official practice or policy of violating the constitutional rights of prisoners by permitting cross-gender supervision, by failing to protect prisoners by hiring officers with histories of sexual misconduct, by failing to train officers from engaging in sexual misconduct or sexual harassment, by condoning searches of the opposite gender, by failing to supervise and discipline sexually deviant officers, by retaining such officers by tolerating such conduct when it was known by supervisors, and by failing to investigate and remedy such claims. The following sections will examine the liability issues which emerge from these two levels of claims.

Sexual Assaults of Officers on Prisoners

Although correction officers may not be able to absolutely guarantee the safety of prisoners from attacks by other prisoners, they cannot tolerate the sexual assault of a prisoner by an officer. There is no more repugnant conduct to a female prisoner and for the community to learn about than an incident when an officer sworn to uphold the law has sexually assaulted her. Given the custodial environment of the prison and the power a correction officer possesses over prisoners, the Sixth Circuit Court of Appeals characterized such conduct as a "shocking abuse of power" in *Pelfrey v. Chambers* (1995). While such conduct is rare in the correctional facility, a number of incidents have generated civil lawsuits.

In *Riley v. Olk-Long* (2002) a female prisoner brought a Section 1983 action alleging she had been raped by a correction officer. The appellate affirmed a lower court's ruling that the officer did indeed rape the prisoner and that liability therefore attached. The appellate also affirmed that the warden and the director of security were deliberately indifferent to the substantial risk of harm to the prisoner. In one incident, the correctional officer asked the female prisoner if he could watch her and another female prisoner have sexual relations. In a later incident, the officer attempted to reach under the prisoner's nightgown but she backed away. Over a period of time the officer continued to harass the prisoner and on one occasion grabbed her from behind and rubbed up against her while fondling her breasts. The prisoner did not report these incidents to supervisors, thinking she would not be believed and fearing reprisal by the officer through disciplinary actions. Later, the officer entered the prisoner's cell and had forcible intercourse with her. She began performing oral sex on the officer because she feared she would get pregnant. Another female prisoner witnessed the incident and reported it to correctional officials, who conducted an investigation. Administrators allowed the officer to resign and charged him with sexual misconduct with a prisoner. He pled guilty, and the jury awarded the prisoner $15,000 in compensatory damages and $30,000 in punitive damages.

In *Goode v. Correctional Medical Services* (2001) a female brought civil rights claims against prison officials, the medical contractor, and the contractor's nursing personnel for excessive force, sexual assault, and Eighth Amendment violations resulting from an obstetric examination. The health care employees performed an unauthorized internal exam and hugged and kissed the prisoner during the examination. As a result of the exam, the prisoner bled, her blood pressure rose, and she went into labor four weeks early. The court found that the prisoner stated a legitimate Eighth Amendment claim.

Administrators who have developed and implemented appropriate procedures and training can insulate themselves from liability in this area. In *Daniels v. Delaware* (2000) a female prisoner who had been raped by a correction officer and had become pregnant filed a Section 1983 lawsuit and a claim involving the Violence Against Women Act against prison officials. The district court granted summary judgment to the officials, stating that the prisoner failed to establish a valid claim that the officials were deliberately indifferent to her health and safety. The court noted that the department conducted full investigations into the incident and into other incidents when the officer had taken female prisoners outside their cells after lockdown. The court ruled that there was no evidence that the incident concerning the plaintiff involved sexual misconduct and that the officials had disciplined the officer. The court ruled that departmental supervisors were not deliberately indifferent to the training needs of the officers since they had provided the officers with the necessary training consistent with the American Correctional Association training materials. The officer had received numerous hours of training in cultural awareness, sexual harassment, the proper treatment of prisoners, and the department's code of officer conduct which prohibited sexual contact between officers and prisoners. Moreover, the court stated that the level of training provided to the officer was adequate to meet what is necessary under the Eighth Amendment and that national training standards do not set forth constitutional minimums but are instructive in recommending training goals.

A court's decision indicating an active administrative response in this area is found in *Stockman v. Lowndes County, MS* (2000). One week after her confinement in the detention center, a female detainee attempted suicide and was moved to an observation cell near the officers' station where she could be monitored more closely. Two days later, a male detention officer instructed a female officer to take a lunch break in another part of the jail. While another male officer stood lookout, the officer entered the female detainee's cell and raped her. Around two months later the detainee reported the rape, and an investigation by the sheriff found that the two officers had been placed on administrative leave. Based on the findings of the investigation, the two officers were terminated, and the assaulting officer pled guilty to criminal charges of rape. The detainee filed a lawsuit alleging that her constitutional rights had been violated by the sheriff because of his deliberate indifference in failing to protect her from the officers and in failing to train them regarding sexual misconduct between detainees and officers.

Prior to the incident, the sheriff had instituted policies on the treatment of detainees, sexual misconduct between officers and detainees, and the supervision of female prisoners by male officers He had also arranged for several training seminars on the subject. The court granted summary judgment to the sheriff, finding that there was no evidence of deliberate indifference to the safety of female detainees in the detention center. While male officers were permitted limited surveillance of female detainees, such conduct did not intrude upon the detainees' rights, did not pose a substantial risk of harm to detainees, and did not create the desire of the officer to rape the detainee. There had been no other sexual attacks in the detention center prior to this incident and the court noted that the sheriff had promulgated operational policies governing the care of detainees and had provided extensive training on the subject. The court ruled that the detainee failed to demonstrate either a pattern of similar incidents in which other prisoners had been sexually assaulted or injured, or a custom or practice reflecting deliberate indifference to the constitutional rights of prisoners.

When administrators can demonstrate that they have designed a system of protective mechanisms for the welfare of all prisoners—such as policies, practices, codes of conduct, the training and supervision of officers, and disciplinary measures against officers after an investigation—the courts are likely to grant summary judgments for the administrators. An officer acting outside the law, the policies, and the training in this regard is likely to be terminated, to be prosecuted, and to lose in a civil action.

In two similar cases, *Cain v. Rock* (1999) and *Barney v. Pulsipher* (1999), the courts followed the same line of reasoning as in *Daniels* and *Stockman*. *Cain* and *Barney* involved random sexual assaults of female detainees by detention officers. In both cases liability attached against the two officers and the sheriffs were granted summary judgment. In *Barney* the court held that the sheriff was not deliberately indifferent to the practices of hiring officers or in providing policies for and training of male officers in supervising female detainees. In *Cain*, the issues of policy, hiring, and training emerged, and the court found that the plaintiff had not proved administrative negligence regarding these issues. The additional issue of cross-gender supervision was addressed only in *Cain* when the detainee claimed that allowing male officers to supervise female detainees violates the Fourteenth Amendment. The court found that there is no constitutional violation involved in the policy of cross-gender supervision and that therefore such a claim cannot withstand a valid Section 1983 action. (Liability of cross-gender supervision will be discussed below.)

Compare, however, the court's ruling in *Women Prisoners v. District of Columbia* (1994). Female prisoners filed a class action suit against the prison officials, claiming their Eighth Amendment rights had been violated. Their suit included claims of sexual harassment, sexual assault by male officers, vulgar sexual remarks by officers, lack of privacy in their cells, a refusal by some officers to announce their presence in the housing units of female prisoners, and inadequate confinement conditions and health care services for female prisoners. The court found that these claims amounted to malicious, wanton, and unnecessary infliction of pain, in violation of the Eighth Amendment. Deliberate indifference was demonstrated, the court stated, since the officials had known about the conditions, the inadequate medical services, and the risk of danger to female prisoners yet had done nothing to address them. The court ordered the department to correct the deficiencies and ordered the officials to write and implement new policies dealing with harassment of female prisoners, sexual assaults on prisoners, the investigation of such complaints, the internal monitoring of complaints and investigations, and the provision of training for all departmental employees. The training was required quarterly for the duration of the court order.

Cross-Gender Supervision

An emerging area of correctional litigation facing administrators and officers in detention centers and prisons is the issue of cross-gender supervision. Two basic questions emerge from this type of litigation: Do male and female officers have a right to gender-neutral employment in housing units of the opposite gender? Under the Fourth Amendment, can prisoners expect privacy which precludes officers of the opposite gender from searching and observing/supervising them? (The legal issue of searching prisoners and the various types of searches performed in the confinement setting are addressed in more detail in Chapter 10.)

As discussed previously in this chapter, correction officers are obligated to provide a level of custody and security which reasonably protects prisoners in their care. Security of any correctional facility is of paramount concern to correctional authorities, officers, prisoners, and the community. This means that security measures like surveillance, searches, close supervision of prisoners, and security patrols must be routinely performed to minimize the risks of violence, contraband, escapes, weapons, drugs, arson, property damage, and assaults. Prisoners have asserted that such activities performed by officials of the opposite gender violate their rights to privacy. While the courts have attempted to find a balance between the right of officers to supervise prisoners of the opposite gender and the privacy rights of the prisoners, there is much disagreement concerning ways of applying such legal rights.

In *Dothard v. Rawlinson* (1977) the United States Supreme Court addressed the question of sex discrimination in prison. The Court upheld the prison authorities' position that being male was a Bona Fide Occupational Qualification (BFOQ) in contact-officer positions in a maximum custody prison in Alabama because violence there was the order of the day. The prison environment was characterized as a "jungle" because the prison was overly populated with violent prisoners and sex offenders. Therefore, female officers were banned from working in prisoner-contact positions owing to the high frequency of assaults. The Court noted that the BFOQ must be reasonably necessary to the normal operation of the prison. Justices Marshall and Brennan strongly dissented, commenting that women officers would not make the situation in the prison any worse than what male officers were experiencing.

The Court's decision, however, has had little effect on employment opportunities for women working in prisons, because, since the 1970s, more women have been employed as officers in male prisons and in jails. Some courts have forbidden policies that prohibit female officers from working in male housing units. In *Griffin v. Michigan Department of Corrections* (1982) the court held that, under Title VII, being male was not a required BFOQ for an officer to work within the male cellblock. The court further held that, when feasible, women working in a male housing unit could serve as a viable rehabilitative and stable influence on male prisoners. However, the court, in *Torres v. Wisconsin Department of Corrections* (1988), upheld the prison superintendent's decision to prohibit male officers from working in female prisons to enhance rehabilitation. The dissenting judge stated that the presence of male officers in female prisons was "valuable" to prisoners preparing to return to the community and that the idea of rehabilitation as a justification has all but been discarded in American corrections.

In *Bell v. Wolfish* (1979) the United States Supreme Court held that judicial intervention in the matters of sentenced prisoners is more restrictive than intervention in the matters of pretrial detainees in detention centers. However, concerning the matter of cell searches and privacy issues in jails, the Court held that there is no distinction between pretrial detainees and sentenced prisoners and that therefore a detainee has no reasonable expectation of privacy. The Court further held that pretrial detainees do not pose a lesser security threat than convicted prisoners and in some cases may pose a greater risk to jail security and order.

Generally, the courts have deferred to correctional officials in security concerns, as long as there is a rational basis and a legitimate penological objective for the policy and practice (*Turner v. Safley* 1987). In *Turner*, the United States Supreme Court determined that four factors must be considered in determining the validity of the policy: (1) a valid connection between the policy and the governmental interest, (2) alternative means of implementing the policy (3) the impact of the policy, and (4) the availability of ready alternatives to the policy.

This area of the law is not settled, but, as mentioned above, generally the courts have deferred to correctional officials as long they can demonstrate a reasonable and legitimate correctional objective. Generally, the courts have held that some viewing of prisoners in states of undress does not violate the Constitution if it is reasonable, if it is the exception rather than the rule, and if it is done for a legitimate purpose. Most courts have been willing to recognize the necessity for occasional observation of prisoners by officers of the opposite gender, particularly of male prisoners by female officers. Moreover, infrequent and casual viewing of prisoners by officers of the opposite gender does not violate a prisoner's privacy right when such viewing is necessitated by security needs.

In *Oliver v. Scott* (2002) a male prisoner brought a claim against the administrator and officers alleging constitutional violations arising from cross-gender observation, strip searches, and a lack of privacy partitions in male showers. The appellate court upheld a lower court's granting of summary judgment, ruling that any minimal right to bodily privacy possessed by the prisoner did not preclude cross-gender surveillance and that such surveillance, in the absence of partitions in the male showers, did not violate the prisoner's constitutional rights. The court noted that a period of confinement in jail did not override the right of surveillance by members of the opposite sex. Further, the court held that the prisoner failed to specify the unconstitutional policy that correctional officers had allegedly violated by engaging in cross-gender strip searches and monitoring of prisoners.

Contrast, however, the court's ruling in *Ashann-Ra v. Com. of Virginia* (2000). The court denied summary judgment to correctional officers when a male prisoner claimed that female prison officers regularly observed the male prisoner's genitals and other private parts of the anatomy while he showered. While the court ruled in favor of the prisoner, it stopped short of agreeing that such viewing of prisoners by female officers created emotional distress, sexual dysfunction, and psychosomatic injuries in violation of his protected right to privacy.

The courts have generally supported policies which permit a patdown search of male prisoners by female officers. In the cases *Smith v. Fairman* (1982), *Madyun v. Franzen* (1983), *Grummett v. Rushen* (1985), *Timm v. Gunter* (1990), and *Canell v. Armenikis* (1993), the courts held that conducting clothed patdown searches did not violate the rights of male prisoners. The court in *Grumett* noted that the patdown searches of male prisoners' groin areas by female officers did not unduly interfere with the prisoners' rights, since the searches did not involve intimate contact with the prisoners' bodies. The court in *Timm* went further, stating that a prison policy of female officers searching male prisoners is no different from a policy of male officers searching male prisoners, including the genital and anal areas. The court held that the policy was reasonable, that officers were trained to conduct searches in a professional manner, and that the touching of the genital and anal areas was brief and incidental. Moreover, the court in *Canell* stated that the gender of the officer is irrelevant as long as there is justification to view or search the prisoner and the officer behaves appropriately.

The more problematic issue in cross-gender litigation, however, has emerged when female prisoners assert that male officers have violated their rights when the officers observe them in states of undress or when the prisoners are searched. Some courts appear somewhat reluctant to support male officers viewing female prisoners in states of undress and conducting bodily searches. In *Jordan v. Gardner* (1993) the court rejected a prison policy allowing male officers to perform clothed searches of female prisoners. A female prisoner had brought a claim challenging the constitutionality of a policy that allowed cross-gender clothed searches. Sitting en banc, the appellate court found that the policy of allowing male officers to search female prisoners was a violation of the Eighth Amendment. The court found that conducting random, nonemergency, suspicionless clothed body searches of female prisoners constituted cruel and unusual punishment. The court noted that the policy inflicted "pain"—in violation of the Eighth Amendment—since many of the female prisoners claimed that they had been sexually abused prior to their confinement and that unwanted touching by men would cause psychological trauma. The court found that such searches were not performed in emergency situations, were unnecessary to ensure prison security, and did not ensure equal employment for male officers.

The impact of the *Jordan* decision by the Ninth Circuit Appellate Court struck down a policy that would permit male officers to routinely conduct clothed searches of prisoners. This decision however, may be not be broadly applied. The decision in *Carl v. Angelone* (1995) recognized that the need to provide security measures may outweigh the privacy concerns of female prisoners. Correctional officers sued the prison director, claiming discrimination for having initiated a policy of allowing only men to work in male institutions and only women to work in female institutions. The director transferred all male officers working in female prisons to male institutions and implemented the same policy for female officers, based on a BFOQ. The court denied the director's motion for summary judgment and stated that he could not assert qualified immunity based on an alleged BFOQ in order to minimize the conflict between the privacy interests of prisoners and the nondiscrimination requirement of Title VII. The court also held that there is no rule per se that makes it illegal for male correction officers to conduct routine or random body searches of female prisoners.

While some courts have voiced reservations about male officers viewing and searching female prisoners, the court in *Carlin v. Manu* (1999) concluded that such a policy did not violate the female prisoners' constitutional rights. Female state prisoners challenged patdown searches that were performed by male officers. The court granted summary judgment for the officers, noting that performing such searches was not clearly identified as unlawful under existing law and that the searches were unusual in that they had been caused by the emergency removal of the prisoners to a male prison: Female prisoners had flooded the cells and had to be evacuated temporarily. Further, in *Drummer v. Luttrell* (1999) the court held that strip-searching and handcuffing a female prisoner during a unit search did not constitute a due process violation because the action had not imposed a significant or atypical hardship on her. She had been instructed to squat and cough twice, yet she refused to do so. Two male officers were called to intervene, and they escorted her from the shower area wearing only her panties.

Deliberate Indifference and Prison and Jail Conditions

Prisoners have initiated numerous lawsuits claiming that the conditions of their confinement are substandard. Allegations concerning conditions of confinement can include such issues as poor sanitation, living environment, plumbing, ventilation, heating, hygiene, food, overcrowding, noise, and the "totality" of the conditions themselves.

Prison officials are responsible for providing adequate living conditions for prisoners. The Constitution, however, does not mandate "comfortable prisons," and "discomfort in prison is not guaranteed." Nor does the Constitution permit "inhumane prisons" (*Rhodes v. Chapman* 1981; *Farmer v. Brennan* 1994). In *Rhodes,* the United States Supreme Court held that double bunking of prisoners in a cell designed for one prisoner is not cruel and unusual punishment in violation of the Eighth Amendment.

The Court expanded the application of the deliberate-indifference standard to cases of conditions of confinement with its decision in *Wilson v. Seiter* (1991). Wilson had filed a Section 1983 action against Ohio correctional officials claiming that overcrowding, mixing of healthy with physically or mentally impaired prisoners, excessive noise, inadequate heating and cooling, and

Figure 7.2   *Wilson v. Seiter* (1991)

Prisoner Wilson sought monetary damages and injunctive relief in a Section 1983 action claiming that the conditions of confinement violated his Eighth Amendment right to be free from cruel and unusual punishment. He also brought action under the Fourteenth Amendment. He asserted that the totality of conditions—including overcrowding, excessive noise, inadequate heating and cooling, improper ventilation, lack of storage space, unsanitary dining facilities, and his being housed with the mentally impaired—violated his rights. The lower courts rejected Wilson's claim and he appealed to the United States Supreme Court.

The Court granted certiorari to assess whether the deliberate-indifference standard applied to conditions of confinement in accordance with the cruel and unusual punishment clause of the Eighth Amendment. In a 5-4 decision the Court held that if conditions of confinement deprive a prisoner of basic human needs, those conditions are not actionable unless the correctional official has acted with a sufficiently culpable state of mind in allowing those conditions to exist. The Court ruled that the appropriate standard to apply to such actions is that of deliberate indifference, which satisfies the Eighth Amendment's state-of-mind requirement. The decision in *Estelle v. Gamble* (1976) dictated this decision.

This case is significant because it grants more authority to correctional officials in operating their facilities. Also, it makes it more difficult for prisoners to prevail in such actions since they must prove that officials had a culpable state of mind— meaning that officials had intended, through the conditions, to punish prisoners under the Eighth Amendment. Prisoners must show that correction officials were deliberately indifferent to the conditions in question and therefore intended harm to the prisoners. It is unlikely that prisoners will prevail in such a claim.

a lack of sanitation violated his Eighth and Fourteenth Amendment rights to be free from "cruel and unusual" punishment. The Court noted that "deliberate indifference" is the sole standard for evaluating allegations of inadequate prison conditions. The Court also stated that prisoners filing such claims must show a culpable state of mind on the part of the official. In other words, prisoners must show that corrections officials had "intent" to continue such deplorable prison conditions. The Court's decision is significant since it makes it more difficult for prisoners to prevail in such actions (Figure 7.2).

In *Canell v. Multnomah County* (2001) a pretrial detainee brought a Section 1983 claim alleging that the conditions of his confinement in the detention center had violated his constitutional rights. The detainee claimed that double bunking him with other prisoners and failing to shower and debug him and other prisoners in order to prevent communicable diseases had violated his rights. He also alleged that he had experienced such illnesses and harms as toe fungus; brief denials of food, sanitation, and water; nose sores; cold winter temperatures, and being forced to share a cell with a prisoner with AIDS. The court granted summary judgment for the sheriff, stating that the prisoner had not suffered constitutionally significant harms which would support a Section 1983 claim.

A prisoner brought a *pro se* complaint against correctional officials alleging unconstitutional conditions of confinement in *Davis v. Scott* (1998). The appeals court held that the prisoner's confinement for three days in a crisis management cell, which he alleged had blood on the walls and excrement on the floor, did not constitute a deprivation so extreme as to violate the prisoner's rights under the Eighth Amendment. The court noted that the prisoner had cleaning supplies available to him. In *Geder v. Godinez* (1995) an Illinois prisoner confined at Statesville Prison filed a claim for cruel and unusual conditions of confinement. He alleged he was confined in conditions that included defective pipes, sinks, and toilets; improperly cleaned showers; a broken intercom system; stained mattresses; accumulated dust and dirt; and infestation by rats and roaches. The district court granted summary judgment for the correctional officials. The court concluded that whether the conditions were viewed separately or cumulatively, they were insufficient to establish a deprivation of human needs which would constitute a violation of the Eighth Amendment. The court further noted a lack of evidence that prison officials knew of and consciously disregarded an excessive risk to prisoner health or safety. Prison conditions are not unconstitutional under the Eighth Amendment simply because they are restrictive or harsh.

In *Dixon v. Godinez* (1997) a prisoner brought a Section 1983 action claiming that the conditions of his protective custody cell violated his Eighth Amendment right to be free from cruel and unusual punishment. The lower court granted summary judgment to correctional officials. On appeal, the appellant court ruled that poor ventilation in the prisoner's cell during the summer did not violate the Eighth Amendment, since the cell had a window which opened and an electric fan. The prisoner's claim that the rank air in the cell exposed him to diseases and caused respiratory problems was not supported by medical or scientific evidence. Further, the appellate court affirmed a lower court's holding in *Beverati v. Smith* (1997) that conditions in an administrative segregation cell did not violate his constitutional rights. The court found that the conditions within the segregation cell block were not atypical, although they allegedly included cells infested with vermin; cells smeared with human feces and urine and flooded with water; unbearably hot temperatures; cold food in small portions; infrequent receipt of clean clothing, bedding, and linen; the prisoners' inability to leave cells more than three or four times per week; denial of outside recreation; and denial of educational or religious services.

Frequently conditions-of-confinement actions contain multiple claims, alleging that the "totality" of prison conditions is cruel and unusual, violating prisoner rights. In *Simpson v. Horn* (1998) a prisoner brought a Section 1983 lawsuit against a correctional commissioner and other officials claiming that the prison was overcrowded, in violation of his Eighth Amendment right to be free from cruel and unusual punishment. He also asserted that the classification system for double-cell assignments violated the equal protection clause of the Fourteenth Amendment. The court found that the alleged deficiencies in the prison were not cruel and unusual and granted summary judgment to correctional officials. The court noted that prison officials have the right, acting in good faith and in particular circumstances, to take into account racial tensions in maintaining security, discipline, and good order in prisons and jails. The court found housing two prisoners in a cell designed for one prisoner does not, per se, violate the Eighth Amendment protection against cruel and unusual punishment, but it may do so if it results in deprivations of essential food, medical care, sanitation, or other conditions intolerable for human confinement. The prisoner had alleged that as a result of overcrowding, prisoners were not provided with adequate furniture, cleaning supplies, laundry service, ventilation, bedding, clothing, recreational equipment, or telephones. He also alleged that food was served cold 85 percent of the time and that the dining hall was not kept clean or free of vermin.

Detention centers holding pretrial detainees and sentenced offenders have been prime targets for litigation claiming inadequate jail conditions. In *Benjamin v. Fraser* (2001) county officials had entered into a consent decree to work toward correcting deficiencies within the jails of New York, prior to the passage of the PLRA. Correctional officials requested to terminate the consent decree, which covered fourteen jails that confined over 10,000 detainees. The court agreed to terminate the decree on some of the provisions but failed to do so on others. The court found that the temperatures in the jails violated due process, noting that extremes in temperatures presented health risks and did not meet constitutional standards. The court held that the mere presence of vermin in the jails did not rise to a level of a due process violation, distinguishing between vermin "activity" and "infestation." The conditions of the sinks and toilets did not violate the rights of prisoners, nor did the preparation of food violate health codes since there had been no reports of food-borne illness and adequate sanitary practices were in place. Due process violations were found in the inhumane conditions of unsanitary cells, inadequate lighting, excessive noise, unsanitary mattresses, dirty and clogged ventilation registers, and dirty clinic areas. The court found that correctional officials had been deliberately indifferent to these conditions, since the consent decree had been in place for years and little progress had been made to remedy the problems.

Conditions or confinement which pretrial detainees were forced to endure were actionable in *Antonelli v. Sheahan* (1996). The court determined that pretrial detainees had stated a valid claim when they had asserted that the jail served rancid food, provided no exercise, failed to protect the detainees from extreme cold, lacked sufficient lighting, and allowed incessant noise at night over a lengthy period. The court also noted that a pest infestation claim was not defensible by showing two pest control sprayings within sixteen months in places where the problem had been persistent and prolonged and resulted in physical harm. The court concluded that the confinement of pretrial detainees must be related to a legitimate and an objective goal and that there can be no intent to punish.

The Ninth Circuit Appellate Court affirmed the lower court's decision not to enjoin correctional officials from placing mentally disturbed or suicidal prisoners in safety cells in *Anderson v. County of Kern* (1995). The court heard testimony that mentally disturbed and suicidal prisoners were violent and dangerous to themselves, requiring temporary placement in a safety cell. In some cases prisoners were so violent they had to be shackled to a toilet grate for protection against suicide. The court agreed with the testimony and also held that the deprivation of sinks, urinals, and beds for short periods of time during violent episodes was constitutionally justifiable because the prisoner was confined to safety cells for only short periods. Likewise, in *Robeson v. Squadrito* (1999) there was no Eighth Amendment violation for overcrowded jail conditions, where the mattress on the dayroom floor was not sanitarily maintained, minimal exercise did not threaten health, diet was minimally adequate, and there was no deliberate indifference to safety.

SUMMARY

Claims concerning failure to protect, conditions of confinement, and sexual misconduct have emerged as critical litigation areas facing correction officials and officers. Depending on the status of the prisoner, the courts will apply either the Eighth and Fourteenth Amendment standards when evaluating the case. Failure-to-protect and conditions-of-confinement claims will be scrutinized within the purview of the "deliberate indifference" standard under the Eighth Amendment. The plaintiff must show that the correction official knew that a substantial risk of harm existed for the prisoner. This standard is a high hurdle for the plaintiff prisoner to clear and is even more difficult for him or her to clear with the passage of the Prison Litigation Reform Act.

Despite the tough standard of deliberate indifference, prisoners occasionally prevail in these lawsuits. Therefore, as in other areas of liability, correction administrators should take deliberate steps to ensure that appropriate policies and procedures are in place which address these common areas of prisoner litigation. Officials can not totally eliminate all prisoner-on-prisoner sexual or physical assaults within the prison or detention center and are not guarantors of absolute safety of prisoners within their custody. Security procedures, however, should be in place which will minimize the risk of such assaults. Such procedures are frequently implemented through polices of formal/informal counts, routine searches, scheduled activities, classification and housing assignments, checks on special-threat groups, intelligence gathering, restricting mass movements of prisoners in institutions during certain periods of the day, close supervision of prisoners, the use of segregation for unmanageable or assaultive prisoners, and the use of protective segregation for prisoners requiring additional safety. Officers must be informed of these directives and trained in these security protocols, and they must work toward ensuring that the safety of all prisoners is a paramount job function. Officers should work toward keeping abreast of the potential risks of breaches of safety and security within their facilities.

Cross-gender supervision is also emerging as a critical liability area. The law is unsettled in this area, but many courts defer to correctional authorities when the authorities assign officers of one gender to supervise prisoners of the opposite gender. Some courts distinguish between prisoner privacy and prisoner modesty. Correctional administrators should develop and enforce policies that support officer employment rights. At the same time administrators should ensure that policies are implemented that direct officers in properly supervising all prisoners, that direct officers in proper search-and-surveillance methods, that emphasize a code of professional officer conduct, that deal with sexual conduct with prisoners, that keep officers accountable, and that address progressive discipline for all personnel who violate such policies.

Clearly, the key factors in supervising prisoners, regardless of gender differences, are professionalism and the performance of duties within the framework of the law, agency policies and procedures, and training. In other occupations society expects the person to act professionally when performing various functions of the job. Correctional personnel should be no less concerned about acting with the highest levels of integrity when they are in contact with prisoners.

Maintaining a systematic approach to these areas and keeping abreast of the legal changes impacting this topic can assist correction officials in averting future liability.

REFERENCES

Camp, C., and G. Camp. 2002. *The 2001 corrections yearbook (1996–2000)*. Middletown, CT: Criminal Justice Institute.

Collins, W. C., and A. W. Collins. 1996. *Women in jail: Legal issues*. Longmont, CO: National Institute of Corrections.

General Accounting Office. 1999. *Women in prison: Sexual misconduct by correctional staff*. Washington, DC: United Sates General Accounting Office.

Harrison, P. M., and A. J. Beck. 2003. *Prisoners in 2002*. Washington, DC: Bureau of Justice Statistics. U.S. Department of Justice.

Henderson, J. 1990. *Protective custody management in adult correctional facilities: A discussion of causes, conditions, attitudes, and alternatives*. Washington, DC: National Institute of Corrections.

Ingram, J. D. 2000. Prison guards and inmates of opposite genders: Equal employment opportunity versus right to privacy. *Duke Journal of Gender Law and Policy* 4: 1–42.

Moss, A. 1999. Sexual misconduct among staff and inmates. In *Prison and jail administration: Practice and theory*, edited by P. M. Carlson and J. S. Garrett, 189–95. Gaithersburg, MD: Aspen Publishers.

Silver. I. 2003. *Police civil liability*. Newark, NJ: Matthew Bender Publishers.

Souryal, S. 1999. Corruption of prison personnel. In *Prison and jail administration: Practice and theory*, edited by P. M. Carlson and J. S. Garrett, 171–77. Gaithersburg, MD: Aspen Publishers.

Vaughn, M. 1996. Prison civil liability for inmate-against-inmate assault and breakdown/disorganization theory. *Journal of Criminal Justice* 24: 139–52.

Vaughn, M., and R. V. del Carmen. 1995. Civil liability against prison officials for inmate-on-inmate assault: Where are we and where have we been? *The Prison Journal* 75: 69–89.

Cases Cited

Anderson v. County of Kern, 45 F. 3d. 1310 (9th Cir. 1995)

Antonelli v. Sheahan, 81 F. 3d 1422 (7th Cir. 1996)

Ashann-Ra v. Com. of Virginia, 112 F. Supp. 2d 559 (W.D. Va. 2000)

Barney v. Pulsipher, 143 F. 3d 1299 (10th Cir. 1999)

Bell v. Wolfish, 441 U.S. 520 (1979)

Benefield v. McDowell, 241 F.3d 1267 (10th Cir. 2001)

Benjamin v. Fraser, 161 F. Supp. 2d 151 (S.D.N.Y. 2001)

Benner v. McAdory, 165 F. Supp. 2d 773 (N.D. Ill. 2001)

Beverati v. Smith, 120 F. 3d 500 (4th Cir. 1997)

Cain v. Rock, 67 F. Supp. 544 (D. Md.1999)

Canell v. Armenikis, 840 F. Supp. 783 (D. Or. 1993)

Canell v. Multnomah County, 141 F. Supp. 2d 1046 (D. Or. 2001)

Carl v. Angelone, 883 F. Supp. 1433 (D. Nev. 1995)

Carlin v. Manu, 72 F. Supp. 2d 1177 (D. Or. 1999)

Daniels v. Delaware, 120 F. Supp. 2d 411 (D. Del. 2000)

Davis v. Scott, 157 F. 3d 1003 (5th Cir. 1998)

Dixon v. Godinez, 114 F. 3d 640 (7th Cir. 1997)

Dothard v. Rawlinson, 433 U.S. 321 (1977)

Dowling v. Hannigan, 995 F. Supp. 1188 (D. Kan. 1998)

DeShaney v. Winnebago Department of Social Services, 489 U.S. 189 (1989)

Drummer v. Luttrell, 75 F. Supp. 2d 796 (W.D. Tenn. 1999)

Estelle v. Gamble, 429 U.S. 97 (1976)

Farmer v. Brennan, 511 U.S. 825 (1994)

Freeman v. Godinez, 996 F. Supp. 822 (N.D. Ill. 1998)

Geder v. Godinez, 8 F. Supp. 1078 (N.D. Ill. 1995)

Goode v. Correctional Medical Services, (2001)

Griffin v. Michigan Department of Corrections, 654 F. Supp. 690 (D. Mich. 1982)

Grummett v. Rushen, 779 F. 2d 491 (9th Cir. 1985)

Holt v. Sarver, 309 F. Supp. 362 (E.D. Ark. 1970)

Iwanski v. Ray, 44 Fed. Appx. 370 370 (10th Cir. 2002)

CHAPTER 8

LIABILITY AND WRONGFUL CUSTODIAL DEATHS

*The question is not whether the officers did all they could have,
but whether they did what the Constitution requires.*

Williams v. Kelso (2000)

A vexing problem has emerged for detention centers and prisons as they are increasingly confining the mentally impaired and individuals who have a substance abuse history or who are under the influence of a substance at time of admission. With some frequency this population has become violent and assaultive against officers or other prisoners and exhibits self-injurious behaviors, necessitating the use of higher levels of force and/or less-than-lethal force equipment. Such behaviors generally require several officers to restrain the prisoner. In many of these altercations the prisoner is physically controlled and restrained without sustaining injuries. In some cases, however, the prisoner may have been maximally restrained in a restrictive position, commonly referred to as the "hogtied position"(hands and legs restrained and connected by a strap or other device, legs bent back toward the hips and placed on the prisoner's stomach); or may have been placed in a restraint chair or in a "four-point" restraint position. Annually a small number of these prisoners die while in custody after having displayed violent behaviors.

In a majority of these cases, the person has been controlled and restrained, and within minutes, officers may notice the once combative person is now unresponsive. Emergency procedures may be initiated and/or medical assistance summoned, whereupon it is determined that the individual is dead, all within a few minutes or hours of the event.

Moreover, periodically a portion of this population has attempted or successfully committed suicide while confined. The estate of the deceased prisoner will generally file a civil action claiming that correctional personnel were deliberately indifferent in protecting the prisoner from himself/herself, were indifferent to his/her mental or medical health needs and/or were in some way negligent in performing their duties, which led to the prisoner's death. It is highly common for the estate to file a wrongful death claim against the agency administrators, the officers involved, and the governmental entity.

This chapter describes the potential civil liability issues commonly associated with wrongful custodial deaths following restraint incidents and deaths due to prisoner suicides. Custodial deaths are rare but may occur in either a detention center or a prison. Research indicates a sudden death after a violent restraint and a prisoner suicide are more likely to occur in a detention facility (Ross 2001). The liability issues involving standards of care in state courts are examined, as well as the standards for use of force, restraints, medical care in accordance with actions stemming from claims of negligence and Section 1983. Sudden in-custody deaths after a use-of-force confrontation are statistically rare but are emerging as a critical area in correction litigation. While many of these lawsuits are settled out of court, those cases decided by trial yield a number of legal issues worthy of concern for police officers and administrators. A custodial death will normally produce a civil lawsuit by the estate attempting to demonstrate that the officers and governmental entity should be held responsible for the wrongful death.

PLAINTIFF ASSERTIONS OF WRONGFUL CUSTODIAL DEATHS

A lawsuit filed concerning a wrongful custodial death will allege that the agency as a whole was intentionally negligent, grossly negligent, and deliberately indifferent to the needs of the deceased. The lawsuit will generally assert that the department's customs, policies, and procedures (or lack thereof) were the "proximate cause" of the death. The plaintiff will attempt to show that the department ignores industry standards, historically ignores problems in the agency, and typically fails to correct constitutional deficiencies.

The claim may also assert that the department fails to keep abreast of changes in the profession and that a death or a lawsuit occurs before the agency makes necessary changes. Generally the following allegations are made against public officials in a sudden wrongful death (which are not mutually exclusive): Excessive force was used by the responding officers; officers assaulted and battered the deceased; the officers' use of restraints contributed to the decedent's death; the officers were grossly negligent or deliberately indifferent to the medical and/or psychological needs of the deceased the officers failed to assess/monitor the medical condition or to provide/summon medical assistance for the deceased; the officers failed to transport the deceased to the nearest hospital or to summon medical assistance; the officers failed to follow departmental policy; the decedent in a maximum restrained position was transported in a vehicle, an action which contributed to his death; officers violated the decedent's constitutional rights; officers acted outside the scope of their authority; and officers conspired to injure or cause the death of the deceased.

The claim may also assert that administrative personnel and/or the agency failed to provide officers with policies which would direct them in responding to "special needs" prisoners (those drug-induced or mentally impaired), failed to provide officers with training in properly responding to and using force-control techniques on "special needs" prisoners, failed to provide officers with appropriate equipment to perform their duties, failed to supervise their officers, failed to train supervisors, negligently entrusted equipment to their officers without training or competency evaluation, condoned excessive-force measures with prisoners, failed to articulate directives in recognizing problems of "special needs" prisoners, failed to develop protocol for responding to violent prisoners' medical/psychological needs, failed to conduct an internal investigation or failed to conduct an independent investigation of the death, conspired to cause the death of the deceased, and covered up the death with a less-than-adequate internal investigation. Each case will obviously comprise numerous variables for the plaintiff to attack. In any lawsuit not all initial allegations will withstand judicial scrutiny. Agency personnel should, however, be prepared to justify and defend each claim.

Negligence Components

Wrongful death torts, usually established by law and found in all states, arise whenever a death occurs as a result of an officer's unjustified action (del Carmen 1991). The standard applied in negligence torts is whether the officer's act or failure to act created an unreasonable risk to another. When correction officers exercise custodial control over a person, they have a duty to provide reasonable care (*Thomas v. Williams* 1962; *Wagar v. Hasenkrug* 1980; *Abraham v. Maes* 1983). This means that the officers have a legal duty to take reasonable precautions to ensure the health and safety of persons in their custody, render medical assistance as warranted, and treat detainees humanely. Establishing negligence is difficult. In order to prevail in a claim of negligence, a plaintiff must establish four components: legal duty, breach of duty, proximate cause of injury, and actual injury.

Legal duties require officers either to act or refrain from acting in particular situations. Such duties may arise from laws, customs, judicial decisions, and various agency regulations (Kappeler, Vaughn, and del Carmen 1991).

Once the plaintiff has proven that a legal duty was in place, the plaintiff must demonstrate that the officer breached the legal duty by failing to act in accordance with it. Courts recognize that correction officers are only liable to specific individuals and not the general public. There must exist some special knowledge or circumstance that sets the individual citizen apart from the general public and shows a relationship between that citizen and the police (Kappeler 2001). Next, if the plaintiff can show that the officer owed a duty and breached that duty, it must be established the officer was the proximate cause of the harm or the damage. A close causal link between the officer's negligent conduct and the consequent harm to the detainee must be proven. Such a link may be determined by asking, But for the officer's conduct, would the plaintiff sustained the injury, damage, or death? Finally, to maintain liability, it must be proven that actual damage or injury was incurred as a result of the officer's negligent conduct.

These components provide the structure in which a state tort claim for negligence in a wrongful custodial death will be examined. "Proximate cause" is defined differently by many courts. It may be enough to show that the officer's behavior or omission to act rose to a level which caused the injury or death of the detainee.

Special Duty of Care

Courts have also established that an officer may owe a special duty when he or she has reason to believe that the detainee presents a danger to himself. The concept of special duty is based on two factors: (1) the officer's knowledge of the detainee's mental state and (2) the extent to which the condition renders the detainee unable to exercise ordinary care. If it is foreseeable that a circumstance shows a detainee's condition creates a hazard and if there is a reasonable anticipation that injury or damage to the detainee is likely as a result of an act or omission by the officers), a general duty of care is required of police, and this duty becomes a special duty that may lead to liability if the duty is breached. If an officer possesses sufficient knowledge of a detainee's mental or intoxicated condition and the detainee is rendered helpless, a special duty to render care may exist.

A special duty of care creates higher responsibilities and may include cases of unexpected custodial deaths. In *Fruge v. City of New Orleans* (1993) the estate brought a wrongful death claim for a diabetic detainee who had appeared to be intoxicated. The detainee was placed in an adjustment cell, where he was later observed to be foaming at the mouth. He was transported to the hospital and died two hours later. The attending doctor stated that he had a moderately enlarged liver, which can cause sudden death. The court found that officers were negligent in their decision to incarcerate since they owed a duty to protect the prisoner from harm and preserve his safety. The court concluded that the city had failed in its responsibility (i.e., had breached its duty) by not ascertaining the prisoner's medical condition and transporting him to a hospital. The detainee's intoxication triggered the need for a higher degree of care by officers.

The court acknowledged that officers have a duty to provide emergency medical assistance to those in their custody. The court rejected, however, the idea that drug abusers fall into the same category as the elderly and the mentally ill, since drug abusers have a responsibility to advise the police that they have consumed drugs (i.e., self-inflicted harm requires self-care responsibility). The plaintiff failed to prove that the officers were the proximate cause of the death of the detainee by delaying medical care, and comparative fault was used as the defense for the officers: "a policy of individual responsibility for voluntary behavior."

The estate in *Brown v. Lee* (1994) brought a wrongful death claim when the deceased died in the police lockup from an overdose of methylenedioxy-methamphetamine (i.e., "ecstasy"). The plaintiff asserted that the sheriff had a duty to obtain medical treatment for him. The lawsuit alleged negligent failure to provide medical care and negligence in monitoring detainees in the lockup. The deceased had been arrested on charges of disturbing the peace because he had been walking in the middle of traffic, sweating and grimacing. The arresting officer detected the odor of alcohol and during transport asked him if he had used the drug ecstasy. He denied any drug use, although he acted "hyper" and was sweating. The detainee said he was fine during booking. Medical attention was offered, but he refused and was placed in a cell.

During the night a trusty noticed that the decedent was experiencing breathing difficulties and was shaking, and he called for the officers. Responding officers found the detainee dead. An autopsy revealed that he died from a drug overdose. The court acknowledged that officers owe a duty to provide care for a detainee and that they owe a higher degree of care to an intoxicated person who cannot care for himself or herself. However, because the detainee had denied being under the influence of the drug and had denied medical care when it was offered and because even an overdose of the drug is infrequently fatal, the court dismissed the claim, stating that it is "unreasonable to impose a duty on the sheriff to provide medical treatment to every intoxicated detainee."

As these cases show, the courts determine a special duty on a case-by-case basis. The courts expect correctional entities to provide a level of care and caution when taking custody of detainees who exhibit signs of intoxication and mental illness. While a plaintiff may be able to prove that the officer owed a duty and breached the duty, he or she must next prove that the officer was the proximate cause of the injury or death. Providing such proof is not a simple endeavor since there are considerable differences among the courts' interpretations of "proximate cause." In these cases of unexpected death, one method of determining whether the officer was the proximate cause of the death is to ask the question: But for the officer's action, would the detainee have died? Careful consideration must be given to the decedent's medical and psychological history and his or her condition in the hours prior to and during the arrest to determine the true cause of death. In some incidents the officer's action/inaction may be a significant factor and may rise to a level of culpability, resulting in liability. The courts will determine the degree of knowledge the correction officers had at the time or had later obtained relative to the detainee's condition and resultant death. Many courts will evaluate the case based on the totality of circumstances. Other courts, however, will consider the knowledge that the officers possessed about the prisoner who exhibited symptoms associated with sudden deaths and whether the death was foreseeable.

Wrongful Custodial Death Claims under Section 1983

Wrongful death actions are recognized as lawful in all states; therefore, such laws may be utilized in a Section 1983 action. Section 1983 authorizes the application of any state remedial law consistent with the purposes of Section 1983 to any situation for which federal civil rights laws do not provide appropriate remedy (Silver 2003). Wrongful-death claims may be filed under Section 1983 when the death resulted from excessive force or failure to attend to medical needs or from any other constitutional violation and when the conduct of the defendants was the proximate cause of the death under intentional tort principles (*Wright v. Collins* 1985).

Depending on the confinement of the prisoner (in a detention center or a prison), unexpected custodial death cases filed under Section 1983 are evaluated within the purview of the Eighth and Fourteenth Amendments. Detainee deaths in detention centers generally are examined in accordance with the standards of "shocks the conscience" (*Johnson v. Glick* 1973) and "deliberate indifference" (*Estelle v. Gamble* 1976). The death of a convicted prisoner is assessed in accordance with the Eighth Amendment standard of cruel and unusual punishment (*Hudson v. McMillian* 1992) and the standard of "deliberate indifference" (*Estelle v. Gamble* 1976). Pertinent issues and common claims in these cases include excessive force; inappropriate use or abuse of restraints; failure to render medical/psychological care; failure to train, supervise or direct the officers involved in the case; and policies and customs issues which are alleged to have violated the decedents' constitutional rights. Prisoner behaviors consistent with the inability to provide care for themselves, such as intoxication or mental illness, pose a particular dilemma for responding officers. The following Section 1983 case analysis of wrongful deaths in correctional custody reveal how the courts determine liability.

Excessive Force and Restraint Claims

A majority of sudden-death restraint incidents involve violent behaviors of a prisoner requiring responding officers to use higher levels of physical-control measures and less-than-lethal force equipment or implements. As a result, the primary claims filed against the responding officers are allegations of excessive force.

In *Bozeman v. Orum* (2002) the estate of the deceased detainee brought a Section 1983 claim against the sheriff and several officers alleging the force used had caused his death, thereby violating his Fourteenth Amendment right concerning the use of excessive force. The detainee had become violent in the jail and the officers had threatened to "kick his ass" if he did not cease his behavior. He continued his violent actions, the officers apparently punched or slapped the detainee, and he subsequently died as the result of officers' actions. The court granted summary judgment to the officers and sheriff, noting that some level of force was necessary to restore order when the detainee was having a mental breakdown in his cell. The court noted that the sheriff had provided adequate training in the proper use of force, including training in positional asphyxia, and was therefore not liable for failing to train or supervise the officers.

Associated with excessive-force allegations is a second level of claims which often asserts that the police maximally restrained the deceased, which purportedly contributed to his death. The assertion is frequently made that the deceased died as a result of "positional, postural, restraint, compressional or mechanical asphyxia," because he had been placed in the "hog-tied" or restrictive position. The claim may also assert that the individual died from asphyxia owing to the weight of the officers on his body for an extended period during control and restraint. These allegations may be further supported by results of an autopsy or an independent autopsy conducted by a pathologist hired by the estate claiming that the method of restraint contributed to the asphyxia which caused the prisoner's death. Moreover, this assertion will attempt to prove excessive force by contending that officers had used restraints without deference to the obvious medical needs of the prisoner.

One of the first litigated custodial death cases involving the use of restraints in a detention facility was *Lozano v. Smith* (1983). During a patdown, Lozano (who was mentally impaired) struck the arresting officer and violently fought with the two officers. One officer struck him in the head with a flashlight, causing a severe injury. Lozano was handcuffed and transported to the jail. At booking he initiated another fight, and several detention officers fought with him and placed him in a padded cell. Later officers transported him to the emergency room for treatment, and he was released by medical personnel back to the jail. He was placed in a cell and shortly afterward began ramming his head into the cell bars. He was again transported to the hospital, where he stayed for two days. He was then released back to the jail and placed in the padded cell. Within a few hours, Lozano began ramming his head into the cell door, causing his head to bleed severely. Lozano had been hitting the door with such force that he broke the glass. The sheriff called a doctor and was informed the doctor would be there shortly and would give Lozano a sedative. The sheriff instructed several detention officers to enter the cell to control and restrain Lozano, who was screaming and beating his head against the wall. Officers sprayed mace into the cell first, but it failed to disable Lozano.

Fearing that Lozano would use a piece of glass to harm himself or them, officers rushed into the cell. One officer placed Lozano in a headlock, while other officers restrained his arms and legs. Lozano grabbed one officer's genitals and began hitting him in the stomach. After a lengthy struggle, officers were able to control and retrain Lozano with handcuffs, hands behind his back. Lozano continued to struggle and a security belt was placed on him. The officers moved Lozano to another cell, but once inside the cell Lozano rammed his head into the wall. Officers took him to the ground and held him down as he continued to kick and scream. An officer left to obtain leather restraints to secure Lozano's legs. Before the officer returned, an officer with medical experience entered the cell and noticed Lozano's skin turning blue and observed that he was not breathing. The officer initiated a heart massage and medical personnel responded and continued the massage, though unsuccessfully. The doctor then responded and pronounced Lozano dead. An inquest determined that the death was accidental. The autopsy was performed and the pathologist found 115 injuries to Lozano's body, although the pathologist ruled that a significant number were self-precipitated by Lozano. Two doctors stated, however, that Lozano died as a result of traumatic neck injury, which caused asphyxia, and that the fatal neck injury could have been caused by the headlock placed on Lozano's neck.

Lozano's family filed a Section 1983 claim against the officers for excessive force and claims against the sheriff for failing to train and supervise the officers. Claims of failing to provide medical and psychiatric care were also filed. The court found the sheriff was not liable for Lozano's death nor was he liable for a wrongful failure to supervise his officers. The jury found that the officers failed to act in good faith in using the force techniques to subdue Lozano.

Owens v. City of Atlanta (1986) concerns another example of an early custodial-restraint death. Owens was arrested for drunk and disorderly conduct and became disruptive in a detention cell at the hospital where he had been taken for injuries sustained during his arrest. Officers subdued him and then restrained him to a bench twelve inches wide running along the back of his cell. His arms were crossed in front of him and cuffed to holes along the bench. His ankles were placed in leg irons and stretched and attached to the holes along the wall. This "stretch hold position" was called the "mosses crosses." It was a trained restraint technique used only in situations involving violent detainees. Unable to maintain his balance on the bench, Owens fell forward, his face and shoulders striking the floor and his arms stretched behind him to the bench. When he was discovered, he had a weak pulse and subsequently died. The medical examiner determined he had died of positional asphyxia.

The appellate court affirmed the lower court's summary judgment in favor of the officers. The court noted that the restraint method was not inherently dangerous and that the officers had been trained in its use and had used it before without problem. The officers' action did not rise to a constitutional violation. The court also noted that the agency was not deliberately indifferent to the medical needs of Owens, nor were they indifferent to the training needs regarding the use of the restraints.

New medical research has assisted in dispelling the myth regarding the association of positional asphyxia with "hog-tying." Prior theories had linked the restraint process to the cause of death in several cases. It was thought that the restrained position restricted the ability to breathe properly, thereby asphyxiating the person. In *Price v. County of San Diego* (1998) an arrestee who had a history of methamphetamine use fought violently with police, was restrained in the hog-tied position, stopped breathing, and died two days later in the hospital. A Section 1983 claim for violation of constitutional rights, wrongful death, and excessive force was filed, along with state negligence claims. One medical examiner argued in court that restraint asphyxia contributed to the decedent's death, while another medical examiner testified that the hog-tying procedure did not dangerously affect oxygen levels or contribute to the arrestee's death, based on new medical research concerning restraint asphyxia (Chan et al. 1997). The research revealed that one's oxygen levels were not compromised by being restrained in the hog-tied position after a violent struggle.

Based on the medical research, the judge ruled that "hogtying, in and of itself, did not cause the arrestee's death and that the deputies did not use excessive force." The judge further "acknowledged that the consequences of abusing drugs led to a heart attack, which more than anything killed him" (at p. 920). The case was dismissed. This case is important since medical research has debunked past theories that hog-tying causes positional asphyxiation. The court concluded that hog-tying an individual in and of itself is not considered to be excessive force.

In *Grayson v. Peed* (1999) the appellate court affirmed summary judgment for the sheriff and detention officers in a restraint-death incident when physical force and pepper spray were used and the detainee was placed in a four-point restraint position (i.e., supine, with ankles and wrists restrained to a bed). The estate of the deceased detainee charged under Section 1983 that the sheriff had failed to supervise and train the officers in the proper use of force and equipment, thereby violating the constitutional rights of the prisoner. During booking, the intoxicated detainee acted irrationally and began yelling and screaming. He was strip-searched and placed in a cell, and a struggle ensued. Officers used pepper spray to control him, and he calmed down. The next morning he became violent again, and an extraction team of five officers forcibly removed him to another cell after he had refused to cooperate. He was sprayed and punched several times by officers during the cell extraction. He was restrained, relocated, and placed in a four-point restraint position. He was monitored and within minutes he appeared unconscious and was found "fine" by medical personnel. Shortly thereafter, an officer noticed he was not breathing. CPR was initiated and he was transported to the local hospital, where he expired. He died of congestive heart failure as a result of an enlarged heart.

The appellate court granted summary judgment to the sheriff and officers, ruling that their use of force was necessitated by the detainee's behaviors and was used in good faith to control the detainee. The court also noted that the sheriff was not deliberately indifferent to the medical needs of the detainee. The court stated that there was a trained medic on hand during booking and during the encounter and that he responded appropriately once the need for medical care had become apparent. Further, the court noted that the detention facility had been accredited by the American Corrections Association and the National Commission on Correctional Health Care for ten years and that no actionable deficiencies in the policies, customs, or training were evident.

The jury returned a verdict of "no cause" for action in *Love v. Bolinger* (1998). During a hearing to determine the competency of a bipolar individual to stand trial, the detainee became agitated and rushed the judge's bench. Five officers struggled with the detainee and sprayed him twice with pepper spray. Once he was finally subdued, two sets of handcuffs were secured to his wrists, with his hands in front. He was escorted from the courtroom and down one floor to a padded cell in the detention center. The detainee continued to struggle during the escort and fought with officers, kicking them once they placed him in the cell. While officers were removing the handcuffs, one officer noticed he had stopped breathing and began CPR, while another officer summoned medical personnel. Within several minutes paramedics responded and continued life-saving efforts. A pulse was restored but it stopped during transport to the hospital, where he was pronounced dead. The estate filed a Section 1983 action claiming he died of positional asphyxiation from a choke-hold and from the officers' having placed their weight on him in the cell. Two other pathologists reviewed the autopsy and each determined he had died of an enlarged heart. For five days the jury listened to the officers' and expert witnesses' testimony. They found in favor of the officers, claiming they had not used excessive force or caused the death of the decedent.

Deliberate Indifference to Obvious Medical/Psychological Needs

Beyond the claims of excessive force and improper use of restraints, allegations for failure to recognize behaviors and medical symptoms commonly associated with sudden custodial deaths will be filed. The duty to protect a detainee from harm and to provide reasonable medical care is premised partially on the notion that the government is responsible for these individuals because it has deprived them of the ability to look after themselves (Silver 2003). The duty commences upon confinement, whether in a jail or in a prison. The assertion may be made that officers were deliberately indifferent to the medical/psychological needs of the prisoner. This legal claim may be framed within the context of the Fourteenth Amendment in accordance with the U.S. Supreme Court's decision in *City of Revere v. Massachusetts General Hospital* (1983). In this case the Court concluded that municipalities have a constitutional duty to obtain necessary medical care for detainees in their custody. Failing to obtain such care may rise to a level of deliberate indifference.

The applicable standard in regard to medical-care issues is deliberate indifference pursuant to *Estelle v. Gamble* (1976). The plaintiff must establish specific omissions sufficiently harmful to prove deliberate indifference to serious medical needs. To hold officers liable, the plaintiff must show that they intentionally denied or delayed access to treatment or interfered with treatment. The Court in *Estelle* held that an inadvertent failure to provide adequate medical care does not rise to a constitutional violation.

Correction officers, however, are not considered absolute insurers of health to those in their custody. The courts do not hold detention/correction officers to the same level of care as a medically trained physician, although officers have a responsibility to determine the medical or psychological well-being of a person in their custody. The plaintiff may attempt, however, to prove that officers failed to provide for medical needs—an attempt which was made in *DeShaney* v. *Winnebago County of* (1989). In this case the United States Supreme Court recognized that a special relationship can exist between the state and a person giving rise to a constitutional duty by the state to assume some responsibility for the person's medical needs only "when the State takes a person into its custody and holds him against his will" (at p. 1005). Confining prisoners in a detention center or prison can be classified as having a "special relationship" with prisoners. There are three primary components which must be considered in determining whether a "special relationship" may exist for medical purposes: Officers (1) created the danger to which plaintiffs were exposed, (2) knew of the impending danger, and (3) had custody of the plaintiff. Hence, liability for officers may attach when the need for medical care of a prisoner in their custody has been created after a force situation (e.g., baton strikes, physical control techniques, restraint, and so forth) and the person has sustained an injury, and when officers knew that the person needed medical assistance through verbal inquiry or assessment or requests made by the individual. With this in mind, officers should take reasonable precautions to assess and monitor the condition of the prisoner and summon medical care as warranted after a violent force-restraint confrontation.

In many of these violent-restraint situations, the prisoner is mentally impaired, has had a history of taking antipsychotic medication but has not taken it recently, or is currently abusing other chemicals. In many of these incidents the prisoner's overall health is extremely poor: The prisoner may have a diseased heart and defects of other internal organs. Officers also encounter individuals who are under the influence of a chemical at the time of booking and become violent or shortly after a period of incarceration require restraint and suddenly die.

In *Smith* v. *Wilson County* (2000) Smith died of cocaine intoxication in the detention center, and his family filed a Section 1983 action for failing to provide medical care at the time of Smith's arrest and while Smith was confined. Smith had resisted arrest for failing to stop at a stop sign. Officers noticed he was chewing something and attempted to remove it. Smith stated he had swallowed a marijuana cigarette, and then said it was rock cocaine, and then marijuana. The arresting officer asked if he wanted medical attention. Smith refused, and he was transported to the police department for processing. At the station, Smith informed the lieutenant that he had not swallowed cocaine. The lieutenant instructed the officer to take Smith to the magistrate. The magistrate set Smith's bond, and Smith did not complain about needing medical care nor did he appear to be under the influence of drugs. Unable to post bond, he was booked into the detention center. He was placed in a holding cell and shortly afterward became agitated and began yelling. Officers moved him to an isolation cell and Smith stated that the "rock of cocaine he swallowed is killing me." Smith then stated he had swallowed only a marijuana cigarette. Officers did not summon medical personnel since Smith did not appear to need medical treatment.

During a standard security check three hours later, Smith was found unconscious in his cell. Medical personnel were summoned and life-saving efforts were initiated but unsuccessful, and Smith was pronounced dead at the hospital, approximately five hours after he had been arrested. The autopsy revealed that Smith had not suffered any "acute external injuries." The pathologist determined the cause of death to be cocaine intoxication, which had caused an idiosyncratic reaction of the heart since Smith's heart had been enlarged from extensive cocaine abuse.

The family filed a legal action claiming the arresting officers used excessive force in taking Smith to the ground and were deliberately indifferent in failing to provide medical care, in violation of his Fourth and Fourteenth Amendment rights. The court awarded summary judgment to the arresting officers. Under the Fourteenth Amendment the family also filed claims against the detention facility officers and the sheriff for wrongful death, for officers' failing to recognize and respond to a medical emergency, and for the sheriff's failing to train, supervise, and direct officers in the care of intoxicated prisoners. The court also granted summary judgment to the detention personnel, finding no evidence that the officers or the sheriff were deliberately indifferent to Smith's medical needs.

Failure to Train Officers

A frequent claim in unexpected-death actions are allegations that police supervisors failed to train officers. The assertion is made that officers have not been instructed or trained properly by the supervisor or agency and thus lack the skills, knowledge, or competency required in a range of actions and observations, such as using appropriate force measures including restraints and other equipment, recognizing the hazards of drug-induced violent behavior, recognizing obvious medical or psychiatric behaviors, recognizing the risks of hog-tying, and responding to "special needs" prisoners (i.e., those who are intoxicated or mentally impaired).

Section 1983 claims of this nature will focus on the United States Supreme Court case *City of Canton v. Harris* (1989). The Court established that the inadequacy of police training may serve as a basis for Section 1983 liability only when the failure to train amounts to deliberate indifference to the rights of persons with whom the police come into contact. The plaintiff must show that the custom or policy of the department was to ignore officer training and that this failure to train was the moving force behind a constitutional violation. In custodial-death cases, the plaintiff must show that the alleged lack of training in regard to the use of force and restraints and the alleged lack of medical/psychiatric care for "special needs" prisoners is closely related and actually caused the officers' deliberate indifference to the serious medical needs of the prisoner.

In *Swans v. City of Lansing* (1998) the jury found in favor of the plaintiff, who had died in a detention cell. Upon being admitted into the detention center, Swans kicked the booking sergeant in the head and fought with officers. He was restrained with handcuffs, but the officers were unable to secure him in a restraint chair. He was forcibly moved to a cell where he continued to fight violently with the officers. In the cell, five officers and a lieutenant attempted to further restrain him with a Kick-Stop restraint strap, like a strap they had used in numerous other situations with violent detainees. The strap broke and the officers restrained Swans with additional handcuffs and leg-irons connected to his ankles. The officers left Swans on his side/ stomach, monitored him by closed circuit television, and returned to the cell within ten minutes. The officers found Swans lying in urine and unresponsive. They moved him to the hallway, removed the restraints, initiated CPR, and summoned medical personnel. Medical personnel found no pulse, continued life-saving efforts, and transported him to the hospital, where he was pronounced dead. An autopsy revealed that he had died of cardiac dysrythmia caused by postural asphyxia during custodial restraint. The jury determined that the officers had used excessive force and misused the restraints and that administrative personnel had failed to train, supervise, and direct officers in how to properly respond and restrain mentally impaired detainees. The jury awarded $10 million to Swans' estate.

The use of restraints may be considered unreasonable force if they were used inappropriately in regard to the need, if officers were not trained in their proper use, or if officers failed to follow the department's restraint policy. There must be proof that a particular violation of a federal right was a "highly predictable" consequence of the failure to equip police officers with specific tools to handle recurring situations. The question that emerges from these restraints deaths is whether or not deaths from asphyxia are highly foreseeable or whether or not they are predictable consequences of restraining persons who are prone while hog-tied. The question also emerges of whether supervisors are deliberately indifferent to the training of their officers in the use of restraints with "special needs" prisoners.

The *Price* case is illustrative of these questions as the court, relying on scientific evidence regarding "hog-tying," found that the restraint procedure in and of itself is not excessive force and that it did not cause asphyxia. The court found that drugs caused the individual's death and not the restraint procedure. The Swans case, however, reveals how a jury may view this phenomenon, despite the reliable scientific research showing that maximally restraining a violent mentally impaired person is not in and of itself deadly force. In analyzing these cases, courts will review the totality of the circumstances: the cause of death, the extent of the person's medical or psychiatric condition, the restraints authorized and the methods used, the officer's perception of safety, and the resistive behaviors requiring further immobilization of the person. As seen in these case examples, the courts are split in their opinions as to whether the hog-tying procedure should be considered excessive force. This type of restraint litigation is still emerging and changes in court interpretations may be forthcoming.

PRISONER SUICIDES

A suicide by a prisoner or pretrial detainee poses a serious problem for detention and prison personnel. Suicides are more likely to occur in detention facilities than in prison. Ross (2001) reported in a twenty-year study of in-custody deaths in detention facilities that suicides are the second leading cause of death, behind deaths as a result of natural causes and ahead of deaths as a result of AIDS.

Civil litigation in this topic area has increased since the 1970s, and millions of dollars have been awarded as a result of an attempted or actual suicide. However, the trend of prevailing plaintiffs has declined during the 1990s. These civil actions normally assert that the confining agency and its officers failed to take the proper measures to prevent such an incident.

A wrongful death claim resulting from a prisoner suicide may be brought under Section 1983 or, as described earlier, under state tort law. In accordance with Section 1983, the plaintiff's claim will invariably allege that the defendant was deliberately indifferent to the deceased by failing to properly screen the prisoner upon reception into a detention facility failing to recognize signs of symptoms of suicide, failing to train detention personnel, failing to protect the prisoner from himself by providing a safe environment (i.e., an environment without deficiency in design and structure), failing to properly search the prisoner and seize items which might be used to commit suicide,, failing to "watch" the suicidal prisoner on a continuous basis, and failing to provide mental health services—to mention a few (Cohen 1992).

A typical complaint will allege multiple theories of liability. In *Vinson v. Clarke County, Alabama* (1998), for example, an intoxicated detainee hanged himself in his cell within thirty minutes after his confinement. An autopsy revealed Vinson's blood alcohol level was .21 percent, well over the .1 percent legal limit. The jail did not have a policy of screening newly admitted detainees, and the cell was not monitored by closed circuit TV. The estate filed a Section 1983 lawsuit against the officer and the sheriff in their individual and official capacities, claiming that Vinson's Fourteenth Amendment rights had been violated. Specifically, the estate claimed that the officer was deliberately indifferent to Vinson by allowing or causing him to suffocate by strangulation in [his] custody, by failing to modify the bars so that detainees would be unable to hang themselves from them, by failing to initiate screening of special-needs prisoners, by failing to install video monitoring equipment. The estate also claimed that the officer knew or should have known that Vinson was a suicide risk and that the officer inadequately monitored the jail cells and failed to take precautions to remove dangerous items from the detainee's cell. Finally, the estate alleged that the sheriff was deliberately indifferent to providing training for his officers. The court found the officer immune from liability since he was not indifferent to the needs of Vinson, because the detainee had not presented any signs that would lead an officer to conclude that he was a serious harm to himself. The court also granted summary judgment to the sheriff, finding that the sheriff's practices did not violate the detainee's constitutional rights.

Suicide and Deliberate Indifference

A frequent issue in most cases of prisoner suicides is what standard of review should apply. In Chapter 8, the deliberate-indifference standard was described and applied to various correctional issues. As mentioned, deliberate indifference originated in *Estelle v. Gamble* (1976), which involved medical-care issues of state prisoners under the Eighth Amendment. In *Bell v. Wolfish* (1979) the U.S. Supreme Court held that pretrial detainees at the very least possess the same rights as convicted prisoners. While the Court has never specifically recognized a prisoner's right to protection from self-harm, the principles and analyses of *Bell* and *Estelle* have been applied to prisoner suicide cases.

Consider, however, the *Farmer v. Brennan* (1994) decision (concerning a prison case) in which the United States Supreme Court held that in order for liability to attach in civil rights actions against correctional personnel, deliberate indifference to a prisoner's safety and health must be based on evidence that they were subjectively aware of the risk. Correctional officials are not absolute guarantors of the safety of prisoners, but they cannot ignore obvious risks or dangers to prisoners in their custody. The officials must be aware of the facts from which the inference could be drawn that a serious risk of harm exists. Although *Farmer* was not a suicide case per se, it is instructive in that it was a deliberate-indifference case involving issues of "knew or should have known" and should strengthen the ability to defend suicide cases involving issues of knowledge. In *Hare v. City of Corinth* (1996), the Fifth Circuit applied *Farmer* standards to a pretrial detainee suicide claim. The court ruled that the duty not to be deliberately indifferent was minimally established. A check on the prisoner who threatened suicide while in withdrawal from the drugs consumed prior to arrest was made by an officer, although he failed to remove a blanket from the cell. The officer's belief that the detainee was too weak to tear it was objectively reasonable.

To prevail in a Section 1983 suit for violation of rights under the Fourteenth or Eighth Amendment, the plaintiff must establish that the defendant displayed deliberate indifference to a "strong likelihood" of suicide rather than a mere possibility. The lower courts generally apply the Fourteenth Amendment to pretrial detainees and the Eighth Amendment to convicted prisoners confined in a prison. However, lower courts have applied the Eighth Amendment to cases of suicide in detention facilities. The plaintiff must prove that officials were deliberately indifferent to the prisoner's serious needs. Deliberate indifference is more than making a mistake. In suicide cases, deliberate indifference means (1) that officials should have known or that it was known that the prisoner was a suicide risk and that steps were not taken to prevent the suicide; and/or (2) that the officers and agency were deliberately indifferent to the prisoner's serious medical or mental health needs (Plitt 1997).

In *Popham v. City of Talladega* (1990) the court applied the "strong likelihood" test of deliberate indifference in a suicide case of an intoxicated pretrial detainee. The estate brought a Section 1983 action against city and jail officials claiming that their son had the right to be protected from committing suicide while confined, that officials had failed to properly monitor him, and that officers had not been properly trained to recognize suicidal symptoms. Popham had been placed in a holding cell, and his belt, shoes, socks, and the contents of his pockets were removed. His cell was monitored by closed-circuit television, and he was periodically monitored physically. The last physical check on him occurred at 11:00 pm, and at 5:00 am he was discovered hanging from his cell bars with his jeans.

The appeals court affirmed the lower court's decision that jail personnel were not deliberately indifferent since they were unaware of any suicidal tendencies.

The court held that suicides in custody are analogous to issues involving an alleged failure to provide medical care and that deliberate indifference is the proper standard of review in such cases, regardless of the status of the prisoner. The deliberate-indifference standard as applied to suicide cases requires a strong likelihood, rather than a mere possibility, that self-infliction of harm will occur. Standard procedures were followed by personnel, and a failure to train officers in screening for suicidal tendencies did not provide a basis for imposing liability. Further, in *Thornton v. City of Montgomery* (1999) the court ruled that detention officers and administrators were not liable for a mentally impaired detainee's death from asphyxiation, which was either suicide or an accidental death caused by his illness. The officers' conduct did not rise to the level of deliberate indifference, because there was no "strong likelihood" of suicide.

Likewise, in *Sanders v. Howze* (1999) the Appellate Court of the Eleventh Circuit followed the same line of reasoning as in *Popham*. After the lower court denied summary judgment, the appellate court reversed the decision and held that jail officials were entitled to qualified immunity in the suicide of a detainee. Several weeks after his confinement, the decedent removed the razorblade from a disposable razor and cut his wrists. He was transported to the local hospital, as per jail policy, and was later transferred to a state hospital where he remained for several months. He returned to the jail and was placed in general population, where within two days he used a pencil to reopen his earlier wound. He was again transported to the local hospital and treated. He was transferred to the state hospital a second time and later released back into the jail and placed in an observation cell. The county petitioned the court for a psychiatric evaluation, but before the request was granted the detainee hanged himself with a bed sheet. The court ruled that jail officials were not deliberately indifferent to the needs of the detainee and followed established policy in responding to him.

Suicidal Risk Factors

The question as to whether a detainee's past or current behaviors indicate a suicidal "profile" often arises. The question posed is asserted by the plaintiff in many custodial suicide legal actions. The claim is that the decedent "fit" the profile and officers failed to recognize it and therefore should be held liable. In an attempt to establish a foundation for such an argument, the plaintiff will cite many studies suggesting that the decedent characterized the "typical suicide" in custody.

The use of a profile is highly controversial, and the research of literature on suicide points toward patterns and risk factors that correctional personnel should observe. It is important to recognize that there does *not* exist a defin-

Figure 8.1   Prisoner Suicide Awareness Factors

- Nature of arrest/transport from transporting officer.
- Mental state/mental health history of prisoner.
- Prisoner expresses feelings of hopelessness.
- Prisoner expresses he is thinking about killing himself.
- Prisoner's past history of suicide attempts.
- Prisoner's intoxicated state.
- The prisoner shows signs of depression.
- The prisoner shows concern about a loss: a job, family, position in community, etc.
- The prisoner's behaviors: anxious, afraid, angry, acting strange.
- Prior arrests and convictions.
- History of taking medication.
- Prisoner charged with a "shocking" crime.

itive profile of potential custodial suicide about which all researchers agree (Plitt 1997). With any research there are methodological problems which can skew data in one direction. A significant problem in the suicide research is that studies all examine the suicide without fully comparing the decedent to other confined prisoners (Kennedy and Homant 1988). In other words, why didn't other detainees in the same facility also commit suicide? Does one "profile" fit all prisoners in all locations across the country? Such questions are often ignored in many studies. Rather than claiming that a prisoner fit a certain profile and therefore committed a jail suicide, it would be more precise to state that a suicide happened to occur while a detainee was confined in a jail. Thus, a "typical suicide" does not exist in the confinement setting. What should be addressed are factors which may alert correctional personnel to potential risks of a detainee suicide and what constitutes awareness of suicide (see Figure 8.1). While such factors are not inclusive of every possible factor and may not apply to every detainee, they may be useful in training correctional personnel about behaviors of all detainees, may be useful in housing assignments, and may be useful in determining potential medical care for the detainee. Understanding behaviors of all detainees in a detention or correctional setting can assist personnel in being more proactive in reception procedures, removing items from a cell or from the detainee which could be used to commit suicide, utilizing particular cells and housing assignments, and monitoring procedures and services provided to prisoners. That a detainee merely fits a "suicide profile" independent of other factors does not prove that the prisoner was likely to commit suicide and therefore does not support liability against correctional personnel.

In *Estate of Frank v. City of Beaver Dam* (1996) the estate of the decedent confined in jail who committed suicide brought a Section 1983 action against a detention officer. The court dismissed the case, holding that the officer was entitled to qualified immunity since he had not been deliberately indifferent to the rights of the detainee. The court noted that although one officer had been informed that the detainee had exhibited severe mood swings during transport to the jail, the detainee did not make any threats, cause any disturbances, stagger, slur his speech, or do anything bizarre that would cause the officer to believe he was suicidal. The court determined that the detainee's quiet behavior as he walked to the cell and his unresponsiveness to questions asked by the officer did not suggest he was in imminent danger to himself. The court did note that once the detainee was placed in his cell, he later ate breakfast and engaged in a telephone conversation.

The Eighth Circuit court of appeals affirmed a lower court's decision to grant summary judgment for jail officials after a detainee committed suicide in *Liebe v. Norton* (1998). The court found that detention officers were not deliberately indifferent to the detainee's health and safety since they had classified him as a suicide risk, had taken precautionary measures by placing him in a holding cell, had removed his shoes and belt, and had periodically checked on him. The intake officer classified the detainee as a "suicide risk" because he had admitted to previously attempting suicide and was taking clonazepam and valium. Officers checked on the detainee at intervals ranging from seven to twenty-one minutes but did not turn on the audio system in the holding cell. The detainee used his long-sleeved shirt to hang himself from an electrical conduit in the cell. The family asserted that the officers had failed to supervise their son and that the county had failed to test officers on its policy manual regarding custodial suicides. The court found that the county was not deliberately indifferent to the training of officers, since the policy manual outlined their duties step by step.

The issue of suicide risk was examined in *Payne for Hicks v. Churchill* (1998) by the Seventh Circuit Court of Appeals. The family brought a wrongful death action involving a suicide of their son against city jail officials. The appellate court affirmed the lower court's dismissal on the suicide issue but remanded the case on an excessive-force claim. According to the court, the detainee's intoxication, his tattoo questioning life, and his angry cursing did not indicate an obvious, substantial risk of suicide. The court found that failing to monitor the arrestee or to recognize the risk of suicide constituted negligence, at most. The decedent was admitted to a holding cell at 1:00 am and died of suffocation after hanging himself with a blanket before 4:00 am.

In *Gregoire v. Class* (2000) the estate of a state prisoner who had committed suicide filed a Section 1983 action against prison officials for failing to adequately respond to the prisoner's alleged behaviors indicating the potential of suicide. The prisoner's former wife called the prison case manager in the housing unit, informing him that the prisoner was planning suicide. The former wife failed to inform the case worker that the prisoner had attempted suicide in the past, that he had made previous threats to commit suicide, and that he had been formerly treated for depression. The case manager checked on the prisoner thirty minutes after the phone call. Officers found the prisoner hanging in his cell. The court granted summary judgment to the case manager and prison officials, ruling that they were not deliberately indifferent to the prisoner's suicidal risks in violation of his Eighth Amendment.

Conversely, in *Comstock v. McCrary* (2001) a state prisoner who had been placed on suicide watch and who was released back to the general population later committed suicide, and his family sued. A prison psychologist had determined that the prisoner presented a risk of suicide and placed him on a suicide watch. Several days later the psychologist released him from the watch without making any reasoned assessment of the prisoner's suicide risk, despite knowing that other prisoners had targeted him as a "snitch." The court denied summary judgment, concluding that there was sufficient evidence which established that the psychologist subjectively perceived, and was deliberately indifferent to, the risk that the prisoner might commit suicide.

Compare, however, the court's ruling in *Pelletier v. Magnuson* (2002). A state prisoner committed suicide and the family filed a Section 1983 for failing to prevent the prisoner from harming himself and for allegedly tampering with or destroying documents relating to the medical care of the deceased prisoner. The court granted summary judgment to the health care providers, a supervisor, a social worker, a medical doctor, and a licensed psychiatrist. The court noted that the psychiatrist was not deliberately indifferent for not knowing that the prisoner was psychotic and suicidal at all times.

Allegations of Failure to Train

As described earlier, a claim of failure to train officers by administrators will frequently emerge in a wrongful-death lawsuit. The same claim is commonly asserted in suicide litigation. The plaintiff will cite *City of Canton v. Harris* (1989), alleging that the agency was deliberately indifferent by failing to train officers in suicidal tendencies and recognition of them, in policy issues, in monitoring procedures, in how to obtain medical or mental health care, and in resuscitation procedures, to mention a few. (As discussed below, the training standard of deliberate indifference is a high hurdle for the plaintiff to overcome.)

For example, in *Smith v. Blue* (1999) a juvenile in a county detention facility hanged himself with a bed sheet, and his family filed a Section 1983 claim. The court found the county liable for violating the Fourteenth Amendment rights of the detainee in failing to protect him from his own suicidal ideations. The youth had been diagnosed as suffering from attention deficit disorder and the diagnosis had been confirmed at the time of intake. During his four-month confinement he threatened suicide and physically harmed himself on several occasions. His behavior worsened, and he was placed in isolation yet allowed to retain a bed sheet, a towel, T-shirts, and shoes with laces. One evening he was found dead, hanging with a bed sheet from a loose sprinkler head. Records revealed that security checks had been made every fifteen minutes. Further investigation, however, revealed that officers had prelogged security checks at the beginning of a shift, and officers testified that this was the practice of the jail. The youth's body had been hanging for over an hour, indicating that rounds had not been made every fifteen minutes. The court found that the supervisors' condoning of such a practice constituted deliberate indifference to the training of the officers.

Further, in *Owens v. City of Philadelphia* (1998) the federal district court denied summary judgment to the defendants, ruling that the training program was deliberately indifferent to detainees' needs. According to the court, the detainee's statement to an officer that he felt "schizy" and that he was "going to hurt myself" raised questions on issues of knowledge and deliberate indifference. The court held that it was not necessary to show that an officer believed harm would actually befall the detainee; rather, the plaintiff need only show that the official acted or failed to act despite his knowledge of substantial risk of serious harm. The officer had summoned a psychiatrist knowing that she intended to issue a pass for the detainee to go to the mental health unit but failed to note in the log book the detainee's statement about harming himself. There was nothing in the record that indicated the pass was ever issued. The court further found that the officials' alleged conduct as policy makers with respect to inadequate training to prevent suicide by pretrial detainees was actionable under Section 1983.

The issues of a county's suicide prevention policy and a failure to train emerged in *Yellow Horse v. Pennington County* (2000). The detainee was placed on a suicide watch, and a detention officer, after evaluating the detainee and reviewing his eating, social, and sleeping habits, as well as the charted progress made by other officers during the watch, released him from the watch, according to facility policy. The detainee later committed suicide. The family sued and the lower court granted summary judgment for county officials. The appellant court affirmed, finding that the county's suicide prevention policy did not show deliberate indifference to the rights of detainees and that it was, in fact, a reasonable approach to preventing suicide, since it included prisoner processing and screening, documented extensive officer training, and annual policy review. The court applied the *Farmer* decision to the case and concluded that the officers were not indifferent to the known risks of suicide.

In *Boncher ex rel. Boncher v. Brown County* (2001) the court determined that compliance with state minimum standards regarding suicide prevention and that the decisions made by officers with no special training did not constitute evidence of deliberate indifference. A detainee had been admitted to the jail for a domestic violence charge. He had a long history of alcoholism and had attempted suicide three times in the past, although this history was unknown to the admitting officers. Thinking he was a "happy drunk," the officers placed him in a general population cell, where he hanged himself with a bed sheet within forty-five minutes. The appellate court affirmed summary judgment for the county, stating that even though the officers had little training in suicide awareness, they did conduct an initial screening and there was no evidence they were deliberately indifferent.

Summary

Two emerging areas of liability have been described, which have increased allegations of wrongful deaths. Sudden deaths in correctional custody are a rare occurrence after a use of force confrontation, but the liability potential for a wrongful death can be critical. Officers and administrators possess a broad range of responsibilities concerning detainees in their custody. They are not absolute guarantors of health, but under theories of negligence and Section 1983 provisions, they do owe a duty of care for those prisoners in their custody who otherwise cannot care for themselves.

Based on case analysis, correctional and detention agencies can insulate their officers and themselves from liability by taking a proactive stance in considering the following policy and training recommendations. Deaths after a violent-restraint struggle allege excessive force, and therefore administrators are encouraged to first review and revise their use-of-force policy to insure that officers are directed in using "reasonable" force measures. Policy should direct officers in the proper escalation and deescalation in a variety of physical-force techniques and equipment based on the behaviors manifested by the prisoner. Included in the force policy should be a section devoted to the use of authorized restraints. This section should direct officers in utilizing department-issued restraint devices that specify how to further restrain combative and "special needs detainees." If the agency uses a restraint chair to restrain combative and self-injurious prisoners, specific procedures should address when the chair may be used, the duration of the restraint, and monitoring protocols.

Procedures need to be revised or developed which direct officers in responding to the mentally or chemically impaired (i.e., special-needs detainees). This policy should be structured within state standards for dealing with detainees who require medical or psychiatric treatment or hospitalization. The policy should direct officers in how to respond to this population, when to summon backup officers or a supervisor, when to summon medical or psychological assistance, and to what facility such detainees should be transported. Proper response and precautions employed with detainees at risk commences with policies that direct officers in making justifiable decisions when encountering such persons.

In compliance with the *Canton* decision, administrators are also encouraged to provide officers with regular training relevant to the policies identified. In many jurisdictions, police encounter "special-needs" individuals with recurring frequency. Regular training should be provided in assisting officers in responding to "special-needs" individuals, in recognizing behaviors/symptoms associated within custody deaths, such as those of the mentally ill and the intoxicated. Realistic training should be routinely provided for officers which addresses skill competency and use-of-force decision making in all authorized physical control tactics and restraint equipment. Further training should be regularly provided to officers in how to assess the medical/psychiatric condition of detainees, how to monitor the needs of detainees in restraints, and when to summon medical assistance for those detainees involved in a violent-force confrontation. Administrators are encouraged to require officers to maintain certification in First Aid and CPR in order that officers may recognize and respond to medical emergencies. Finally, periodic training which addresses the critical issues to be put into an incident report should be provided.

If an agency experiences an in-custody death or suicide, the administrator should immediately contact its risk manager and its legal counsel and ensure that a thorough internal investigation is conducted. Consideration of utilizing an independent agency to conduct the investigation is advisable. Moreover, the administrator is encouraged to initiate immediately an ongoing file by compiling all relevant polices, officer incident reports, training files of personnel involved, autopsy reports, attending-physician reports, emergency medical personnel reports, investigation reports, statements of all witnesses, photos and videos of the incident scene, all taped radio communications throughout the incident, and a time line of the incident events.

Liability concerns regarding custodial suicides were also addressed. The standard of court review in these cases is whether there was a strong likelihood that the detainee or prisoner would commit suicide and whether officials were deliberately indifferent to a substantially known risk of harm. It is common for the plaintiff to allege that the decedent fit a suicide profile and that officers failed to recognize the symptoms within such a profile.

While a "typical" suicide profile is nonexistent, the review of cases illustrates that detention agencies are likely to prevail in this type of litigation when proactive measures have been instituted and followed by agency personnel. It is important to underscore that maintaining a detention or correctional facility requires an understanding of prisoner behaviors and that guidelines should be developed which direct officers in the performance of their duties in order to provide an orderly and safe operation. Not all custodial suicides can be prevented, but many can be averted through proper planning and careful adherence to a system of fundamental correctional strategies. This system should include a two fold approach: policy development and training. Administrators are encouraged to develop intake screening procedures for admitting all prisoners. Policies for classifying and housing prisoners should be in place, based on the need of the prisoner at the time of admission and as a prisoner's needs change throughout confinement. Policies should direct officers in monitoring all prisoners and in watching those who have been determined to require closer observation. Procedures should outline when officers should summon supervisory assistance and when they should summon medical or mental health professionals, based on demonstrated behaviors of the prisoner. Administrators should ensure that all directives are in compliance with state minimum standards and legal decisions for confining prisoners.

Moreover, all personnel having contact with prisoners should be trained in such policies which direct decisions in responding to and supervising prisoners. Training should involve recognizing and understanding human behavior and common prisoner behaviors, particularly behaviors of the mentally impaired and the chemically addicted.

References

Chan, T., G. Vilke, T. Neuman, and J. Clausen. 1997. Restraint position asphyxia. *Annals of Emergency Medicine* 30: 578–86.

Cohen, F. 1992. Liability for custodial suicide: The information base requirements. *Jail Suicide Update* 4: 1–9.

del Carmen, R. V. 1991. *Civil liabilities in American policing: A text for law enforcement personnel.* Englewood Cliffs, NJ: Brady.

del Carmen, R. V., and V. Kappeler. 1991. Municipal and police agencies as defendants: Liability for official policy and custom. *American Journal of Police* 10: 1–17.

Kappeler, V. 2001. *Critical issues in police civil liability.* 2nd ed. Prospect Heights, IL: Waveland Press, Inc.

Kappeler, V., M. Vaughn, and R. V. del Carmen. 1991. Death in detention: An analysis of police liability for negligent failure to prevent suicide. *Journal of Criminal Justice* 19: 381–93.

Kennedy, D. B., and R. J. Homant. 1988. Predicting custodial suicides: Problems with the use of profiles. *Justice Quarterly* 5: 441–56.

Plitt, E. A. 1997. *Police civil liability and the defense of citizen misconduct.* Chicago, IL: Americans for Effective Law Enforcement.

Ross, D. L. 2001. Assessing in-custody deaths in jails. *American Jails* 25, no. 4: 13–26.

Silver, I. 2003. *Police civil liability.* Newark, NJ: Matthew Bender Publishers.

Cases Cited

Abrhams v. Mayes, 436 So. 2d 1099 (La. Dist. Crt. App. 1983)

Bell v. Wolfish, 441 U.S. 520 (1979)

Boncher ex. rel. Boncher v. Brown County, 272 F. 3d 484 (7th Cir. 2001)

Bozeman v. Orum, 199 F. Supp. 2d 1216 (M.D. Ala. 2002)

Brown v. Lee, 639, So.2d 897 (La. App.1994)

City of Canton v. Harris, 489 U.S. 378 (1989)

City of Revere v. Massachusetts General Hospital, 463 U.S. 239 (1983)

Comstock v. McCrary, 273 F. 3d 693 (6th Cir. 2001)

DeShaney v. Winnebago County Department of Social Services, 489 U.S. 189 (1989)

Estate of Fank v. City of Beaver Dam, 921 F. Supp. 590 (E.D. Wis. 1996)

Estelle v. Gamble, 429 U.S. 97 (1976)

Farmer v. Brennan, 511 U.S. 285 (1994)

Fruge v. City of New Orleans, 613 So. 2nd 811 (La. Dist. Ct. App. 1993)

Grayson v. Peed, 195 F. 3d 692 (4th Cir. 1999)

Gregoire v. Class, 236 F. 3d 413 (8th Cir. 2000)

Hare v. City of Corinth, 74 F. 3d 633 (5th Cir. 1996)

Hudson v. McMillian, 503 U.S. 1 (1992)

Johnson v. Glick, 481 F. 2d 1028 (2nd Cir.1973)

Liebe v. Norton, 157 F.3d 574 (8th Cir.1998)

Lozano v. Smith, 718 F. 2d 756 (5th Cir. 1983)

Love v. Bolinger, IP 95-1465-C-B/S, Ind. (1998) [unpublished]

Monell v. Department of Social Services of NY, 436 U.S. 658 (1978)

Owens v. City of Atlanta, 780 F. 2d 1564 (11th Cir. 1986)

Owens v. City of Philadelphia, 6 F. Supp. 2d 373 (E.D. Pa. 1998)

Payne for Hicks v. Churchill, 161 F. 3d 1030 (7th cir. 1998)

Pelletier v. Magnuson, 201 F. Supp. 148 (D. Me. 2002)

Popham v. City of Talladega, 908 F.2d 1561 (11th Cir. 1990)

Price v. County of San Diego, 990 F. Supp. 1230 (S.D. Cal.1998)

Pyka v. Village of Orland Park, 906 F. Supp. 1196 (N.D. Ill. 1995)

Sanders v. Howze, 177 F. 3d 1245 (11th Cir. 1999)

Simpson v. Hines, 903 F. 2d 400 (5th Cir. 1990)

Smith v. Blue, 67 F. Supp. 2d 686 (S.D. Tex. 1999)

Smith v. Wilson County, No. 5:98-CV-842-BO (3) (E.D. N.C., 2000) [unpublished]

Swans v. City of Lansing, 65 F. Supp. 2d 625 (W. D. Mich. 1998)

Thomas v. Williams, 124 S.E.2d 409 (Ga. App. 1962)

Thornton v. City of Montgomery, 78 F. Supp. 2d 1218 (M.D. Ala. 1999)

Tindall v. Multnomah County, 570 P.2d 979 (Or. App. 1977)

Vinson v. Clarke County, Ala. 10 F. Supp. 2d 1282 (S.D. Ala. 1998)

Wagar v. Hasenkrug, 486, F. Supp. 47 (D. Mont.1980)

Wright v. Collins, 766 F.2d 841 (5th Cir. 1985)

Williams v. Kelso, 201 F. 3d 1060 (8th Cir. 2000)

Yellow Horse v. Pennington County, 225 F. 3d 923 (7th Cir. 2000)

CHAPTER 9

LIABILITY ISSUES SURROUNDING SEARCHES AND SEGREGATION

The Fourth Amendment proscription against unreasonable searches does not apply within the confines of the prison cell.

Hudson v. Palmer (1984)

Prisons and detention facilities incarcerate an involuntary population that has demonstrated a propensity for violating the law, antisocial behaviors, and often violent conduct. The importation theory explains prisoner behaviors by examining preprison associations, experiences, and behaviors (Garrit 1961; Toch 1977)—many of which are explained by sociodemographic or psychological factors. The model suggests that prisoners have learned to respond to various stressors in their lives through violent means and is exhibited in their interactions with others prior to a period of confinement. Once prisoners are confined in the prison or detention center, they "import" their learned "street" behaviors into the correctional facility and continue their "con-wise" behaviors throughout their interactions with other prisoners and correctional personnel. Many believe, "once a con, always a con."

Recognizing that a change in a prisoner's address, from the community to that of a prison, does not necessarily change behavior, correctional officials must ensure that proactive security and order maintenance measures are in place. Once incarcerated, most prisoners quickly learn the prisoner "code" by taking on the manners of survival within the facility. Prisoners will hoard all types of materials and contraband in their cells, attempt to abuse drugs, gain access to or make weapons, devise escape plots, and develop ways/devices with which to attempt escape. Administrators need to remain alert to reduce the access to or actual possession of contraband items in order to increase the safety and security of prisoners and personnel that work in the facility.

Performing searches of prisoners is a fundamental task of correction officers and is a primary method of ensuring that contraband remains in check. Full access to cells and other areas of the prison to conduct unannounced and random searches is important to maintain security, to deter the stock-piling of drugs and weapons, and to thwart any escape plots. Searches are also used to maintain adequate levels of sanitation within the correctional facility. Many correction departments have instituted a policy of requiring officers to perform between five and ten personal prisoner patdown and cell searches daily. On an irregular basis, officers conduct a search of the total facility in an attempt to eliminate the introduction of contraband. Searches in a corrections facility are governed by the requirements of the Fourth Amendment.

There are five types of searches generally performed in a corrections institution. Clothed patdown frisks or searches of prisoners and cell searches are the most common forms of searches. Clothed frisks are commonly used before and after a visit, before entering and leaving a secure area, and prior to leaving a work or school assignment. Cell searches are performed generally by housing unit officers. These involve the complete search of items and property in the prisoner's cell. Strip searches of prisoners require the prisoner to remove all of his/her clothes and items in pockets; involve the visual inspection of the inside of the mouth, as well as the ears, nose, and anal and genital areas; and require the prisoner to run his/her hands through his/her hair without the officer touching the prisoner. These searches are commonly performed when a prisoner is being admitted into the prison facility, when a prisoner is admitted into a segregation unit and/or an observation cell, when a prisoner is being transported outside the facility, in some cases after a visit, and when a prisoner is believed to be in possession of dangerous contraband. The policy of many correction agencies, when feasible, is to have an officer of the same gender as that of the prisoner conduct the strip search. When feasible, strip searches should be conducted away from the observation of others. A blanket policy requiring the strip searching of all incoming detainees in a detention center is unconstitutional, although requiring incoming detainees to change from street clothes to jail attire is not.

Body cavity searches are an extension of strip searches and involve the probing of body cavities to determine the concealment of contraband. Body cavity searches are to be performed by a designated health care professional. When feasible, correctional personnel of the same gender as that of the prisoner being searched may be present during the search. Body cavity searches require reasonable suspicion that the prisoner is concealing contraband in an orifice of the body. Some agencies require a search warrant prior to conducting a body cavity search. Facility searches generally involve the lockdown of all prisoners in their cells in order to perform a total search of all cells, housing units, buildings, yard, dining room, and other areas of the facility.

Equally important to the efforts of keeping contraband in check, correction officials must have a system in place which underscores control and order maintenance of unmanageable prisoners. A prisoner disciplinary policy establishes a regulation on prisoner conduct, attempting to keep limits on acceptable prisoner behavior (Cripe 1999). A disciplinary system should be written down and should specify to prisoners unacceptable behaviors, the sanctions for possible misconduct, the procedures for handling misconduct, how the disciplinary process works, and the appeal process. All officers need to be trained in how to implement the disciplinary system. Prisoners may be disciplined for rule violations and for violating the law, but such administrative responses or sanctions must be consistent with due process stipulations in accordance with the Fourteenth Amendment.

Similar to other areas of liability, prisoners have challenged the constitutionality of how correction officials and officers conduct searches and enforce sanctions of the disciplinary system. These issues have been addressed in several United States Supreme Court decisions and have been interpreted and applied by the lower courts since the late 1970s. This chapter addresses the landmark cases which direct officials in performing these correctional functions and the potential liability issues facing them.

SEARCHES

In part, the Fourth Amendment protects the right of the people to be secure in their persons, houses, papers, and effects against unreasonable searches and seizures. The focus of the amendment is the protection from an unreasonable search and seizure and the inference of the right of the people to be secure from the intrusion of the government into their houses and effects. The legal question for correction personnel is: What triggers a Fourth Amendment protection for prisoners who have been lawfully incarcerated in a correctional facility? Moreover, since the detention center or the prison is not a prisoner's "home," does the prisoner have an expectation of privacy and how is an unreasonable search or seizure defined in the corrections context?

In three separate cases, the United States Supreme Court has addressed two major types of searches: prisoner cell searches and strip searches of all prisoners after a contact visit. Using the Fourth Amendment, the Court has established guidelines for lower courts to apply when examining issues pertaining to searches of detainees and convicted prisoners. Two of the decisions address searching pretrial detainees in jails, and the other decision involves searching the cells of convicted prisoners.

In *Bell v. Wolfish* (1979) pretrial detainees of a Federal Correctional Center filed a class action suit challenging the constitutionality of the conditions of their confinement, including the strip and body cavity searches. Detainees were required to expose their body cavities for visual inspection as part of a strip search after a contact visit with a person from outside the facility. Correction officials testified that such searches were necessary to discover and to deter the smuggling of weapons, drugs, and other contraband that could breach the security of the facility. The district court upheld the strip search, but banned the body cavity search absent probable cause to believe the prisoner was concealing contraband. The appellate court affirmed, finding that there was only one documented case when contraband was discovered during a body cavity search.

Applying the intrusiveness/balancing test, the United States Supreme Court approved a policy of strip searching all detainees in the detention facility. The Court, however, admitted the policy gave it "pause" when it considered that some officers may abuse such a practice. Such abuse the Court held, cannot be tolerated, and the searches must be conducted in a reasonable manner and not for "punishment." The importance of providing security of the facility, however, outweighed the concern of abusing the practice. The Court noted that a person confined in a detention facility has no reasonable expectation of privacy with respect to his room or cell and that the Fourth Amendment provides no protection for such persons. A search warrant is not required prior to conducting the search. The *Bell* decision also approved the random search of a detainee's cell.

The Court again addressed searches of detainees and convicted prisoners in two 1984 decisions. In *Block v. Rutherford* (1984) the Court reviewed the claims of detainees who challenged policies of random cell searches and of strip searches after contact visits in the Los Angeles County jail. The detainees brought a class action lawsuit complaining that they should be present during a cell search and that they themselves should not be strip searched after contact visits. Rather than filing the claim under the Fourth Amendment, the detainees claimed that such practices violated their due process rights under the Fourteenth Amendment. The policy at the jail allowed random cell searches when detainees were out of their cells during meals, showers, recreation, or other activities. The district and appellate courts supported the detainees' claims, but the Supreme Court reversed the lower courts. Relying on their decision in *Bell*, the Court upheld the jail policies of conducting random cell searches and of conducting strip searches after contact visits. The Court determined that detainees had no right to observe cell searches.

On the same day the Court also ruled on a convicted prisoner's challenge of cell searches in prison, in *Hudson v. Palmer* (1984). Palmer filed a Section

1983 lawsuit after an officer had searched his cell looking for contraband. During the "shakedown," the officer discovered a ripped pillow case in a trash can near Palmer's bunk. Misconduct charges were lodged against him; he was found guilty, was reprimanded, and was ordered to reimburse the state for the cost of the pillow case. The district court rejected Palmer's Fourth Amendment claim, but the Fourth Circuit Court of Appeals reversed. The appellate court held that the Fourth Amendment affords prisoners with "limited privacy rights" regarding searches and that officials must have a "reasonable belief" that prisoners are in possession of contraband. The Supreme Court granted certiorari.

The Court examined the issue of whether a prisoner has an expectation of privacy in his cell, consistent with Fourth Amendment protections. The Court noted that while persons imprisoned for crime enjoy many protections of the Constitution, it is also clear that imprisonment carries with it the circumscription or loss of many significant rights. The Court held that society is not prepared to recognize as legitimate any subjective expectation of privacy that a prisoner might have in his prison cell and that, accordingly, the Fourth Amendment proscription against unreasonable searches does not apply within the confines of the prison cell. The Court emphasized that a balancing of interests must be considered when evaluating the reasonableness of a search in prison. The prison shares none of the attributes of the privacy of a home, an automobile, an office, or hotel room, and therefore the Court struck the balance in favor of security within the facility. Unfettered access to prison cells by prison officials is imperative if contraband is to be ferreted out and sanitary conditions maintained. The Court, therefore, reversed the appellate court's holding and concluded that prisoners do not have a reasonable expectation of privacy under the Fourth Amendment. The Court also stated that searches that were conducted for harassment purposes and not supported by penological objectives were actionable.

Cell Searches

As in other areas of liability, even though the Supreme Court has established case law through a decision, some lower courts strictly apply the decision, while other courts hold that prisoners have limited privacy rights. For example, in *Carter v. McGrady* (2002) a state prisoner filed an action alleging his rights were violated when he was unlawfully subjected to an unnecessary cell search and discipline in retaliation for "jailhouse" lawyering. Disciplinary action resulted after a cell search revealed that the prisoner had engaged in overt misconduct by hiding credit cards and stolen property and by storing paperwork and letters that had been used for fraud and deception. The appellate court affirmed the district court's summary judgment for officials, holding their actions were legitimately related to penological objectives, and thus precluding a retaliation claim. The Fourth Amendment does not provide an expectation of privacy precluding cell searches.

In *Ballance v. Young* (2000) a state prisoner brought a claim that his Fourth Amendment right to be free from an unreasonable search and seizure was violated when a correction officer seized several items of personal property from his cell. Consistent with prison rules, officers confiscated a notebook containing clippings. The metal parts of the notebook posed a risk of being used as a weapon, and razors and other contraband could be concealed inside the notebook. The court granted summary judgment to the officials, stating that the confiscation was reasonable in light of security concerns and that the prisoner did not have a right to privacy in his cell. Likewise, in *Barstow v. Kennebec County Jail* (2000), the court granted summary judgment to the sheriff when a detective searched a pretrial detainee's cell and found evidence that supported a crime of terrorizing a cellmate. The prisoner claimed his Fourth and Fourteenth Amendment rights of due process had been violated when the detective did not first obtain a warrant to search his cell. The court held that the Fourth Amendment did not apply to the search, that the detective had probable cause to search the cell, and, citing the *Bell* decision, that the detective did not need a search warrant prior to searching a cell.

Compare, however, the holding of the court in *U.S. v. Rollack* (1999). A pretrial detainee's mail was seized during a cell search. The district court held that a detainee has a reasonable expectation of privacy concerning his mail when a search is performed or initiated by officials and when the search is unrelated to security concerns. The court ruled that a detainee has an expectation of privacy concerning his mail when searches do not target concealed weapons, drugs, or other items clearly related to security inside the facility.

Consider the court's decision in *Scher v. Engelke* (1991), after an officer had performed unnecessary and harassing searches. Over the course of nineteen days, an officer conducted ten searches of the prisoner's cell, leaving it in disarray. The court found in favor of the prisoner, noting that such actions constituted cruel and unusual punishment in violation of the Eighth Amendment, even though no physical abuse, pain, or injury was sustained by the prisoner. The court noted that the searches amounted to "calculated harassment" unrelated to prison needs, since the officer had testified that he had no reason to believe that the prisoner had contraband in his cell. The jury awarded the prisoner $1,000 in punitive damages. The court acknowledged that its decision marked the first time a court had used the Eighth Amendment to evaluate a claim of an unreasonable search.

Strip Searches

While the Court in *Bell* held that detainees (and prisoners) may be strip searched after a contact visit, it did not distinguish such a search from searches in other circumstances. This failure to distinguish becomes more than academic and has practical importance for detention personnel. For example, the Court did not address a policy in detention facilities which allows officers to strip search all detainees at time of intake regardless of the charge. The Court denied review of a strip search case in *Ackerman v. Giles* (1985), ruling that the Ninth Circuit Court of Appeals had established that reasonable suspicion must exist before a strip search is conducted at the time of the admission of an arrestee. Failing to establish probable cause to perform a strip search at intake triggers a Fourth Amendment violation (*Giles v. Ackerman*, 1984).

Most of the lower courts have held that a policy which directs officers to strip search all incoming detainees violates the Fourth Amendment for some detainees (*Weber v. Dell*, 1986). *Weber* held that reasonable suspicion must be present for officers to believe that the detainee is concealing weapons or other contraband and that, therefore, a search is necessary before subjecting the detainee to a strip or body cavity search. Beside the *Weber* holding by the Second Circuit, ten other circuits have made the same ruling: the First Circuit, in *Swain v. Spinney* (1997); the Fourth Circuit, in *Clements v. Logan* (1982); the Fifth Circuit, in *Stewart v. Lubbock County* (1985); the Sixth Circuit, in *Masters v. Crouch* (1989); the Seventh Circuit, in *Mary Beth G. v. City of Chicago* (1983); the Eighth Circuit, in *Jones v. Edwards* (1985); the Ninth Circuit, in *Fuller v. M.G. Jewelry* (1991); the Tenth Circuit, in *Hill v. Bogans* (1984); the Eleventh Circuit, in *Justice v. City of Peachtree City* (1992) and in *Helton v. U.S.* (2002).

Skurstenis v. Jones (1999) illustrates the courts' position. A female nonfelony detainee filed a Section 1983 claim against the sheriff and jail personnel claiming she was subjected to a strip search of her pelvic region on admission into the jail in violation of her Fourth and Fourteenth Amendment rights. The district court provided a split decision. The court first held that the strip search was not supported at the time of admission since the officers did not have probable cause to perform the search, but the court granted them qualified immunity from liability on the search issue. The court, however, held the officers liable for touching her exposed pelvic region during an inspection for lice. The touching was conducted by an unidentified male wearing blue jeans and a T-shirt, who was later identified as a worker for the medical services unit. The court found that the pelvic search was not reasonable and was not supported by probable cause.

In *Kraushaar v. Flanigan* (1995) a detainee brought a claim of an improper and unreasonable search when he was admitted to jail for driving under the influence. The appellate court upheld the lower court's judgment in favor of the jail policy. The appellate court held that the officer had probable cause to believe that the detainee had concealed "something" in his pants when he was arrested, based on furtive movements to his waist/belt area. The court stated that the officer did not violate the detainee's rights by having him remove his pants, exposing his underwear.

Definitions of what constitutes a strip search vary and are broadly defined by the courts. Generally, a strip search requires the person to remove all of his or her clothing for a visual inspection of the naked body by the officer *(Doe v. Calumet* 1990). In some cases the person may be required to squat and cough, which is termed by many courts as a visual body cavity search. In *Masters v. Crouch* (1989) the court determined that when a female detainee was required to expose her breast area to a female detention officer, it was considered a strip search. The court in *Mason v. Village of Babylon, New York* (2000) considered requiring a female detainee to lift her bra and panties so that anything hidden inside might fall out—a requirement considered a strip search. Requiring a juvenile detainee to strip down to her panties was considered a strip search in *Justice v. Peachtree City* (1992). If a detainee is required to disrobe and expose or partially expose his or her private body parts, the courts are likely to consider this as a strip search, thus requiring reasonable suspicion to justify the search.

Prisoners have also challenged strip searches. In *Williams v. Price* (1997) death row prisoners filed suit claiming that their Fourth Amendment rights were violated when they were strip searched after recreational periods. The court found that the strip searches, before and after sessions with attorneys and recreational periods, did not violate their Fourth Amendment right to privacy. Also, in *Wilson v. Shannon* (1997) a prisoner in segregation brought a claim against prison officials alleging his constitutional rights were violated in connection with repeated strip searches performed by officers in the segregation unit after a period of exercise. The court granted summary judgment to the officials, noting that such strip searches conducted after exercise were a reasonable security measure taken to prevent weapons and contraband from entering the secure unit and that the prisoner had failed to show that the searches violated his Fourth Amendment rights.

The courts make a distinction between pretrial detainees and convicted prisoners in connection with conducting strip searches. As mentioned above, the *Bell* decision applies to detainees and prisoners after they have returned from a contact visit. The Supreme Court did not make a distinction concerning the length of time the detainee has been confined. The bulk of the strip-search cases allege an illegal search incidental to admission into the detention center and attack "blanket policies" requiring a strip search at intake.

Based on past case applications, reasonable suspicion is the justification for performing a strip search at the time of intake. Strip searches are not prohibited for any reason. If, however, the strip search is incidental to another legitimate detention objective after the person has been admitted, the strip search is justified, just as it would be for a detainee who has been confined for several months. For example, after a detainee has been admitted and processed and the next day receives a contact visit, or if a detainee becomes violent or acts out, requiring him or her to be housed in segregation for hours or days after intake, a policy of requiring a strip search is justified, like the strip search of any detainee exhibiting the same behaviors. The strip search would not be conducted incidental to admission but in response to the detainee's changed status or behavior.

Body Cavity Searches

An extension of the strip search is the body cavity search, which is conducted when there is reason to believe that the person has concealed contraband in a body orifice. Some agencies require a search warrant, and the body cavity search is to be conducted by qualified health personnel. When feasible, an officer of the same gender as that of the prisoner being searched should be present, and the search should be conducted away from other individuals.

In *Rickman v. Avaniti* (1988) the court granted summary judgment to correctional officials, and the appellate court affirmed the implementation of a policy of performing strip and body cavity searches of segregated prisoners when they are leaving their cells. State prisoners filed suit claiming that such a policy violated their Fourth Amendment rights. The appellate court found that such searches were constitutional, given that they were essential to the unit's security demands and that they involved no touching and were conducted in the prisoner's cell. In *Geder v. Lane* (1990) the court found that a prisoner's Fourth Amendment rights were not violated when his rectum was visually searched by nonmedical personnel to determine the presence of contraband after he had returned from a court hearing. The court rejected the argument that the search had to be performed by a "qualified medical person," since the search consisted only of visual inspection and other prisoners were required to submit to such a search.

Prisoners who had been subjected to digital anal searches brought a legal action against the warden and other prison personnel in *Hill v. Koon* (1990). A series of such body cavity searches were conducted on prisoners and the court found that they were constitutionally conducted. There was a legitimate penological need for the searches since there existed reasonable suspicion that the prisoners were smuggling drugs in their anal cavities after contact visits. The searches were performed by a health care professional, out of the view of others; were conducted in a reasonable manner; and therefore did not violate the prisoners' Fourth Amendment rights. One prisoner, however, was required to submit to another anal cavity search and the court determined that this search was unconstitutional. The officials could not demonstrate that the prisoner was concealing drugs in his anal cavity on that particular occasion, even though he had used drugs in the past. The court concluded that the search did not underscore a legitimate penologial objective, and the prisoner was awarded $1,000 in compensatory damages and $3,000 in punitive damages.

In *Roberts v. Rhode Island* (2001) a detainee filed an action against a policy that required all male detainees committed to the state to be subjected to strip and body cavity searches. The appellate court affirmed the lower court's, holding that such a policy was unconstitutional. When the policy was applied to detainees charged with minor offenses, it was deemed unconstitutional since it was extremely intrusive in nature and institutional security concerns were insufficient to support the blanket policy.

Segregation

Maintaining control and the orderly operation of the correctional facility is critical for the security functions of the facility. There is a need for internal controls and a disciplinary system in every prison and detention facility. Before efforts of rehabilitation and treatment programs can be implemented, security and order within the correctional facility must be established. To that end, rules and regulations must be implemented which outline acceptable and unacceptable prisoner behaviors. The disciplinary system must be fair, impartially implemented, and documented.

Prisoner behaviors need to be controlled in order to maintain equilibrium within the correctional environment. Antisocial behaviors that were part of the criminal lifestyle prior to incarceration continue during confinement. Rules set forth appropriate conduct, and when a prisoner is found to have violated the rules, various punishments may be initiated. A prisoner may temporarily lose privileges like making and receiving phone calls, recreation, visits, and the right to possess personal property. Moreover, for more serious infractions, a prisoner may be placed in administrative segregation (sometimes referred to as "isolation," "the hole," or just "segregation") and may forfeit earned good time And/or the prisoner's security classification may increase, warranting his transfer to higher level of custody.

The United States Supreme Court has examined correctional disciplinary systems and the use of segregation in several cases and has established guidelines for correctional officials when disciplining prisoners. In *Wolff v. McDonnell* (1974) the Court determined the criteria for disciplining prisoners. Prisoners of a Nebraska prison filed a class action suit under Section 1983, claiming that officials violated their Fourteenth Amendment rights by failing to conform to the requirements of due process of law. Legislative action taken in Nebraska had provided that the chief executive officer of the prison was responsible for disciplining prisoners. For serious prison infractions the chief executive officer may place the prisoner in a disciplinary cell and may order a reduction in the prisoner's earned good time. The disposition of each infraction was to be documented in the prisoner's file. Under the Nebraska disciplinary system, the prisoner was informed of the rule infraction charge in a preliminary conference with a prison supervisor and the charging officer; a conduct report was completed; and a hearing was conducted before the prison's Adjustment Committee, consisting of three members; the prisoner had the right to ask questions of the committee.

Prison officials asserted that their disciplinary proceedings addressing serious misconduct were a policy matter and not a constitutional issue. The district court agreed and the appellate court reversed. The Supreme Court noted that the Constitution does not guarantee the provision of "good-time" for satisfactory behavior of a prisoner, since such a provision is legislated by the state. Therefore, the Court held that prisoners do not lose all of their rights because of their convicted and sentenced status. Because a prisoner may lose earned good time, which implies a "liberty interest" (i.e., being considered for early release on parole), due process protections must be implemented which protect the prisoner's rights in disciplinary hearings. Due process generally means "fundamental fairness," but what is fundamentally fair may change as the facts of a situation change. The Court disagreed that the Nebraska system was adequate in protecting the prisoner's rights and held that disciplinary proceedings are not like criminal proceedings but must accommodate certain minimal due process protections. Using parole revocation hearings developed in *Morrissey v. Brewer* (1972) as a model, the Court established five elements that need to be incorporated within disciplinary proceedings/hearings which would ensure the Fourteenth Amendment's due process protections: (1) The prisoner must have advance written notice of the charges no less than twenty-four hours prior to the hearing; (2) the prisoner should be allowed to call witnesses and present documentary evidence in his defense, if permitting him does not jeopardize prison security; (3) the disciplinary committee must be impartial; (4) counsel substitute (prison personnel or other prisoner) will be permitted when the prisoner is illiterate or when the charges are complex; (5) there must be a written statement of the facts determined and the evidence relied upon.

This decision applies only to serious infractions of conduct committed by the prisoner when liberty interests are at stake. The Court stated that the disciplinary proceedings are an administrative function and do not rise to the same level as a criminal proceeding. Therefore, the prisoner does not have the right to an attorney or the right to confront or cross-examine the person bringing the charges.

The issue of whether a prisoner should be afforded counsel during a disciplinary hearing was addressed by the United States Supreme Court in *Baxter v. Palmigiano* (1976). Rhode Island correctional officials charged a prisoner with inciting a disturbance and disruption of prison operations, which may have led to a riot. He was brought before the disciplinary committee and informed that he might be prosecuted for a violation of state law. He was advised that he should talk with his attorney regarding the possible criminal charge, but the committee did not allow his attorney to be present at the disciplinary hearing. He was also advised that he could remain silent but that in doing so he might adversely affect his potential discipline. The prisoner did avail himself to the counsel substitute permitted by prison rules, and he remained silent. He was found guilty by the disciplinary committee and assessed thirty days punitive segregation. He filed a Section 1983 lawsuit, claiming officials violated his Fourteenth Amendment due process rights by not permitting him the right to an attorney during the disciplinary hearing.

Relying on its decision in *Wolff*, the Supreme Court refused to give prisoners more due process rights. The Court again noted that disciplinary misconduct proceedings are less than a criminal trial and that therefore the same due process protections do not apply. Correctional authorities were not in error in failing to provide the prisoner with counsel at the time of the disciplinary hearing. In regard to the prisoner's remaining silent during the hearing, resulting in adverse consequences, the Court held that, on its face, it is not an invalid practice. The appellate court had concluded that requiring a prisoner to admit to a crime in a prison disciplinary hearing violated the prisoner's Fifth Amendment right to avoid self-incrimination. The Court rejected this argument and stated that if a prisoner was forced to admit guilt, the prisoner would be granted immunity in a criminal prosecution. Thus, *Baxter* holds that prisoners are not allowed an attorney in a prisoner disciplinary hearing, consistent with the *Wolff* decision, and that a prisoner's remaining silent during the hearing may be used against him.

In *Hutto v. Finney* (1978) the United States Supreme Court affirmed a lower court's decision that set a limit of thirty days during which a prisoner could be confined in punitive segregation. After several hearings, the district court in Arkansas found the entire correctional system violated the Eighth Amendment rights of prisoners. The district court found that prisoners' claims of correctional practices, including indefinite punitive segregation, violated the prisoners' rights and that the officials had acted in bad faith. The court issued an order outlining remedial corrections and limiting the duration that a prisoner may be housed in punitive segregation, and awarded the prisoner's attorney $20,000. Correctional officials appealed and the Court granted certiorari.

The Court affirmed the district court's limitation on the use of punitive segregation. The district court had held that punitive segregation may be used to punish and correct misbehavior but may not be used indefinitely and therefore set a time limit. The Court found no error in the limitation requirement as a result of the past poor record of the Arkansas Department of Corrections. The Court also emphasized that the limitation presents little danger of interference with prison administration, since the Commissioner of Corrections testified that prisoners should not ordinarily be held in punitive isolation for more than fourteen days. Awarding attorney's fees was ruled as valid and consistent with the Civil Rights Attorney's Fees Award Act of 1976.

The United States Supreme Court distinguished between administrative segregation and punitive segregation in *Hewitt v. Helms* (1983). After quelling a prison riot in a state correctional facility in Pennsylvania, an investigation by the state police, revealed that Helms had participated in the riot, and he was placed in restrictive confinement. The next day a misconduct report was written, charging that Helms had assaulted a correction officer and had conspired to disrupt the normal operations of the facility by taking control of the control center. A hearing committee, four days later, considered the case and found him not guilty, as a result of insufficient evidence, but it continued his placement in restrictive confinement. A second misconduct report was filed against Helms for assaulting a second correction officer. Helms and an officer testified at the disciplinary hearing. The committee found Helms guilty, assessed six months of administrative segregation, and dropped the first misconduct charge. Helms filed a legal action claiming his Fourteenth Amendment rights of due process had been violated.

The Supreme Court held that formal hearings like those used in prison disciplinary cases (*Wolff*) are not required prior to placing a prisoner in administrative segregation. The Court determined that correctional officials, in performing an investigation and a hearing, satisfied the minimum due process requirements for placement of a prisoner in administrative segregation. An informal, nonadversarial evidentiary hearing is sufficient for placement in administrative segregation in order to decide if the prisoner presents a security risk and to complete an investigation regarding a prisoner's involvement in an alleged misconduct. The Court emphasized that the mechanics of due process are not the same for prisoners in disciplinary proceedings as they are for free citizens. Administrative segregation is the type of confinement prisoners can reasonably anticipate receiving at some point during their incarceration. The Court stated that prison officials should be accorded wide-ranging deference in the adoption and execution of policies and practices that in their judgment are needed to preserve internal order and discipline to maintain institutional security.

The Court made a distinction between punitive segregation and administrative segregation. Punitive segregation is used for punishing a prisoner for violating a prison rule, while the purpose of administrative segregation is to protect a prisoner. Both confinements isolate the prisoner from the general population, but, unlike punitive segregation, a formal process is not required for administrative segregation. Placement in punitive segregation requires providing the prisoner with notice of the charges and an opportunity to present his view of the circumstances.

The question addressed by the Court in *Superintendent (of the Massachusetts Correctional Institution at Walpole) v. Hill* (1985) was: How much evidence is required to support a finding of guilt during a prison disciplinary hearing? The disciplinary hearing committee found two prisoners guilty of assaulting another prisoner and ordered that they each forfeit one hundred days of earned good time. They were placed in administrative segregation for fifteen days. During separate hearings, the disciplinary committee reviewed the charging officer's report and heard testimony. The officer stated that he did not actually observe the two prisoners assaulting the other prisoner. The officer observed the assaulted prisoner with blood coming from his mouth and his eye swollen. The prisoner could not identify his assailants. The officer observed three prisoners leaving the area, two of whom were the prisoners charged with the assault. Health care personnel informed the officer that the prisoner had indeed been assaulted. The two prisoners maintained their innocence of the assault. The injured prisoner gave a written statement indicating that neither of the charged prisoners had assaulted him. The charged prisoners filed a lawsuit with the State of Massachusetts Superior Court claiming that their Fourteenth Amendment rights had been violated because the hearing committee had no evidence to support its finding that the prisoners had committed the assault. The Superior Court and the State Supreme Court found in favor of the prisoners and ordered that their disciplinary records be cleared of the assaults and that their good time be restored. The United States Supreme Court decided to hear the case.

Massachusetts law held that before prisoner good time can be forfeited, a "modicum" (small portion) of evidence must exist to support the forfeiture. Such a level of evidence was required to prevent arbitrary deprivations without ensuring due process and because such loss of good time implied a liberty interest of the prisoner. The Court held that the requirements of due process are satisfied if some evidence supports the decision of the prison disciplinary board. The Court noted that the correction officials complied with the *Wolff* standard by documenting the evidence relied upon to determine the guilt of the two prisoners. The Court also noted that due process only requires some evidence to support the finding of a disciplinary board. The evidence may be described as meager, but the record was not so devoid of evidence that a finding of guilt was otherwise arbitrary. Therefore, the Court ruled that only a modicum of evidence is required to support a disciplinary committee's finding of guilt of a prisoner charged with misconduct. This decision diminishes the constitutional rights of prisoners.

In the controversial decision of *Sandin v. Conner* (1995), the United States Supreme Court reconsidered their previous ruling in *Wolff*. Conner, confined in a Hawaii prison, was charged with the serious misconduct of obstructing a correction officer in the performance of his duties when Conner refused to comply with a strip search. At his disciplinary hearing, the committee denied his request to call witnesses to confirm his innocence. He was found guilty and assessed thirty days punitive segregation. He filed an administrative appeal and a Section 1983 lawsuit. Before the case was heard by the district court, the deputy warden ruled in favor of the prisoner's appeal, expunging his record of the misconduct charge. The district court entered summary judgment for correctional officials but the appellate court reversed, finding that the prisoner had been deprived of his state-created liberty interest, which had emerged from the misconduct report. The Supreme Court granted certiorari.

The Court reversed, abandoning its prior holding in *Wolff*, finding that it was too mechanical and cumbersome. The Court held that placement in segregation (administrative or punitive) does not invoke a "liberty interest" thereby triggering a due process right. Conner had incorrectly asserted that any state action taken for punitive purposes encroaches upon a liberty interest under the Due Process Clause even in the absence of any state regulation. However, Conner's confinement in disciplinary segregation did not present a liberty interest invoking due process. The Court determined that discipline by correction officials in response to a wide range of misconduct falls within the expected parameters of the sentence imposed by a court of law. The purpose of prison discipline is to effect prison management and rehabilitation goals, and the Court concluded that such discipline does not ordinarily impose any sanction or retribution beyond that contained in the sentence being served. As long as the imposed discipline does not add to the sentence or go beyond conditions imposed by the sentence, the disciplinary action does not create a liberty interest.

Moreover, the Court held that nothing in the Hawaii Parole Board's code requires the Board to deny parole in the face of the prisoner's misconduct record. The parole board may consider a myriad of factors when deciding to grant a release on parole, and the prisoner is afforded due process protections during the parole hearing process. Hence, the Court concluded that neither the practice of the correctional officials nor the Due Process Clause afforded Connor a protected liberty interest that would entitle him to procedural protections set forth in *Wolff.*

Lower Courts Application

As seen in the above case review, the Supreme Court has examined a wide scope of constitutional issues pertaining to prisoner confinement in segregation over the past thirty years. The Court has come almost full circle in its position prior to the *Wolff* decision by inserting its decision into *Sandin.* The Court has also distinguished between administrative and punitive segregation, and the lower courts have taken several opportunities to apply the case law with varying interpretations.

In *McClary v. Kelly* (1998) a state prisoner filed a Section 1983 lawsuit alleging that his confinement in administrative segregation for over four years violated his due process rights. Medical experts testified that the total isolation of administrative segregation confinement had a negative affect on the prisoner's mental health since he had been deprived of the social opportunities that other prisoners were provided. The district court found that the hardships experienced by the prisoner in segregation were atypical and significant when compared to those of other prisoners in general population. The court found that the state had, by regulation, granted the prisoner a protected liberty interest in remaining free of administrative segregation but that those regulations, when properly followed, satisfy the limited due process rights a prisoner has under the Due Process Clause of the Fourteenth Amendment.

In *Fraise v. Terhouse* (2002) state prisoners filed a Section 1983 action challenging their classification status and treatment as members of a "Security

Threat Group" (STG, or gang). Prisoners were placed in a special housing unit. The appellate court affirmed the lower court's decision to grant summary judgment to correctional officials. The appellate court determined that the STG policy did not violate the prisoners' equal-protection rights or their due process rights by placing them in "special housing." The court determined that officials had a legitimate and neutral objective in maintaining order and security in the prison and had proper grounds to conclude that these prisoners were core members of an STG since they were recognized leaders of the Five Percent Nation and the officials had documented the group's activities. The court found no violations of the prisoners' due process rights because the prisoner group had demonstrated a propensity for violence. The court concluded that the prisoners were not deprived of a protected liberty interest by their confinement in the special housing unit, since the placement did not impose any atypical hardships on them.

Prisoners have challenged the practice of denying the calling of witnesses at disciplinary hearings. In *Hoskins v. McBride* (2002) a prisoner filed an action challenging revocation of good-time credits following a disciplinary hearing. The court denied the petition, ruling that prison officials did not deny the prisoner due process by failing to compel witnesses to name a "certain offender" named in a tip regarding drug trafficking or by denying him permission to view security tapes and other physical evidence. The court noted that while prisoners have the right to call witnesses for disciplinary hearings when the right does not create a security risk within the institution, that right is not an unlimited right.

One state prisoner prevailed against correctional officials on claims of denying him the right to call a witness during a disciplinary hearing in two separate legal actions. In *Williams v. Wilkinson* (2000) the prisoner had been charged with testing positive for marijuana, but he stated that another prisoner had provided the urine sample for the drug test. The court found that officials had disallowed witnesses to testify indicating that another prisoner had indeed provided the urine sample and that the substance abuse coordinator for the prison had also been denied the opportunity to testify. The court ruled that such denials violated the prisoner's due process rights. In *Williams v. Wilkinson* (2001) the same prisoner filed another action challenging the denial to call a witness during a disciplinary hearing. The prisoner again had been charged with a substance abuse violation and been denied the opportunity of calling witnesses on his behalf. The court granted the prisoner an injunction barring the denial of witnesses owing to the belief regarding their credibility.

Prisoners have also filed claims asserting that correctional officials violated their due process rights by basing a misconduct hearing on insufficient evidence. In *Wright v. Coughlin* (1998) a state prisoner confined in punitive segregation filed a Section 1983 action claiming he was deprived of his due process rights during a hearing. The appellate court upheld the lower court's decision to grant summary judgment to the correctional officials, ruling that the hearing officer's denial of the prisoner's request to view videotape and to call witnesses did not violate due process. The prisoner had been placed in disciplinary segregation for five-and-half months. The court also found that the absence of periodic confinement reviews did not implicate a liberty interest arising from the due process clause and that the length of the disciplinary confinement did not implicate a liberty interest protected by the due process clause.

A state prisoner filed a habeas corpus petition in *Sylvester v. Hanks* (1998) seeking to overturn a prison disciplinary committee's finding that he had actively participated in a prison riot. He was charged with conspiracy to incite a riot and ordered to three years' confinement in disciplinary segregation. The district court denied the petition and the appeals court affirmed. The appellate court found "some evidence" which supported that the prisoner had participated in the riot and found that due process did not require the prison to compel unwilling witnesses to give testimony at hearings that concerned only the prisoner's custody status and not his length of confinement. Compare, however, the court's ruling in *Burnsworth v. Gunderson* (1999). A prisoner was found guilty of escape by a prison disciplinary board. The prisoner filed a Section 1983 action claiming that the board deprived him of his due process rights because of insufficient evidence. The district court found no due process violation but ordered the conviction expunged from the prisoner's files. The appeals court upheld the decision, holding that due process was violated when the board convicted the prisoner of escape with no "shred of evidence." The court agreed that the conviction should be expunged from the prisoner's file.

Most courts have concluded that the *Sandin* decision does not apply to pretrial detainees. Pretrial detainees who allegedly violate jail rules are constitutionally entitled to certain procedural protections before being placed in disciplinary segregation. The reasoning is that since pretrial detainees have not been sentenced, the possibility of segregated confinement cannot implicitly fall within the terms of the prison or jail sentence (Krantz 2003). Affording due process protections can prevent unconstitutional attempts to punish detainees for crimes for which they have not been convicted.

In *Rapier v. Harris* (1999) a pretrial detainee filed a Section 1983 claim against the sheriff and officers alleging they had deprived him of his due process rights by "punishing" him with placement in segregation for 270 days of his confinement. The appeals court upheld a lower court's granting of summary judgment to the sheriff and officers. The court agreed that a detainee may be punished for misconduct but that such punishment can only be imposed after affording the detainee some sort of procedural protection. Jail officials had placed the detainee in segregation for misconduct without a notice or hearing or any other process. During confinement the detainee was denied periodic showers, writing materials, and commissary privileges. But the court held that the detainee was not deprived of anything necessary for his sustenance.

In *Benjamin v. Kerik* (2000) correctional officials petitioned the court to terminate a consent decree under the Prison Litigation Reform Act. The court granted the petition, noting that officials did not inflict punishment upon pretrial detainees by subjecting them to restrictive housing, because the disciplinary due process policy of the jail was required to be implemented within seventy-two hours of the infraction leading to the housing assignment. Also, in *Benjamin v. Fraser* (2001) the appellate court agreed with prisoners that when officials place them in restrictive housing or use restraints, procedural protections need to be in place—which include a hearing, a written decision, a timely review of appeal regarding placement in restrictive confinement or restraints, and the opportunity to seek further review based on good cause.

In *Resnick v. Adams* (1999) a presentence detainee submitted a habeas corpus petition seeking to recover forfeiture of his good time lost to violating a random drug screening of his urine. He tested positive for morphine and lost twenty-seven days of good time. The court dismissed the petition, stating that the sanction for violating detention rules was not prohibited. The court found that the sanction was not excessive in light of the seriousness of the violation. In *Edwards v. Johnson* (2000) an appellate court dismissed a detainee's Section 1983 action when she sued for having been placed in disciplinary segregation for fifteen days. At her disciplinary hearing it was determined she had violated facility rules when she had unauthorized contact with visitors of the facility. She had handed out flyers to a touring group which called the facility a terrorist concentration camp. The appellate court stated that being placed in segregation after a hearing did not violate her due process rights.

TRANSFERS OF PRISONERS

Frequently prisoners' violations of prison rules are so persistent or their behaviors are so violent that an increase to a higher level of security classification is warranted. Questions emerge as to what constitutional rights prisoners may possess regarding involuntary transfers to a higher-custody prison. Due process safeguards have been examined in conjunction with United States Supreme Court decisions. In *Meachum v. Fano* (1976) the disciplinary committee determined in a hearing that several prisoners had been involved in a series of fires set within the medium-custody institution over two-and half months. The committee recommended that one prisoner be placed in administrative segregation for thirty days and that the other prisoners be transferred to a maximum-custody prison. The transfers were reviewed and approved by prison administrators, and the prisoners filed a Section 1983 action claiming that their due process rights were violated because they had been transferred to a less desirable prison without an adequate hearing. The prisoners contended that the transfer had created a grievous loss, and the appellate court agreed.

The United States Supreme Court overturned the appellate court's decision, holding that the Constitution does not require that the state have more than one prison for convicted felons; nor does the Constitution guarantee that the convicted prisoner will be placed in any particular prison if, as is likely, the state has more than one correctional institution. The Court opined that the due process clause of the Fourteenth Amendment does not protect a prisoner from transfer from one prison to another. Transfer from one prison to another may occur for a variety of purposes, one of which may be misconduct, and such rationale is vested in prison officials. The Court further noted that confinement in any of the state's institutions is within the normal limits or range of custody which the conviction has authorized the state to impose. As long as the transfer of a prisoner is a discretionary-under-agency policy, the due process clause of the Fourteenth Amendment does not require a hearing prior to a transfer to a prison where conditions are less than favorable.

In *Montanye v. Haymes* (1976) the Court further considered the question of providing a hearing prior to transferring a prisoner to another prison within the same state for disciplinary reasons. Haymes had been assigned to work in the prison library at the Attica prison in New York. He was removed from his job for circulating a petition of other prisoners which expressed that eighty-two prisoners had been denied legal assistance. The next day he was informed that he was being transferred to another maximum-custody institution without loss of good time nor with any other disciplinary measures. He filed suit claiming retaliation and a violation of his due process rights as a result of the prison officials' failure to provide a hearing prior to the transfer.

Consistent with their decision in *Meachum*, the Court ruled that a prisoner transferred to a prison of similar security status is not entitled a hearing prior to the transfer. Ostensibly the Court maintained that the reason for the transfer to another state prison is irrelevant, except when a transfer is made for punitive purposes or when the discipline implied in the transfer does not invoke the due process clause of the Fourteenth Amendment requiring a hearing. Since the Court had already ruled that a hearing was not required to transfer a prisoner from a less secure prison to a more secure one, it is only logical that a hearing not be required regarding the transfer of a prisoner to a prison of the same security level.

In *Fermin-Rodriguez v. Westchester County* (2002) a prisoner filed suit against jail personnel and federal officials for violating his alleged liberty-interest rights. The prisoner claimed that the conditions in the jail were inferior to those of the state prison. The district court dismissed the action, holding that the prisoner had no liberty interest in being returned to a state prison from the county jail and that a delay in the transfer to state detainee status did not violate due process. The court stated that officials have discretion to transfer a prisoner from one facility to another.

In *Dodson v. Reno* (1997) a prisoner in a federal pretrial detention center filed a *Bivens* action against correctional officials challenging his transfer to the segregation wing of a federal prison which housed gang members who threatened his life. The district court found the transfer reasonable since it provided a higher level of security and granted summary judgment to correctional officials. The court noted that the transfer did not violate the prisoner's Eighth Amendment rights and that the prisoner was not entitled to an injunction barring officials from transferring him to any prison in the United States.

An involuntary transfer of a prisoner from a prison to a mental health facility, however, requires due process protections under the Fourteenth Amendment since a "liberty interest" is implied. In *Vitek v. Jones* (1980) the Supreme Court held that certain procedural protections must be in place prior to transferring a mentally impaired prisoner to a mental health facility. Jones had set fires in his cell, burning his mattress and severely burning himself. He was transferred to a burn unit of a private hospital for treatment and then transferred to the security unit of a state mental hospital. Under Nebraska statute, if a designated physician or psychiatrist finds a prisoner suffers from a mental disease or defect and cannot be provided with proper treatment in prison, the Director of Corrections may transfer the prisoner to another facility for treatment or examination. Jones was diagnosed as suffering from a mental defect and the transfer was ordered. Jones filed a legal action challenging the transfer without a hearing, in violation of his due process rights under the Fourteenth Amendment.

The Court, wary about potential abuse of mentally impaired prisoners, ruled that a hearing is required prior to an involuntary transfer to a mental health facility. The Court opined that a criminal conviction and a sentence of imprisonment extinguish an individual's right to freedom from confinement for the term of the sentence, but they do not authorize the state to classify him as mentally ill in order to subject him to involuntary psychiatric treatment without first affording him due process protections. Because it is stigmatizing in many ways, an involuntary transfer to a mental health facility for treatment requires the following process:

1. the prisoner must be given written notice that a transfer to a mental health facility is being considered;

2. a full hearing must be held—after a reasonable time, so that the prisoner can prepare for it;

3. the prisoner must be allowed to present witnesses at the hearing and to cross-examine other witnesses;

4. the hearing must be conducted by an independent decision maker;

5. a written statement must be made by the fact finder of the evidence relied upon and of the reasons for ordering the transfer;

6. legal counsel must be appointed for the prisoner if he or she cannot afford one; and

7. the prisoner must be given timely notice of all the above rights.

Procedural protections were addressed in *U.S. v. Frierson* (2000). In the absence of the prisoner, a district court conducted a hearing and ordered the prisoner to be involuntarily committed to a medical center for treatment of a mental illness. The prisoner appealed and the appellate court reversed the lower court's decision. The court ruled that the prisoner had a statutory right to attend the hearing and that a telephone call to the prison and the prisoner's nonresponsiveness to an officer's efforts to get him to the phone did not provide the prisoner with the requisite opportunity to participate in the hearing. The court also held that the prisoner was not given timely notice about the time of the hearing.

SUMMARY

As seen in the case discussion in this chapter, the United States Supreme Court continues to constrain many prisoner rights and increases the power and authority of correctional officials. In *Hudson*, the Court held that prisoners have no privacy rights in their cells and, in *Block*, that prisoners do not have the right to be present during a search of their cells. The prison or detention cell does not hold the same privacy standard as the home of a free citizen. Unrestricted access to prison and detention cells is a critical security element, and cell searches are important to maintaining the safe operation of the facility. The courts do make a distinction between pretrial detainees and sentenced prisoners concerning strip searches. As a rule, pretrial detainees may not be strip searched at the time of detention intake, unless there is evidence of reasonable suspicion. This policy, however, can change at any point throughout the detainee's confinement, based on his or her behaviors. While the Supreme Court allows unrestricted freedom to search prisoners and their cells, unreasonable searches which are performed merely to harass prisoners or which are unsupported by a legitimate penological objective may increase the risk of liability. To the extent feasible and practical, strip searches should be performed by an officer of the same gender as that of the prisoner. If a situation arises when a strip search is performed by an officer of the opposite gender of the prisoner being searched, the rationale for conducting the search should be documented.

The Court understands the legitimate correctional need for the use of segregation and has made a distinction between administrative and punitive segregation. A liberty interest no longer exists as it applies to disciplinary sanctions, under *Sandin*, but the disciplinary process in prison still requires the *Wolff* safeguards to be implemented by hearing committees. The decision applies equally to disciplinary hearings in detention facilities. Only a "modicum of evidence" is required to find a prisoner guilty of serious misconduct in a disciplinary hearing under the *Wapole* decision.

The Court further restricted the rights of prisoners through its decisions in *Meachum* and *Montanye*. A choice of a particular prison is not made by the prisoner but by correctional officials based on the needs of security and other factors. Decisions to transfer a prisoner to a prison of a higher level of custody or to a prison of the same level of custody do not equate to a constitutional review. The Court, however, took a different position in its holding in *Vitek*. The involuntary transfer of a mentally impaired prisoner implies a liberty interest, and due process safeguards must be followed. The prisoner must be found to suffer from a mental defect by medical personnel and must be provided a hearing and afforded counsel; also, officials must follow the Court-established criteria for such a transfer. Disciplinary hearing boards and transfer committees of the mentally impaired can defend against potential liability by adhering to these legal parameters.

REFERENCES

Cripe, C. 1999. Inmate disciplinary procedures. In *Prison and jail administration: Practice and theory,* edited by P. M. Carlson and J. S. Garrett, 208–18. Gaithersburg, MD: Aspen Publishers.

Garritt, D. L. 1961. The prison as a rehabilitation agency. In *The prison*, edited by D. Cressey. New York: Holt, Rinehart, and Winston.

Krantz, S. 2003. *The law of sentencing, corrections, and prisoners' rights*. St. Paul, MN: West Publishing.

Toch, H. 1977. *Living in prison: The ecology of survival*. New York: Free Press.

Cases Cited

Ackerman v. Giles, 105 U.S. 2114 (1985)

Ballance v. Young, 130 F. Supp. 2d 762 (W.D. Va. 2000)

Barstow v. Kennebec County Jail, 115 F. Supp. 2d 3 (D. Me. 2000)

Baxter v. Palmigiano, 425 U.S. 308 (1976)

Bell v. Wolfish, 441 U.S. 520 (1979)

Benjamin v. Fraser, 264 F.3d 175 (2d Cir. 2001)

Benjamin v. Kerik, 102 F. Supp. 2d 157 (S.D.N.Y. 200)

Block v. Rutherford, 468 U.S. 576 (1984)

Burnsworth v. Gunderson,179 F. 3d 771 (9th Cir. 1999)

Carter v. McGrady, 292 F. 3d 152 (3rd Cir. 2002)

Clements v. Logan, 455 U.S. 942 (1982)

Dodson v. Reno, 958 F. Supp. 49 (D. Puerto Rico 1997)

Doe v. Calumet City Illinois, 754 F. Supp. 1211 (N.S. Ill. 1990)

Edwards v. Johnson, 209 F. 3d 772 (5th Cir. 2000)

Fermin-Rodriguez v. Westchester County Jail, 1919 F. Supp. 2d 358 (S.D.N.Y. 2002)

Fraise v. Terhouse, 283 F. 3d 506 (3rd Cir. 2002)

Fuller v. M.G. Jewelry, 950 F. 2d 1437 (1991)

Geder v. Lane, 745 F. Supp. 538 (C.D. Ill. 1990)

Giles v. Ackerman, 746 F. 2d 614 (9th Cir. 1984)

Helton v. U.S., 191 F. Supp. 179 (D.D.C. 2002)

Hewitt v. Helms, 459 U.S. 460 (1983)

Hill v. Bogans, 735 F. 2d 391 (1984)

Hill v. Koon, 732 F. Supp. 1076 (D. Nev. 1990)

Hoskins v. McBride, 202 F. Supp. 2d 839 (N.D. Ind. 2002)

Hudson v. Palmer, 468 U.S. 517 (1984)

Hutto v. Finney, 437 U.S. 678 (1978)

Jones v. Edwards, 770 F. 2d 739 (1985)

Justice v. City of Peachtree City, 961 F. 2d 188 (11th Cir.1992)

Kraushaar v. Flanigan, 45 F. 3d 1040 (7th Cir. 1995)

Mary Beth G. v. City of Chicago, 723 F. 2d 1263 (1983)

Mason v. Village of Babylon, New York, 124 F. Supp. 2d 807 (E.D.N.Y, 2000)

Masters v. Crouch, 872 F. 2d 1248 (1989)

McClary v. Kelly, 4 F. Supp.2d 195 (W.D.N.Y 1998)

Meachum v. Fano, 427 U.S. 215 (1976)

Morrissey v. Brewer, 408 U.S. 471 (1972)

Montanye v. Haymes, 427 U.S. 236 (1976)

Rapier v. Harris, 172 F. 3d 999 (7th Cir. 1999)

Resnick v. Adams, 37 F. Supp. 2d 1154 (C.D.Cal. 1999)

Rickman v.Avaniti, 854 F. 2d 327 (9th Cir, 1988)

Roberts v. Rhode Island, 239 F. 3d 107 (1st Cir. 2001)

Sandin v. Conner, 515 U.S. 472 (1995)

Scher v. Engelke, 943 F. 2d 921 (8th Cir. 1991)

Skurstenis v. Jones, 81 F. Supp. 2d 1228 (N.D. Ala. 1999)

Stewart v. Lubbock County, 767 F. 2d 153 (1985)

Superintendent, Massachusetts Correctional Institution at Walpole v. Hill, 472 U.S. 445 (1985)

Swain v. Spinney, 117 F.3d 1 (1997)

Sylvester v. Hanks, 140 F. 3d 713 (7th Cir. 1998)

U.S. v. Frierson, 208 F. 3d 282 (1st Cir. 2000)

U.S. v. Rollack, 90 F. Supp. 2d 263 (S.D.N.Y. 1999)

Vitek v. Jones, 445 U.S. 480 (1980)

Weber v. Dell, 804 F. 2d 796 (2nd Cir. 1986)

Williams v. Price, 25 F. Supp. 2d 605 (W.D.Pa. 1997)

Williams v. Wilkinson, 132 F. Supp. 601 (S.D. Ohio 2001)

Williams v. Wilkinson, 122 F. Supp. 2d 894 (S.D. Ohio 2000)

Wilson v. Shannon, 982 F. Supp. 337 (E.D. Pa. 1997)

Wolff v. McDonnell, 418 U.S. 539 (1974)

Wright v. Coughlin, 31 F. Supp. 2d 301 (W.D. N.Y. 1998)

CHAPTER 10

CORRECTIONAL SUPERVISOR LIABILITY

> *The administration of a prison, we have said, is at best*
> *an extraordinarily difficult undertaking.*
> *Wolff v. McDonnell* (1973)

Judicial intervention has been the principal agent in forcing change in the nation's prisons and jails. The extent of this involvement by the federal judiciary in overseeing major changes in the nation's prisons is perhaps second in breadth and detail only to the court's earlier role in dismantling segregation in the nation's public schools (Feely and Hanson 1990). Judicial activism is the norm in the contemporary prison, and many correctional systems are under judicial scrutiny to change and improve conditions. Prison litigation has become broad in scope, involving numerous state and local programs, from education and environmental protection to personnel issues.

Since the 1970s, correctional executives have received intense scrutiny from the judicial system regarding their managerial activities. As prisons have become overcrowded, violent, racially polarized, and financially strapped, administrators have seen not an expansion of their powers but their role reduced from a that of "prison czar to a well constrained manager" (Hawkins and Alpert 1989). Still required to maintain order and security within the prison, correctional administrators must do so with limited budgets, with less authority, and within legal mandates and potential liabilities. While most correctional actions occur behind the fortress walls of the prison, the media, the public, interest groups, and the judiciary are keenly interested in the incarceration, treatment, and punishment of prisoners.

The contemporary prison administrator has unique liability concerns that previous administrators did not have to confront thirty years ago. Prison administrators have previously reported their concerns over judicial regulations which impact their job effectiveness, their satisfaction in the job, officer morale, weakened officer and administrative authority with prisoners, and violence in prisons (Feely and Hanson 1990; Cullen et al. 1993; Flanagan, Johnson, and Bennett 1996). However, current research on prison liability reveals that administrative liability ranks among the top five most frequent areas for prisoner lawsuits. Ross (1997) reported that in a twenty-five-year study of published Section 1983 judicial decisions from 1970 to 1994, prison and jail administrators prevailed in only 46 percent of prisoner claims citing administrative deficiencies. He also reported that administrative liability accounted for the third most commonly litigated category (behind failure-to-protect and medical-care claims) in which monetary awards were granted to a prevailing prisoner. In a risk management study of civil liability claims of 57 out of 83 county detention facilities in Michigan, Ross (2001) found that administrative liability ranked fourth out of twenty civil litigated categories of claims filed by detainees but ranked low in regard to monetary awards granted. Correctional administrators need to be aware of their potential management liability.

The purpose of this chapter is to examine the potential liability issues for the correctional administrator in directing employees. This discussion focuses specifically on federal Section 1983 civil litigation that names the correctional administrator as defendant for failing to properly fulfill administrative functions in directing, controlling, hiring, assigning, training, retaining, and disciplining employees. Case examples and strategies for reducing liability exposures will be discussed.

MANAGERIAL DUTIES AND POTENTIAL FOR LIABILITY

Correction administrators, like other executives of an organization, are responsible for planning, controlling, organizing, budgeting, staffing, directing, reporting, and supervising employees (Archambeault and Archambeault 1982; Phillips and McConnell 1996). Additional managerial competencies endemic to prison administrators include, among others, the management of emergencies, decision making, establishing priorities, knowledge of prison security, management of prisoners, knowledge of technology, knowledge of the political process, and management of people (National Institute of Corrections [NIC] 1988; Wright 1994). Of major concern regarding prison administrative competencies is the dynamic area of maintaining knowledge in law and supervisory liability issues. The developing case law in this field strongly suggests that there is a need for administrators and supervisors to know the limits of their jobs and to be more aware of subordinates' competence and performance.

Managing people is central to the effective operation of the prison system. Correction officers exercise legal authority over prisoners. Therefore, correction personnel must exercise a high degree of skill in using their authority and discretion when executing departmental policy and enforcing various aspects of the law. Legal actions against correctional employees frequently emerge from decisions where correctional personnel have implemented a specific policy change that has prohibited or curtailed certain behaviors of the prisoner population. Other prisoner litigation may result from allegations of correctional personnel failing to perform their legally assigned duties, performing the duty in a negligent manner, misusing their authority, using excessive force, or depriving the prisoner of certain constitutional rights.

Prison and jail administrators and correctional supervisors face even greater potential liability. This liability emerges from the managerial function of supervising the actions of employees under their responsibility. Administrators are responsible for numerous managerial functions, and these duties frequently expose administrators to the risk of liability. Any employee action which has been alleged to deprive the prisoner of a protected right may in turn expose the administrator to potential liability. This exposure often places administrators in a position to explain why they should not be held responsible for the employee's conduct. Such situations are frequently difficult to defend and make the administrative chain of command more vulnerable to liability and also heighten the potential for organizational liability.

Virtually every action taken by an administrator in dealing with prisoners and employees entails potential liability and legal consequences. It becomes essential that prison administrators execute their managerial competencies and functions within the context of legal supervisory responsibilities.

This does not suggest that managerial decision making should be impeded by legal paranoia; rather, it implies that the efficient operation of the contemporary prison system should be maintained within working guidelines of potential supervisory liability issues. The duty of prison administrators is to know their potential for liability when they perform their basic managerial functions. Performing the responsibilities of a prison executive not only requires developing managerial competencies to lead the correctional organization but also requires that administrators concomitantly continue to develop legal competencies to reduce their own legal risk and to reduce the risk of the organization from litigation. A thorough understanding of the fundamental liability issues will equip the administrator in accomplishing this objective.

Liability Under Section 1983

Every correctional administrator should be aware of Title 42 United States Code, Section 1983. Since 1978 this has become the primary vehicle by which administrators have been litigated for allegations resulting from their management function. It is the statute used to apply the rights guaranteed by the United States Constitution to the everyday decisions and policies of state and local government agencies. The correctional administrator must be familiar with the law and agency policies in order to avoid liability for violation of constitutional rights (see Chapter 4).

Under Section 1983, neither states nor their agencies may be sued for money since Congress did not intend to include states or state agencies within the meaning of "persons" for purposes of money damages (*Will v. Michigan Department of State Police* 1989). A state and its agencies, however, may be sued for potential injunctive relief to prevent actions in the form of continuous or future constitutional violations against prisoners (*Kentucky v. Graham* 1985). If the plaintiff prevails in an injunctive relief action, the state may be required to pay attorney's fees under 42 U.S.C. Section 1988 (*Hutto v. Finney* 1978).

Foundation for Liability

Frequently plaintiffs' Section 1983 lawsuits include naming the supervisor along with the correction officer. This strategy is based on the theory that the officer acts for the agency and, therefore, what the officer has done reflects agency policy and practice. As a legal strategy, the plaintiff includes the agency and supervisors because the higher the position the employee holds, the closer the plaintiff gets to the deep pocket of the county or state agency. Chances of monetary recovery are increased if supervisory personnel, by virtue of their position, are included in the lawsuit. Moreover, inclusion of administrative and supervisory personnel may also create a conflict of interest in the legal strategy for the defense, hence strengthening the plaintiff's claim against one or more defendants.

Who is the Policy Maker?

In *Monnell v. Department of Social Services of New York* (1978) the United States Supreme Court affirmed that supervisors can be held responsible for acts of their employees,. This decision expanded the meaning of the phrase in

Section 1983, "every person," to include every governmental entity. The supervisor is not liable because an employee has violated the prisoner's constitutional rights but may be liable for abdicating supervisory responsibilities when the employee's failure results in a violation of constitutional rights. Under Section 1983, the doctrine of *respondeat superior* (let the master answer) does not form the basis of liability (*Polk County v. Dodson* 1981). Under the doctrine of *respondeat superior* the master is responsible for the actions of the servant. It does not, however, apply to public employment because public officials are not the "masters" of their employees; they serve the governmental agency.

The *Monnell* decision established governmental liability for behavior of correction personnel when they implement or execute agency-promulgated or agency-adopted policies, or when they implement regulations or conduct which results from a "custom," even though such a custom has not received approval through formal channels (at p. 690).

To establish governmental liability, the plaintiff must establish that there existed a policy or custom and that it was the "moving" force behind the officer's violation of the prisoner's constitutional rights. The courts have enumerated several potential ways liability may be incurred under Section 1983 against supervisors: if they directly participated in the action; if they, after learning of the violation through a report of appeal, failed to remedy a wrong; if they created a policy or custom under which unconstitutional practices occurred or allowed such a policy or custom to continue; and if they were grossly negligent in managing the subordinates who caused the unlawful condition or event (del Carmen 1991; Kappeler 2001).

In *Roman v. Koehler* (1991) a prisoner brought a civil rights action claiming that the commissioner of the department of corrections, a former warden, unnamed corrections officers, and prison health care workers violated his rights by failing to provide "adequate" medical care. The court dismissed the case, stating that in order to sustain a health-care claim, the prisoner must show that his access to physicians was unreasonably delayed or denied or that the prescribed medical treatment was not administered. The court further held that Section 1983 liability can only be imposed on prison officials who were directly and personally responsible for the alleged violation of civil rights.

Frequently the question emerges of who is considered an "official" policy maker. Certainly not all supervisors fall into this category. On two occasions, the United States Supreme Court has ruled on the issue of who is a policy maker for purposes of liability. In *Pembaur v. City of Cincinnati* (1986), the Court held that those public officials who have final policy making authority can render an agency liable under Section 1983 provisions. In *City of St. Louis v. Praprotnik* (1988), the Court held that a governmental entity may be held liable when authorized policy makers "approve a subordinate's decision and the basis for it" (at p. 127). The Court further added that the decision for determining who the official policy maker is for purposes of liability is to be made by examining state law. Generally, prison administrators would fall within this category. In *Marcheese v. Lucas* (1985), the court found the sheriff to be the official agency policy maker and assessed $125,000 against him for failing to train and discipline correction officers after they had beaten a prisoner.

The United States Supreme Court ruled in *McMillian v. Monroe County Alabama* (1997) that the county sheriff was an Alabama state official rather than a county official. In Alabama, the governor and the attorney general, but not the county, generally have authority over the sheriff's department, and therefore Monroe county had no law enforcement authority at the time of the case. Accordingly, when there is no authority to make policy in the area of law enforcement or corrections, no liability will attach.

The Eleventh Circuit Court of Appeals in *Turquitt v. Jefferson County, Ala.* (1998) determined that an Alabama county cannot be held liable in a civil rights case for harms incurred by jail prisoners as a result of improper operation of a jail or negligent supervision of its prisoners because the county has no responsibility in those areas. The court did determine that the sheriff, not the county, is responsible for jail conditions under Alabama law, stating that counties have no duties with respect to daily operations of county jails and have no authority to dictate how jails are operated. The estate of a pretrial detainee who was killed by other prisoners had filed a Section 1983 lawsuit against the county.

Liability can be imposed against supervisors if they establish or enforce a policy or custom that causes a constitutional deprivation. But liability generally cannot be based solely on a single incident of misconduct. In *City of Oklahoma City v. Tuttle* (1985) the United States Supreme Court determined "that proof of a single incident of unconstitutional activity is not sufficient to impose liability...unless it was caused by existing unconstitutional municipal policy, which can be attributed to a municipal policy maker" (at p. 814). Generally, the plaintiff must establish that the deprivation resulted as a matter of continuing agency policy and that the policy was the moving force behind the deprivation.

According to del Carmen and Kappeler (1991), factors which may strengthen a plaintiff's claim of an agency's practices of constitutional abuses may include:

1. frequency of the violation;

2. the extent to which the practice was made routine by employees;

3. the extent to which the practice was accepted by supervisors;

4. the extent to which the action represented shared beliefs of employees;

5. retention of, failure to discipline, or failure to investigate the violating employee; and

6. failure to prevent future violation.

THEORIES OF SUPERVISORY LIABILITY

Standard of Review

Some ambiguity exists among federal courts concerning the level of culpability required for finding liability against supervisors under Section 1983, and this area of liability is still emerging. Occasionally the courts have used the standard of gross negligence but more commonly have used the standard of deliberate indifference for determining supervisory liability.

Deliberate indifference was first established in *Estelle v. Gamble* (1976), when a prisoner sued correction officials over claims of denial of and improper medical treatment of a back injury he had sustained while working on the prison farm. In *Estelle*, the Court held that deliberate indifference involves a conscious intentional decision or choice to inflict unnecessary and wanton pain on a prisoner. Deliberate indifference has been defined, redefined, and expanded over the years by the United States Supreme Court in several correctional cases (*Wilson v. Seiter* 1991; *Farmer v. Brennan* 1994). The standard, which has not been specifically defined, is applied on a case-by-case basis. It generally means that the actor disregarded a known or obvious consequence of his or her actions, consciously chose a course of action in disregard to the harmful outcome, and disregarded a risk of harm of which he or she had been aware. The Court in *Farmer* stated that officials must know that a substantial risk of harm existed as a result of their action or inactions.

Deliberate indifference may be demonstrated by either actual intent or reckless disregard. An administrator acts recklessly by "disregarding" a substantial risk of danger that is either known to the administrator or that would be apparent to a reasonable person in an administrator's position. Mere negligence is insufficient to support a Section 1983 claim. Correctional supervisors are not liable if they can show that they responded reasonably to known risks.

A prisoner brought a Section 1983 claim against correctional supervisors for being deliberately indifferent to his medical needs in *Beckford v. Irvin* (1999). The prisoner had been placed in a mental health unit and confined to a wheelchair since 1984. He was not placed in the center for treatment but because the cell was bigger and could accommodate the wheelchair. Shortly after being placed in the cell, officials took the wheelchair from him and denied him access to it for the majority of his confinement, despite his repeated requests. The jury found in favor of the prisoner, finding that he was unable to participate in outdoor exercise or to take a shower. They awarded the prisoner $125,000 in compensatory damages, for violation of the Americans with Disabilities Act, and punitive damages amounting to $25,000. The court found the award not to be excessive since the supervisors had been deliberately indifferent to the prisoner's medical needs.

There are many forms of potential administrative actions, which may create in their totality evidence of deliberate indifference to constitutionally protected rights. Case law reveals that there are seven general theories from which potential administrative liability emerges: defective hiring practices, negligence in personnel assignments, retaining incompetent officers, as well as failing to direct, supervise, discipline, and train officers. These theories are not mutually exclusive, meaning that the plaintiff will usually allege several areas in which to frame the lawsuit against the administrator. Typically, the officer or officers directly involved in a prisoner incident will be named as primary defendants. Supervisors will also be named in a lawsuit at a secondary level for abdicating their supervisory responsibilities with the errant officers. For example, it is not uncommon for the plaintiff to assert a failure by the administrator in directing, supervising, and properly training an officer in a case alleging excessive force by the officers.

Hiring Practices

Allegations of a faulty system of hiring officers by superiors claim that if the employer had performed a better job in screening applicants, the constitutional violation being alleged would not have occurred. This generally follows the "but for" line of reasoning: But for the hiring of the officer, a constitutional violation would not have occurred.

Liability stems from claims alleging that the administrator failed to conduct a complete background investigation of the employee prior to employment. Liability emerges when an employee is unfit for appointment, when such unfitness was known to the employer or should have been known through a background check, and when the employee's act was foreseeable.

Hiring deficiencies led to liability in *Jones v. Wittenburg* (1977). The sheriff was ordered by the court to provide training and psychological testing of staff. In *Brown v. Benton* (1978) the court found that the termination of an officer was reasonable based on results of background checks.

In *Hirst v. Gertzen* (1982) the family of a prisoner who committed suicide in a jail brought a civil action claiming that their son had been electrocuted. The family alleged that the county officials should be held liable for failing to properly hire and supervise detention personnel. The court determined that the prisoner did indeed take his own life but found that the county had a duty under state law to exercise care in hiring and supervising correctional officers and that such failures resulted in the deprivation of constitutional rights under federal law.

In *Benavides v. County of Wilson* (1992) the court concluded that the sheriff had complied with state requirements when hiring candidates for the position of correction officer. Allegations of deliberate indifference in regard to the improper screening of employees were not supported, even though the prisoner sustained an injury during his confinement. Liability attached in *Parker v. Williams* (1988) when evidence supported the plaintiff's claim against a sheriff for promoting a policy or custom of not conducting reasonable background checks on prospective employees. A former prisoner had been kidnapped and raped by the chief jailer.

For the first time, the United States Supreme Court decided a case involving hiring practices in law enforcement when it reviewed *Bryan County Oklahoma v. Brown* (1997). This case involved an excessive-force claim against a deputy after he had engaged in a pursuit. The plaintiff alleged that the sheriff was deliberately indifferent to the constitutional rights of citizens since he had ignored an alleged past violent history of the deputy and that, therefore, the sheriff's hiring practices were unconstitutional. The Court ruled in favor of the sheriff, stating that the hiring policy was not the moving force behind the incident or behind the plaintiff's injury. The Court further stated:

> [A] finding of culpability simply cannot depend on the mere probability that any officer inadequately screened will inflict any constitutional injury. Rather, it must depend on a finding that this officer was highly likely to inflict the particular injury suffered by the plaintiff. The connection between the background of the particular applicant and the particular constitutional injury must be strong. (at p. 14)

Correctional administrators are encouraged to conduct thorough background investigations and to use psychological examinations prior to hiring employees. There is no magical legal formula for hiring prospective employees. But failing to institute adequate measures and to take reasonable steps in employee selection, or ignoring information regarding the unfitness of a candidate, increases the risk of liability. Hiring procedures must be instituted in compliance with state standards and legal guidelines. Investigators assigned to perform background checks for their agencies must also follow legal guidelines.

In *Morris v. Crawford County* (2002) a detainee brought a Section 1983 action against the sheriff alleging claims of excessive force against a deputy and claims of failing to properly screen the deputy prior to hiring him. The detainee had been arrested and charged with driving while intoxicated and with disorderly conduct. At the detention center he refused to take a breathalyzer test and began yelling and banging on the cell door. Detention officers responded, and according to the detainee, they began to kick him, one officer using a "knee drop" on him which caused an intestinal injury. The detainee claimed the sheriff knew of prior violent acts of the officer but deliberately ignored them at the time of hiring him. The Eighth Circuit Appellate Court affirmed the lower court's summary judgment for the sheriff, finding no "strong" causal connection between the officer's background and the specific constitutional violation alleged by the detainee. The court found that the sheriff was not deliberately indifferent in hiring the officer.

In *Bednar v. County of Schuylkill* (1998) a prisoner filed a Section 1983 lawsuit against a physician alleging deliberate indifference to his medical needs and against the county for failing to perform an adequate background check prior to hiring him. The district court granted summary judgment to both defendants. The court held that the physician's failure to diagnose the prisoner's fractured hip and failure to order an X ray did not constitute deliberate indifference to the prisoner's need for medical care. The court also determined that the facility's administrator was not liable in failing to adequately screen the doctor prior to hiring him, even though five medical malpractice actions had been filed against him and his staff privileges had been suspended at one hospital. These actions had been settled or dismissed prior to employment.

In *Scott v. Moore* (1997) a female pretrial detainee filed a Section 1983 lawsuit against officials claiming that a male correction officer had sexually assaulted her. Charges filed claimed that inadequate staffing at the jail and supervisory failure to conduct background checks of employees prior to employment led to the sexual assault. The appellate court did not find a constitutional violation by the county and held that staffing patterns did not constitute deliberate indifference or create a substantial risk of harm for the detainee. Further, the court held that officials required, as a condition of employment, that officers undergo background investigations, polygraph examinations, and medical examinations. None of these tests revealed any concerns that the officer possessed a proclivity toward sexual deviance. The court noted that the officer had worked without incident as a police officer for four years prior to employment as a corrections officer and that he had been trained in the jail policies and management of prisoners by jail personnel. The officer resigned and pled guilty to the criminal charges.

Negligent Entrustment

Negligent entrustment involves the supervisor's failure to supervise and properly control an employee's custody, use, or supervision of equipment or facilities entrusted to him or her (del Carmen 1991). This theory of liability is different from negligent assignment in that negligent entrustment goes beyond general employee incompetence to specific incompetence in the proper utilization of equipment entrusted to the employee. For example, legal claims may emerge for failing to direct the proper use of an impact weapon in a disturbance which later results in a serious injury or in the death of a prisoner. In *Roberts v. Williams* (1971) a county farm superintendent had given an untrained trusty a shotgun and the task of guarding a work crew. The court held the supervisor liable since the shotgun went off, seriously wounding a prisoner.

Claims stemming from improper entrustment are, however, associated with failure to train. Such claims are based on the philosophy that commensurate training should follow when a supervisor allows an officer to use equipment in the performance of his or her duties. In *Slaken v. Porter* (1984) the court awarded a prisoner $32,000 when evidence supported a claim of excessive force by correction officers when they used high pressure hoses, tear gas, and billy clubs to subdue him while he was in a one-man cell. The officers and supervisory personnel alike were found to be deliberately indifferent to the prisoner's constitutional right to be free from a known risk of harm. Supervisors were found liable since they should have been aware of the propensities for brutality by officers and had the duty to ensure that instruments of control were not misused. In *Norris v. Detrick* (1996) the court found that prison officials properly administered two doses of chloracetaphenone (CN) gas when confronted by a prisoner with known martial arts skills who had refused to return to his cell after numerous orders to do so. The court noted that whether the use of gas is unconstitutional depends on the totality of the circumstances, including provocation, the amount of gas used, and the purposes for which the gas was used.

A detainee brought a legal action against the sheriff for the alleged improper and abusive use of a restraint chair and pepper spray in *Moore v. Hosier* (1998). Upon intake into the detention center, the intoxicated detainee fought with officers. They sprayed him with pepper spray and restrained him in a restraint chair. The detainee claimed that while in the chair he was beaten by the officers and then placed in the shower for decontamination purposes. In ruling in favor of the county, the court found that the sheriff had provided a detailed policy and procedures for training officers in using reasonable force, which included how to properly use the restraint chair and pepper spray.

The test of liability is deliberate indifference. The plaintiff must be able to prove that the officer was incompetent, inexperienced, or reckless, and that the supervisor knew or had reason to know of this. The defense for the supervisor is that proper supervision and training concerning the use and custody of equipment was exercised but that, despite adequate precautions, the act still occurred.

Negligent Assignment

Negligent assignment is the assigning of an employee to a job without first ascertaining employee competence or the retaining of an employee on a job who is known to be incapable of performing job duties. Examples may include assigning a reckless driver to transport prisoners and assigning an officer who has demonstrated instabilities in the past to a gun post. The administrator has a duty not to assign an unfit subordinate to a position and not to leave an unfit subordinate in a position. In *Moon v. Winfield* (1974) liability attached for failure to place a police officer who was unfit for his assignment into a nonsensitive position. The court held the supervisor liable since he had authority to assign or suspend the officer but failed to do either. The supervisor had received five separate misconduct reports within a two-week period as well as a warning that the officer had been involved in a series of actions that indicated mental instability.

In *L. W. v. Grubbs* (1992) an appellate court found supervisors liable when a prison nurse filed a claim for improperly assigning her to work with young violent prisoners when the supervisors knew of their previous violent histories. The court found that the supervisors created a dangerous situation when they assigned the nurse to work by herself with these prisoners and, when left alone, she was raped by one prisoner.

Administrators must pay careful attention to complaints and adverse reports against subordinates. These must be investigated and properly documented. Further, administrators must be generally aware of the competence and weaknesses of subordinates and not assign them to perform tasks for which they lack skill or competency.

Failure to Train

Lawsuits alleging a constitutional injury resulting from the department's policy of failing to provide training to employees are quite common. Many case outcomes have categorically mandated jail and prison administrators to train their personnel or to improve their training programs (*Jones v. Witten-*

burg 1971; *Miller v. Carson* 1975; *Owens v. Haas* 1979). In *Owens*, the Second Circuit Court of Appeals held that while a county may not be liable for mere failure to train employees, it could be liable if its failure was so severe as to reach the level of gross negligence or deliberate indifference. In *Hayes v. Jefferson* (1982) the United States Court of Appeals ruled that a supervisor may be held liable "only where there is essentially a complete failure to train…or training was so reckless or grossly negligent that future misconduct is almost inevitable, or would be characterized as substantially certain to result."

The United States Supreme Court in *City of Canton, Ohio v. Harris* (1989) determined for the first time what standard should be applied to claims of supervisors' failing to train subordinates. The Court held that inadequate training may serve as the basis for liability only where the failure to train amounts to deliberate indifference by policy makers of the agency. The Court emphasized that inadequate training rises to deliberate indifference only when the need for more or different training is obvious and the failure to implement such training is likely to result in a constitutional violation. Liability may not attach for failure to train or improper training without some proof that the department was, or should have been, aware of the need and then made a deliberate decision not to provide training or not to review and/or improve the training provided.

When asserting a failure-to-train claim, the plaintiff must prove the following. First, it must be established whether a training program is adequate to the tasks that the particular employee must perform, and if it is not, whether such inadequate training can justifiably be said to represent agency policy. Second, the failure to train must have been the cause of harm. Third, it is not necessary for a policy regarding training to be unconstitutional in order for liability to attach. Fourth, the plaintiff will generally have to prove that a pattern of incidents has occurred within the agency which demonstrates a problem of failing to train. Fifth, the type of training provided need only be adequate to address a particular matter. Finally, according to the Supreme Court, officers must receive ongoing training in "usual and re-current" situations. For example, regular training should address using force techniques and equipment in situations of self-defense or involving the control of a violent prisoner.

Following the *Canton* decision, a lower court, in *Bordanero v. McLeod* (1989), applied the deliberate indifference standard to a failure-to-train claim in a police arrest situation, which provides an overview of the elements that may give rise to claims of faulty training. An off-duty police officer was beaten in a bar fight. Later the entire night shift of the police department returned with the officer and broke into the bar and the motel rooms that were attached. The officers used bats, ax handles, sledgehammers, mace, and numchucks to enter the premises and beat several patrons severely, killing one. A sergeant refused to intervene. There had been a long-standing custom of breaking down doors without a warrant on felony arrests. Since numerous officers were involved in this situation, the custom of condoning this practice was upheld in court, and the police chief's tolerance of such practices and his failing to respond administratively were attributable to the city. Proof of being deliberately indifferent to training was evidenced by the following elements:

1. contemporary standards of relevant law enforcement duties were not integrated into departmental regulations;

2. there was no in-service training;

3. officers promoted to positions of supervisor were not trained;

4. no operational guidelines were developed;

5. background checks were superficial and psychological examinations were rarely given;

6. personnel performance evaluations were not required;

7. discipline in the department was haphazard and the officers involved in the incident   were not disciplined after they had been indicted;

8. the chief had been previously warned about failing to provide training; and

9. officer requests for training were denied.

Even though the case was one involving police, correctional supervisors can transfer these elements to their setting. Administrators who make it a matter of policy to provide training regularly will avert claims for failing to train their officers.

Since the *Canton* decision, several correctional administrators have been found liable in lawsuits claiming a failure to train. In *Williams v. White* (1990) a prisoner filed a *pro se* complaint against the prison superintendent. The appellate court determined that the prisoner's complaint regarding being placed in solitary confinement without a hearing and placed in a cell without mattress, water, and ventilation was not frivolous. The court held that the superintendent could be held liable in accordance with Section 1983 for operating a prison with unsanitary and inhumane conditions and could be held directly liable for failing to properly train and supervise or control employees. Prison officials were found liable in *Gilbert v. Selsky* (1994) when they failed to train hearing officers in prisoner disciplinary proceedings. The district court found that prison supervisory personnel were personally involved with violations of prisoners' constitutional hearings. In *Women Prisoners v. District of Columbia*

(1994), the district court found prison officials liable for violating the rights of female prisoners who had been subjected to sexual harassment. The court determined that the harassment was the result of a governmental custom and that officials had failed to properly train employees in sexual harassment.

Using the deliberate-indifference standard, a federal district court, in *Coleman v. Wilson* (1995), determined that custodial staff were inadequately trained in signs and symptoms of mental illness, which supported allegations that disciplinary and behavior control measures had been inappropriately used against mentally ill prisoners. The three-hour training course attended by all new officers and the additional in-service training at the institutional level were not sufficient to prevent some officers from using punitive measures to control prisoners' behaviors without regard to the causes of the behaviors.

A Ninth Circuit federal court ruled in favor of prisoners in *Madrid v. Gomez* (1995) on several issues, including failure to train, excessive force, constitutionally inadequate mental services, and deficient medical care. The court held that staffing levels were insufficient, training and supervision of medical staff almost nonexistent, and screening for communicable diseases poorly implemented. Prisoners frequently experienced significant delays in receiving treatment; there were no protocols or training programs dealing with emergencies or trauma; and there were no procedures for managing chronic illness. Prisoners established prison administrators' deliberate indifference, showing that the administrators knew that unnecessary and grossly excessive force was being used against prisoners routinely by officers and that such force posed a substantial risk of harm to prisoners. The court also held that prison officials had known that conditions of isolation presented a substantial risk of excessive harm for the mentally ill and other vulnerable prisoners and that the officials had therefore acted wantonly in violation of the Eighth Amendment.

In *Farabee v. Rider* (1998) a female detainee filed a civil action against the sheriff for malicious prosecution and excessive force. During arrest she was pushed to the ground by the arresting deputy and handcuffed, while the deputy placed his knee in her back. While she was confined in the jail for twelve hours, the deputy allegedly assaulted her and she suffered back and arm injuries. The court denied summary judgment and held that the sheriff owed a duty to protect the arrestee from the risk of excessive force created by his failure to train and supervise deputies.

A youth confined in county juvenile detention center committed suicide, and his family filed a Section 1983 claim against the county and the center's supervisor for violating their son's Fourteenth Amendment right to medical attention. In the case, *Smith v. Blue* (1999), the court found that the supervisor's practice of preentering records of cell checks into the logbook and then avoiding the actual visual checks was so pervasive that it constituted a policy or custom and therefore was the result of inadequate training. Before the youth committed suicide with a bed sheet, he was left unsupervised in his cell after being placed in solitary confinement for failing to follow orders. In the cell, he was allowed to keep a towel, shoes with laces, and a bed sheet. The youth had been confined for four months and had allegedly threatened to commit suicide and to physically harm himself prior to being placed in segregation. Investigators determined that the youth had been dead for at least an hour when he was discovered hanging, thus confirming that recorded cell checks had not been made. Officers stated that it was routine practice to pre-record security checks indicating they had made rounds every fifteen minutes.

In *Barney v. Pulsipher*, (1998) two former female detainees brought a civil action against a detention officer, the sheriff, and the county commissioners claiming unsanitary jail conditions and that the officer had sexually assaulted them. The detainees had been confined for forty-eight hours. All officials except the detention officer were granted summary judgment. The appellate court affirmed and held that neither the sheriff nor the county was liable for failing to train or inadequate hiring. The court ruled that the detainees did not show that the training provided was the consequence of a deficient training program. The court also determined that the sheriff should not have been expected to conclude that the officer was highly likely to inflict sexual assault on the female detainees if he was hired as a correctional officer. Moreover, permitting the officer to be the sole officer on duty did not impose any liability on the county, where there was no history of such misconduct. The detainees also failed to establish a valid claim of deliberate indifference to the conditions of confinement.

Conducting regular training of correctional personnel and fully documenting that training can assist in defending allegations of inadequate training. In *Vine v. County of Ingham* (1995) the district court held that the sheriff and the county were not deliberately indifferent to a prisoner who died in their custody after consuming methyl alcohol prior to arrest. The court ruled that the sheriff had provided the necessary training to his officers commensurate with state law and that the officers had also received substantial in-service training. The court noted that such claims would apply only if the conduct represents usual or recurring situations with which officers must deal.

In an effort to provide "realistic" training, many agencies have designed scenario-based training, using role players to play the parts of violent, despondent, or riotous prisoners. This type of training can be highly beneficial to officers in decision making and in practicing skills under simulated stress conditions. While such training is recommended and practical, liability can attach against the agency for failing to follow proper safety measures when conducting the scenario.

In *Cole v. State of Louisiana, Department of Public Safety and Corrections* (2002), the State Supreme Court upheld an award of over $1 million in a legal action where the plaintiff correction officer suffered severe injuries incurred in a training exercise. Cole, a tactical team corrections officer, participated in simulated prison riot training exercise and assumed the role as prisoner. Earlier in the day, padded batons were used in the exercises, but during this scenario, unpadded batons were used, and officers wore only helmets for protection. Cole stated that someone unknown forcibly grabbed him and began striking him with the baton with full force about the head, neck, and shoulders. He testified that his helmet came off and that, despite his yelling "code red," which was supposed to stop the action, the aggressor continued to strike him. Testimony revealed that the exercise "just broke down," "it was chaotic," and "there was really no order to it." At the emergency room it was determined that Cole had sustained severe head injuries, including brain trauma, and injuries to his neck and shoulders. The Louisiana State Supreme Court upheld the lower court's ruling that the training was faulty, leading to the intentional act of battery when Cole was struck with the baton. The Court also upheld the awards of $657,000 in general damages, of $157,000 in future medical damages, of $914,390 in lost wages, and of $110,000 in damages for loss of consortium to Cole's wife and daughter.

Failure-to-train litigation has resulted in many judgments against supervisors and is currently the most frequently litigated area in the field of supervisory liability. Training should realistically focus on the essentials of the tasks of correction officers and should target recurring situations and tasks. Emergency preparedness and special-response team training should also be regularly conducted for appropriate personnel, but, as the Cole decision implies, safety measures must be followed. Regular in-service training, designed for administrators and supervisors, should be required. For defense purposes, training seminars need to be tailored to meet job requirements on a regular basis and should be thoroughly documented.

Failure to Direct

Failing to direct refers to a failure to inform employees of the special requirements and limits of the job to be performed. Frequently this is interpreted as a failure of an administrator to promulgate policies and procedures which direct personnel in the specific tasks of the job. In *Ford v. Brier* (1974) the court ruled that failing to establish adequate policies gives rise to civil liability. Examples may include the supervisor's failing to inform employees of the proper procedures for dispensing medication to prisoners or of the limits of force used to restore order during a fight.

A federal district court in *Estep v. Dent* (1996) granted injunctive relief to a prisoner regarding his claim that the prison policy requiring him to cut his ear locks violated the Religious Freedom Restoration Act. Requiring the prisoner to cut his ear locks would substantially violate the tenets of his Jewish faith. The court found that prison officials were deliberately indifferent and failed to establish that the policy was the least restrictive means of furthering its interests in maintaining security.

A federal appellate court in *Vineyard v. County of Murray, GA.* (1993) found that the county was deliberately indifferent to the rights of prisoners to be free from excessive force by deputies who beat prisoners. The court stated that the county's policy of condoning such behavior was the moving force which violated the prisoner's constitutional rights. In *Valencia v. Wiggins*, (1993), liability was assessed against jail officials who acted outside the boundaries of established policy. A prisoner was awarded $2,500 in damages and $27,000 in attorney fees when the court found that officers used excessive force against him in a jail disturbance. An officer struck a handcuffed and compliant prisoner and placed him in a choke hold. The court found that the force and choke hold used violated the jail's policy and therefore constituted malicious and sadistic harm.

In *Miller v. Shelby County* (2000) a prisoner who was assaulted by fellow prisoners brought a civil action claiming that the correctional center's policy of allowing varying security levels of prisoners to engage in recreation at the same time violated his constitutional rights. The court found in favor of the prisoner, finding that the policy posed a substantial risk of harm and that jail officials showed deliberate indifference to the risk posed by the policy. The jail allowed prisoners from varying security levels to take recreation together, including rival gang members. The court noted that jail officials had specific knowledge of the threats against gang members yet took no action to protect the prisoner from the assault. The prisoner sustained permanent injury to his shoulder and the court awarded him $40,000.

The best defensible position for correctional administrators is to establish and maintain a current policy manual for employee direction and institutional operations. Policies and regulations must be written within the framework of "legitimate penological objectives" as determined in the United States Supreme Court's ruling in *Turner v. Safley* (1987). Policies should be reviewed and, if necessary, revised on a regular basis, reflecting the current status of the law. The written policy should reflect not only the theory but the practice of the department. Agency procedures should mirror written job descriptions, specifying the job functions of employees. Employees should be trained and tested in their comprehension of policy content. Each employee should have a current copy of the policy manual, and each employee should inspect it periodically. Correctional supervisors must also be familiar with all policies and must enforce their proper implementation.

FAILURE TO SUPERVISE

One of the primary duties of correctional supervisors is providing day-to-day supervision and control of their employees. Commonly, a claim for failing to properly supervise an employee is attached to a claim for failing to train. It is generally the second most common claim made against a supervisor, following a claim for failing to train.

Allegations of failing to supervise employees involve abdication of the responsibility of overseeing employee activity. Failing to supervise employees properly can lead to litigation for failing to know about employee behavior. Examples include tolerating a pattern of physical abuse of prisoners, racial discrimination, and a pervasive deprivation of prisoners' rights and privileges.

Permitting unlawful activities in an agency may constitute deliberate indifference, giving rise to liability. The usual standard is whether the supervisor knew of a pattern of behavior but failed to act on it. The question then becomes: What constitutes knowledge of a pattern of behavior of an employee? Many courts have established that direct knowledge is required, while other courts state that knowledge can be inferred if a history of violations is established and the administrator had direct and close supervisory control over the employee committing the violation.

In *Treadwell v. Murray* (1995) the court found that the prisoner failed to state a claim of deliberate indifference under Section 1983, based on supervisory liability. As a result, correctional officials prevailed. The prisoner asserted that correctional officials had failed to oversee officers and medical personnel when the officials deprived him of an unsafe rehabilitative environment and initially gave him an inappropriate medical classification.

In *Giroux v. Sherman* (1992), a prisoner was awarded $36,000 in punitive damages after claiming that on four occasions at least eight correction officers beat and tormented him without provocation. Because of the beatings, an old injury was reopened, which required hospitalization. While in the hospital, he was also beaten, and he sustained injuries to the kidney and throat. Supervisory liability was also attached when the court stated that supervisors failed to identify and correct behaviors of the officers. Additional concerns about supervisory liability emerged in *Hudson v. McMillian* (1992), when the United

States Supreme Court learned that a prison lieutenant watched two correction officers beat a handcuffed and nonresisting prisoner and told them not to have "too much fun." The officers were found liable for using excessive force and the lieutenant was found liable for condoning such actions by the officers.

In *Kesler v. King* (1998) former prisoners of Missouri were confined in a private county detention facility in Texas. The prisoners brought a Section 1983 claim against officers, the sheriff, his chief deputy, and the county for excessive force, failing to supervise, failing to train, and failing to screen job applicants. The claim focused on a movement team's action, which was supervised by a lieutenant, in using excessive force—specifically, a stun gun, pepper spray, and canines—to move prisoners from their cells for searches. The incident was videotaped and later shown on *Date Line NBC*. The tape showed a canine biting a compliant prisoner five times, an officer stepping on prisoners as they were forced to crawl, and an officer using a stun gun on other compliant prisoners. The court denied summary judgment to the officials, holding them liable for abdicating their supervisory responsibilities.

Courts hold that a supervisor must be "causally linked" to the pattern of constitutional violations by having knowledge of the pattern and that the failure to act amounts to approval of the pattern and hence tacit encouragement that the pattern continue. Therefore, correctional administrators must not abdicate their responsibility of supervising employees by shutting their eyes upon improper conduct. Performance evaluations, as well as informal appraisals of employee conduct, are to be done periodically to encourage proper conduct. Supervisors should review employee performance firsthand and review all incident reports. Remedial correction of unsatisfactory employee performance should be documented, and employees who chronically fall below the accepted standard should be put on notice that their employment is based on proper adherence to policy and conduct in the workplace. This strategy can assist in reducing potential supervisory liability.

Failure to Discipline and Negligent Retention

Failing to discipline means that the administrator does not investigate complaints about employees and does not take appropriate action as warranted. Allegations can also stem from the supervisor's failing to take action against an employee in the form of suspension, transfer, or termination when the employee has demonstrated unsuitability for the job.

The supervisor has a prescribed duty to take all necessary and proper steps to discipline or terminate a subordinate who is obviously unfit for employment. Unfitness may be determined either from prior acts of gross misconduct or from prior acts of lesser misconduct which indicate a pattern (del Carmen 1991). Supervisory liability may attach when the supervisor knew or should have known of misconduct by exercising reasonable diligence in supervising the employee. No supervisory liability attaches, however, when former acts of misconduct were unknown.

Correctional supervisors have a duty to enforce their legitimate regulations and to follow through with appropriate discipline as warranted. In *Flynn v. Sandahl* (1995) the warden did not violate a correctional officer's due process rights by ordering him to submit to a psychiatric examination after coworkers complained that he had threatened them with physical harm. Any privacy interest of the officer was outweighed by the requirements of maintaining a stable prison workforce.

Administrative liability will be avoided when supervisors fulfill their basic functions of properly enforcing security practices and institutional policies. Prison officials' termination of a correctional officer found sleeping on the job after taking medication for an arthritic knee was not found to be arbitrary or capricious (*Nebraska Department of Correctional Services v. Hansen* 1991). Correctional officials were not found liable when they took prompt effective disciplinary action after a female employee complained of alleged sexual harassment by a correction officer (*Hirschfeld v. New Mexico Corrections Department* 1990).

If the agency's disciplinary system is deficient, supervisory liability may attach. In *Gutierrez-Rodriguez v. Cartagena* (1989), the court held the police administrator personally liable since it found the disciplinary system to be grossly deficient, reflecting a reckless and callous indifference to the rights of citizens. The court found the following procedures inadequate:

1. officers investigated could refuse to testify or give a statement;

2. the agency did not have any provision for remedial training as one of the disciplinary options;

3. the withdrawal of a complaint closed the internal investigation without the agency's having done anything about it; and

4. the immediate supervisors of the officers were not involved at all in the disciplinary process.

Courts have imposed liability for inaction when a superior had known that an employee whose conduct led to a Section 1983 suit had previous knowledge of a policy violation and yet took no corrective actions. A prisoner brought a Section 1983 action against a correctional officer and administrator claiming that he was the victim of excessive force during a cell extraction in *Estate of*

Davis by Ostenfeld v. Delo (1997). The appellate court affirmed the decision for the prisoner, finding that, in violation of the Eighth Amendment, the officer had used excessive force when he struck him in the head twenty-five times while four other officers held him. The prisoner had complied with instructions to lie face down for handcuffing. The court determined that the superintendent had failed to investigate the incident and had failed to take any remedial action, which subjected him to liability. In the past, supervisors had informed the superintendent that the officer had failed to submit use-of-force reports and that there had been persistent complaints about him But the superintendent took no corrective action against the officer. The prisoner was awarded $20,000.

In *Brown v. Youth Services Intern of South Dakota* (2000) the court found egregious behavior on the part of a supervisor who retained an errant counselor involved in a sexual assault of several youths. Several youths of the treatment facility filed a civil action against the counselor's supervisor claiming negligent retention, negligent hiring, negligent supervision, and intentional infliction of emotional distress. The court denied summary judgment to the superintendent and awarded damages to the youths as a result of the alleged sexual assaults. The court noted that the retention of the counselor after repeated reports of sexual abuse constituted extreme and outrageous conduct and a total failure of the superintendent in responding. The court ruled that the administrator should have known of the counselor's alleged propensity for abusing children prior to hiring him.

In *Baker v. Willett* (1999) a prisoner brought a claim of excessive force against a detention officer and a failure-to-discipline action against the sheriff. The court denied summary judgment to the officer, holding that he had deliberately pushed the prisoner off a four-foot table, causing a severe injury to his forehead requiring sutures. The Undersheriff reviewed the incident and interviewed the prisoner, but he did not investigate or discipline the officer. The court dismissed the claims against the county, finding that they could not be held liable on the grounds that the sheriff's department had a practice of not investigating use-of-force complaints or disciplining officers. The court noted that three of five meritorious complaints in the past ten years had been directed toward one officer who had been terminated after disciplinary proceedings.

Clearly, correctional administrators must have workable disciplinary procedures that are adequate and legal. They must protect the rights of both the employee and the complainant. Steps of progressive discipline must be outlined and employees must be made aware of the consequences of employee misconduct. Supervisors must be trained in implementing appropriate disciplinary procedures in order to remedy or correct employee performance.

Complaints regarding employees should be investigated and procedures should be implemented regarding the proper method for conducting the investigation. Supervisory documentation of the investigation and its results should be kept in the employee's personnel file.

Sexual Harassment

Sexual harassment has become one of the most arduous but potentially damaging problems faced by the administrator. Claims of sexual harassment fall within the purview of Title VII of the Civil Rights Act of 1964 under the general prohibition of sexual discrimination in the "terms of and conditions, or privileges of employment." Title VII prohibits employment discrimination based on gender, race, nationality, religion, and age. Failure to react appropriately to sexual harassment claims not only has adverse effects on the agency but also may result in personal supervisory liability and disciplinary action.

An administrator is generally liable for sexual harassment of his/her employees when the harassment results in an adverse employment action such as termination, demotion or unwarranted transfer and when the harassment results in a severely or pervasively hostile work environment. Supervisory liability will not attach when the supervisor can show evidence of acting reasonably to prevent harassment or by acting promptly to correct the behavior. Supervisors must also be diligent in investigating prisoner complaints regarding correctional officers' misconduct in this area.

The courts are increasingly reviewing cases of sexual harassment and several cases have emerged in corrections. In *Speer v. Ohio Dept of Rehabilitation and Correction* (1994) the court awarded a female correction officer $7,500 in damages for invasion of privacy because a male supervisor had observed her from the ceiling of a prison restroom. In *Holland v. New Jersey Department of Corrections* (1996), the court awarded $3.74 million to correctional employees who alleged racial and sexual harassment and discrimination in the workplace. Conversely, in *Spicer v. Commonwealth of VA., Department of Corrections* (1995), the Court of Appeals found correction officials not liable for employees who made sexual remarks about a female employee's breasts since the Department had promptly effectively remedied the situation after she had complained.

In two landmark decisions, the United States Supreme Court set the standard for administrative liability in cases alleging sexual harassment. The cases *Faragher v. City of Boca Raton* (1998) and *Burlington Industries, Inc. v. Ellerth* (1998) established the tenet that an administrator is responsible for the misdeeds of an employee when that employee uses the agency relationship to accomplish the misbehavior. In these cases, a supervisor uses his or her authority to further the harassment. In making employment decisions, supervisors act directly as their employers' agents, so employers will always be liable for this (quid pro quo) type of harassment.

The case is much less clear when a supervisor's harassment does not end in an adverse employment decision. The supervisor may still use his or her authority to further the harassment, but the harassment may be no different from that which a regular coworker might commit. Something more than the supervisor's position must be considered before an employer is found liable.

Justice David Souter noted that the primary purpose of Title VII "is not to provide redress but avoid harm" (at p. 1518). In keeping with Congress's intent to prevent sexual harassment, the Court decided to model its rule on the premise that an administrator should be rewarded for making an effort to stop harassment. Along with the administrator's responsibility to thwart sexual harassment, the Court also recognized the victim's responsibility to avoid harm by using the agency's antiharassment policy.

The Court has sent a clear message that Title VII requires employers to try to prevent sexual harassment in the workplace and to provide appropriate discipline as warranted. Such cases require administrators not only to have a sexual harassment policy but also to enforce that policy by promptly correcting any sexually harassing behavior. Supervisors must be thoroughly familiar with the agency's sexual harassment policy and must provide periodic training to all employees.

When the supervisor is on notice of sexual harassment, Title VII requires the administrator to take some action to stop the harassment. This still is not sufficient to avoid liability. The administrator has to prove that the complainant unreasonably failed to prevent or correct the problem by taking advantage of the sexual harassment policy or by correcting the problem in some other way. To meet this component of the defense, administrators must encourage their employees to take advantage of the policy by promptly investigating and documenting all complaints and by preventing retaliation against those who do complain.

A common and recurring theme in many sexual harassment cases includes the claim of a hostile work environment. Such a claim can mean that the work atmosphere encourages or tolerates conduct which interferes with a person's ability to perform work without hindrance or distraction. Examples may include sexual jokes, cartoons, sexually offensive remarks, suggestive photos, racial remarks, inappropriate touching, unwelcomed advances, and/or work promises for sexual favors.

In *Gonzalez v. New York State of Department of Corrections Services* (2000) a female officer brought suit under Title VII for sexual harassment and a hostile work environment. The court ruled in the officer's favor, finding that she had been subjected to a hostile work environment for over one year and that the department had failed to take any action after she had repeatedly complained to supervisory personnel. The court found that the female officer had incurred a pattern of offensive behaviors almost daily, which included male officers' using derogatory terms such as "nigger" and "spic" in her presence and calling her and other female officers "bitches." The court determined that such behavior supported a claim of a hostile work environment in accordance with Title VII and awarded her $100,000.

An African-American detention officer was awarded $100,000 for emotional distress and mental anguish in *Ross v. Douglas County, Nebraska* (2000) for a claim of a hostile work environment. The appeals court affirmed the lower court's ruling, finding that a black supervisor's constant use of racial epithets toward the plaintiff officer created a hostile work environment and that, according to testimony, the warden's actions were carried out for the purpose of retaliation. The officer was permanently assigned to an extremely stressful position after he had filed an employment discrimination charge. The court noted that although the plaintiff alleged only a few specific incidences of racial harassment, this did not preclude the finding that the supervisor's harassment was sufficiently severe to support the plaintiff's claim.

In *Gorski v. New Hampshire Department of Corrections* (2002) a female employee prevailed in a claim that she was terminated from employment as a result of sexual harassment and a hostile work environment under Title VII. She claimed that her supervisors discriminated against her on the basis of her gender and of her pregnancy by making derogatory remarks about her pregnancy that gave rise to a sexually hostile work environment. The appellate court overturned the lower court's decision to grant summary judgment to the department, noting that the employee cited seven separate examples of what she alleged were hostile and abusive comments.

In an attempt to disprove that a prison's alleged lack of security created a "hostile work environment" which caused the death of a female officer by an assault of a prisoner, the appeals court affirmed a lower court's decision of summary judgment for the defendant correctional department in *Sperle v. Michigan Department of Corrections* (2002). The decedent had been murdered in the prison store by a prisoner, and her husband brought suit against the department for failing to prevent her murder and for allowing a sexually hostile work environment. The appeals court found that the husband failed to show that the prison, through any direct act, specifically intended to injure his wife. The court also noted that even if prison officials could have made working conditions safer by providing personal protection devices, adding extra officers, or insuring stricter supervision of prisoners, they did not act in a manner which shocked the conscience of the court and showed they intentionally meant to injure her.

ADMINISTRATIVE DEFENSE

Critical components of administration include planning, controlling, directing, budgeting, and supervising subordinates. Correctional administrators must also be concerned with the ever present liability component which may emerge from fulfilling their basic supervisory functions. The first line of defense against litigation begins with the administrator's making a firm commitment and concerted effort to transform these administrative functions into a proactive risk management program to minimize future lawsuits. Administrators and supervisors represent the best potential for protecting an organization from liability, but the basics must first be in place.

Liability Reduction

By integrating the fundamental components of management with liability risk reduction elements, administrators create a strategy to allow the organization to operate effectively and demonstrate a good faith effort toward reducing liability potential (Ross and Page 2003). The basic elements of a liability risk reduction program include the following:

1. Administrators should consider performing an analysis of agency incidents, complaints, audits, and lawsuits in order to identify problems specific to agency needs. After an assessment has been conducted, supervisors should garner the assistance of legal counsel to determine the latest court decisions (state and federal) that affect prisoner and employee rights.

2. Based on the outcome of the internal assessment, administrators are encouraged to revise outdated policies and develop new policies. Revising existing policy and procedure manuals are essential in complying with court rulings and changes in the law. Once policies are revised or new ones developed, administrators must keep supervisors updated on revisions and on administrative interpretations of them. This will ensure proper implementation and enforcement. It is recommended that agency policies should be reviewed annually by an administrator and revised accordingly. Correctional officials are encouraged to main-

tain current policies and procedures, developed in accordance with state and professional correctional standards.

3. All supervisors and employees should receive training in the policy manual on a regular basis. Moreover, all employees should be trained regularly in the legal dimensions of the job and in frequently performed job tasks. All employees should receive regular competency-based training in all types of physical tactics, equipment, and weaponry commensurate with their duties.

4. Administrators and supervisors must provide proper direction, supervision, and reinforcement of training objectives to ensure that the mission of the agency is being implemented. Administrators must investigate complaints and follow established agency disciplinary procedures as the situation warrants.

5. Written documentation of training, complaints, investigations, and employee disciplinary actions by administrators and supervisors are essential to corroborate management's role in supervising subordinates. Written documentation provides a record of events and incidents, and it establishes a process of reasonable actions taken. It will provide protection to the individual supervisor and the agency in civil litigation.

Summary

While administrative liability under Section 1983 is still developing, it has become a primary source of litigation in corrections. All indications suggest that this area of litigation will continue, and it is incumbent upon administrators to keep abreast of the legal standards imposed upon them. Through decisions of the courts, the days of unfettered supervisory discretion have been replaced with several theories of supervisory liability. Like other areas of correctional liability, deliberate indifference is the standard the courts apply to administrative liability. The standard is applied to claims of failing to train, supervise, and direct, as well as to claims regarding hiring practices, assignments, employee retention, and entrusting employees with equipment.

Judicial intervention has created a mixed blessing for the administrator. Hence, prison administrators should become more proactive in developing their own legal competencies and should maintain a working knowledge of the liability dimensions of their jobs. Moreover, they should be committed to further educating their employees in the legal nature of their responsibilities.

This combined approach will be beneficial in reducing the number of lawsuits and/or successfully defending the next lawsuit.

References

Archambeault, W. G., and B. J. Archambeault. 1982. *Correctional supervisory management: Principles of organization, policy, and law.* Englewood Cliffs, NJ: Prentice Hall.

Cullen, F. T., E. J. Latessa, R. Kopache, X. L. Lucien, and V. S. Burton. 1993. Prison warden's job satisfaction. *The Prison Journal* 73, no. 2: 141–61.

del Carmen, R. V. 1991 *Civil liability in American policing: A text for law enforcement personnel.* Englewood, NJ: Prentice Hall.

del Carmen, R. V., and V. E. Kappeler. 1991. Municipal and police agencies as defendants: Liability for official policy and custom. *American Journal of Police* 10, no. 1: 1–17.

DiLulio, J. J., Jr. 1990. *Courts, corrections, and the Constitution: The impact of judicial intervention on prisons and jails.* New York: Oxford University Press.

Flanagan, T. J., W. W. Johnson, and K. Bennett. 1996. Job satisfaction among correctional executives: A contemporary portrait of wardens of state prisons for adults. *The Prison Journal* 76, no. 4: 385–97.

Feely, M. M., and R. A. Hanson. 1990. The impact of judicial intervention of prisons and jails: A framework for analysis and a review of the literature. In *Courts, corrections, and the Constitution: The impact of judicial intervention on prisons and jails,* edited by J. J. DiLulio, Jr., 12–46. New York: Oxford University Press.

Hawkins, R., and G. P. Alpert. 1989. *American prison systems: Punishment and justice.* Englewood Cliffs, NJ: Prentice Hall.

Kappeler, V. E. 2001. *Critical issues in police civil liability.* 2nd ed. Prospect Heights, IL: Waveland Press.

National Institute of Corrections (NIC). 1988. Competency profile of warden/superintendent. Washington, DC: National Institute of Corrections.

Phillips, R. L., and C. R. McConnell. 1996. *The effective corrections manager: Maximizing staff performance in demanding times.* Gaithersburg, MD: Aspen Publishers.

Ross, D. L. 1997. Emerging trends in correctional civil liability cases: A content analysis of federal court decisions of Title 42 United States Code Section 1983: 1970-1994. *Journal of Criminal Justice* 25, no. 6: 501–15.

_____. 2001. *An analysis of the civil litigation claims in detention facilities insured by Michigan municipal risk management authority: 1994 to 1999.* Unpublished technical report, Livonia, MI.

Ross, D. L., and B. Page. 2003. Jail liability: Reducing the risk by studying the numbers. *American Jails,* January/February, 9–16.

Wright, K. 1994. *Effective prison leadership.* Binghamton, NY: William Neil Publishing.

Cases Cited

Barney v. Pulsipher, 143 F. 3d 1299 (10th Cir. 1998)

Barker v. Willett, 42 F. Supp. 2d 192 (N.D.N.Y 1999)

Beckford v. Irvin, 49 F. supp. 2d 170 (W.D.N.Y 1999)

Bednar v. County of Schuylkill, 29 F. Supp. 2d 250 (E.D. Pa. 1998)

Benavides v. County of Wilson, 955 F. 2d 968 (5th Cir. 1992)

Bordanero v. McLeod, 871 F. 2d 1151 (1st Cir. 1989)

Brandon v. Holt, 469 U. S. 464 (1985)

Brown v. Benton, 425 F. Supp. 28 (W.D. Okl. 1978)

Brown v. Youth Services Intern of South Dakota, 89 F. supp. 2d 1095 (D.S. D. 2000)

Board of the County Commissioners of Bryan County Oklahoma v. Brown, 520 U.S. 397 (1997)

Burlington Industries, Inc. v. Ellerth, 524 U.S. 742 (1998)

Carey v. Phiphus, 435 U. S. 247 (1978)

City of Canton, Ohio v. Harris, 57 U. S. L. W. 4263 (1989)

City of Oklahoma City v. Tuttle, 471 U. S. 808 (1985)

City of St. Louis v. Praprotnik, 108 U.S. 915 (1988)

Coleman v. Wilson, 912 F. Supp. 1282 (E. D. Cal 1995)

Cole v. State of Louisiana Department of Louisiana Department of Corrections, No. 01-C-2123 (2002) (unpublished decision)

Cooper v. Pate, 378 U. S. 546 (1964)

Estate of Davis bu Ostenfeld v. Delo, 115 F. 3d 1388 (8th Cir. 1997)

Estelle v. Gamble, 429 U. S. 97 (1976)

Estep v. Dent, 914 F.Supp. 1462 (W.D. Ky. 1996)

Faragher v. City of Boca Raton, 524 U. S. 775 (1998)

Farabee v. Rider, 995 F. Supp. 1398 (M.D. Fla. 1998)

Farmer v. Brennan, 511 U.S. 825 (1994)

Flynn v. Sandahl, 58 F. 3d 283 (7th Cir. 1995)

Ford v. Brier, 383 F. Supp. 31 (N. D. Ill. 1974)

Gilbert v. Selsky, 867 F. Supp. 159 (S. D. N. Y. 1994)

Giroux v. Sherman, 807 F. Supp. 1182 (E. D. PA 1992)

Gonzalez v. New York State Department of Correction Services, 122 F. Supp. 2d 335 (N.D.N.Y 2000)

Gorski v. New Hampshire Department of Corrections, 290 F. 3d 466 (1st Cir. 2002)

Gutierrez-Rodriguez v. Cartagena, 882 F. 2d 553 (1st Cir. 1989)

Hayes v. Jefferson, 668 F. 2d 869 (6 Cir. 1982)

Hirschfeld v. New Mexico Corrections Department, 916 F. 2d 572 (10th Cir. 1990)

Hirst v. Gertzen, 676 F. 2d 1252 (9th Cir. 1982)

Holland v. New Jersey Department of Corrections, No. 93-1683, 34 (D. N. J. 1996)

Hudson v. McMillian, 503 U.S. 1 (1992)

Hutto v. Finney, 437 U. S. 678 (1978)

Jones v. Wittenburg, 300 F. Supp. 707 (N. D. Oh. 1971)

Jones v. Wittenburg, 440 F. Supp. 60 (N. D. Oh. 1977)

Kentucky v. Graham, 473 U. S. 159 (1985)

Kesler v. King, 29 F. Supp. 2d 356 (S.D. Tex. 1998)

L. W. v. Grubbs, 974 F. 2d 119 (9th Cir. 1992)

Madrid v. Gomez, 889 F. Supp. 1146 (N. D. Cal. 1995)

Maine v. Thiboutot, 448, U. S. 1 (1980)

Marcheese v. Lucas, 758 F. 2d 181 (1985)

McMillian v. Monroe County of Alabama, 520 U.S. 781 (1997)

Miller v. Carson, 401 F. Supp. 835 (M. D. Fla. 1975)

Miller v. Shelby County, 93 F. Supp. 892 (W.D. Tenn. 2000)

Monnell v. Department of Social Services of New York, 436 U.S. 658 (1978)

Moon v. Winfield, 388 F. Supp. 31, (N. D. IL 1974)

Moore v. Hoiser, 43 F. Supp. 2d 978 (N.D. Ind. 1998)

Morris v. Crawford County, 299 F. 3d 919 (8th Cir. 2002)

Nebraska Department of Corrections v. Hansen, 283 233, 470 N. W. 2d 170 (1991)

Norris v. Detrick, 918 F. Supp. 977 (N. D. W. VA. 1996)

Owens v. Haas, 601 F. 2d 1242 (2d Cir. 1979)

Parker v. Williams, 855 F. 2d 763 (11th Cir. 1988)

Patsy v. Board of Regents of Florida, 457 U. S. (1982)

Pembaur v. City of Cincinnati, 475 U. S. 469 (1986)

Polk County v. Dodson, 454 U. S. 312 (1981)

Preiser v. Rodriques, 411 U. S. 475 (1974)

Roberts v. Williams, 456 F. 2d 819 (5th Cir 1971)

Roman v. Koehler, 775 F. supp. 695 (S.D.N.Y. 1991)

Ross v. Douglas County, Nebraska, 234 F. 3d 391 (8th Cir. 2000)

Scott v. Moore, 114 F. 3d 51 (5th Cir. 1997)

Slaken v. Porter, 737 F. 2d 368 (4th Cir 1984)

Smith v. Blue, 67 F. Supp. 2d 686 (S.D. Tex. 1999)

Smith v. Wade, 103 S. Ct. 1625 (1983)

Sostre v. McGinnis, 405 U.S. 978 (1972)

Speer v. Ohio Department of Rehabilitation and Correction, 646 N. E. 2d 273 (1994)

Sperle v. Michigan Department of Corrections, 297 F. 3d 483 (6th Cir. 2002)

Spicer v. Commonwealth of VA Department of Corrections, 66 F. 3d 705 (4th Cir. 1995)

Stokes v. Delcambre, 710 F. 2d 1120 (5th Cir. 1983)

Treadwell v. Murray, 878 F. Supp. 49 (E. D. VA 1995)

Troster v. Pennsylvania State Department of Corrections, 65 F. 3d 1086 (3d Cir. 1995)

Turquitt v. Jefferson County, Ala., 137 F. 3d 1285 (11th Cir. 1998)

Turner v. Safley, 482 U.S. 78 (1987)

Valencia v. Wiggins, 981 F. 2d 1440 (5th Cor. 1993)

Vine v. County of Ingham, 884 F. Supp. 1153 (W. D. Mich. 1995)

Vineyard v. County of Murray, GA, 990 F. 2d (11th Cir. 1993)

Will v. Michigan Department of State Police, 491 U. S. 58 (1989)

Williams v. White, 897 F. 2d 942 (8th Cir. 1990)

Wilson v. Seiter, 501 U.S. 294 (1991)

Women Prisoners v. District of Columbia, 877 F. Supp. 634 (D. D. C. 1994)

CHAPTER 11

CIVIL LIABILITY AND THE IMPACT ON CORRECTIONS

The hands-off doctrine used by the courts for numerous years has been replaced by court intervention since the 1960s. In the past forty years, a prisoner's legal status has changed from that of a "slave of the state" to that of an individual possessing rights while incarcerated to, more recently, that of an individual with more restricted rights. Prisoners are no longer left at the prison gate without the ability of filing lawsuits against their keepers. The previous chapters have illustrated how prisoners have exercised their rights.

Fundamental to the analyses of cases provided within this text are the United States Supreme Court's decisions based on its applications of various constitutional amendments to the correctional setting and the lower courts' applications of those decisions. Moreover, case analysis has identified the major standards of review or principles of law that the Court has established in their precedent-setting cases for future assessment. Over one hundred Supreme Court decisions were described and numerous lower-court applications were presented, covering twenty topics affecting prison and detention personnel. From this review several factors are evident. First, the Court will intervene on behalf of prisoners when clear evidence exists that a fundamental right has been violated. Second, through a majority of decisions since the 1980s, the Court has made it more difficult for prisoners to prevail in a civil lawsuit. Third, the Court will support correction officials' policies and practices when they are supported by a legitimate penological objective. Fourth, lower courts do not always strictly interpret and apply the Supreme Court's decision in the way in which the Court had intended, causing some inconsistencies throughout the varying circuits. Fifth, all Supreme Court decisions have significant impact on the field of corrections for policy makers, supervisors, and officers.

Legal Standards

Significant impact of landmark decisions are the standards the Court establishes—for at least four reasons. First, the Court frequently reviews a matter to resolve an ongoing common and complex situation. Second, in resolving the legal dispute, the Court establishes a standard which provides direction for future review of similar cases, providing some stability in the law. Third, the standard then sets the framework for lower courts with which to apply the decision in cases similar to the original one. Fourth, the standard sets forth the proper response by correctional officials when they are faced with addressing issues of the legal standard.

For example, arguably the most common standard established by the Court in a variety of correctional legal issues is that of "deliberate indifference." This standard addressed correctional officials' responses to medical care issues and was first presented in *Estelle v. Gamble* (1976). The Court determined that when a prisoner submits a claim of failing to provide medical care for a serious medical need, the prisoner must show that officials were deliberately indifferent or consciously chose to ignore a known need expressed by the prisoner. When examining medical or psychiatric care of prisoners, lower courts will apply the deliberate-indifference standard in determining liability. Over the years the Supreme Court has expanded the standard and has applied it to claims of failing to train agency personnel in *City of Canton v. Harris* (1989); to claims regarding conditions of confinement, as described in *Wilson v. Seiter* (1990); to claims of failure to protect, as described in *Farmer v. Brennan* (1994); to claims involving the American Disabilities Act in *Pennsylvania Dep't. of Corrections v. Yeskey* (1998); to claims involving environmental tobacco smoke in *Helling v. McKinney* (1993); and to claims regarding the hiring practices of personnel in *Board of County Commissioners of Bryan County v. Brown* (1997).

The impact of a second standard established by the Supreme Court resolved the issue of using force in corrections in its decision in *Hudson v. McMillian* (1992). For several years confusion surrounded the question: What degree of force is permissible in the prison context? In determining the standard of "sadistic and malicious for the purpose of causing harm," the Court discovered that the standard falls under the Eighth Amendment. The Court also held that merely a "serious injury" was not to be considered in examining a claim of excessive force, since the intent of the officer requires assessment under the standard. The Court further distinguished the standard from its application to pretrial detainees, noting that the standard of "shocks the conscience" is the appropriate principle of law.

Correction Administration

Standards have an important second impact on corrections. Once a case is decided by the Supreme Court, correctional officials should review, revise, or develop an appropriate policy in response. Precedent-setting cases have a direct impact on prisons and detention facilities. The Supreme Court's decision in *Turner v. Safley* (1987) clearly establishes that rules and policies of the correctional agency may restrict a protected right of a prisoner as long the agency can demonstrate a "rationale and legitimate penological objective." Generally, the rationale is supported by security, rehabilitation, and order maintenance factors. Policy sets forth how the agency will apply the case standard and describes what new operational practices may be instituted or prior practices stopped. It also provides direction for supervisors and officers in performing their sworn duties. Changes in the law require correctional administrators and supervisors to keep abreast of the law in order for the agency to provide correctional services consistent with case decisions. Correctional officials must keep correctional supervisors and line personnel abreast of the law, how changes in the law impact policies, and how the legal precedent impacts practices performed by correctional personnel.

A third impact of the Supreme Court's legal standards on correctional law is a natural outgrowth of the policy implications which affect correctional administrators. In Chapter Ten, a detailed review of administrative liability was presented. Since 1978, the term "every person," under Section 1983 litigation, has been applied to correctional administrators. This interpretation means that correctional administrators are not immune from liability. While administrative liability is an area of law that is still emerging, it is clear that a prisoner plaintiff can prevail in a Section 1983 lawsuit when he or she shows that the administrator was deliberately indifferent in managing the correctional agency. The plaintiff must show that the force behind an alleged constitutional deprivation emerged from a policy that was implemented or that failed to be implemented by the administrator. Administrators can also be sued for failing to train, supervise, discipline, and properly hire and assign personnel. The impact of the Court's standard's on correctional administrators is that they must be aware of their own personal liability and take efforts to minimize the risk through taking appropriate management measures.

The three impacts of the Court's standards on correctional liability issues have motivated many correctional administrators to proactively consider new and different management responses. One management strategy now used by many agency administrators to address operational issues and to reduce liability risk exposure is known as "risk management." Risk management is a proactive ongoing process that identifies past losses or circumstances which have exposed the risk of safety, security, and liability for the organization. Through a risk analysis, organizational personnel first identify how common a circumstance or task is and how frequently it occurs and then determine the criticality of performing or not performing the task that had led to the circumstance. The initial process begins with analyses or studies of officer incident reports (over the past three years), investigations, assaults on officers, prisoner assaults on other prisoners, accident reports, riots/disturbances, worker compensations, prisoner grievances, past agency litigation, newly adopted technology/equipment, and recently decided court decisions. Based on the findings of the assessment, the frequency and severity of the circumstance or task should be analyzed to determine how common the circumstance or task is before a risk control strategy is developed.

For example, if an agency wants to develop an officer defensive-tactics training program specific to the agency's need, personnel need to first study the types of encounters within the organization that an officer may face—specifically situations when forced will be used, such as breaking up prisoner fights, acting in self-defense or in defense of another, medical intervention, or cell extraction. Once the type of encounter has been identified, measurements of its frequency of occurrence and its severity should be made. For example, if a number of instances occur requiring a cell extraction when officers or prisoners have been injured, instances which have generated numerous officer-worker compensation claims or grievances or legal claims, thereby causing a reduction in the workforce, and which have also created a number of prisoner lawsuits leading to high awards or settlements, then the frequency and the criticality of the event (e.g., the cell extraction) warrant a risk management response. Such an example portrays officer and prisoner safety issues, security and operational concerns, use-of-force system issues, equipment/technology issues, policy and training issues, legal/liability issues, and budgetary/financial concerns. Clearly, there are high-risk and potentially high-severity concerns facing officers, administrators, and prisoners which can be minimized through a risk management approach. Almost any high-profile, high-liability task and circumstance can be analyzed using this approach.

Risk-control techniques are then developed which can be used to minimize the risk to the organization and to the personnel assigned to perform the task. Because of the nature of the correctional agency, some tasks and resulting circumstances cannot be totally avoided, and therefore, risk avoidance is not always practical. For example, a state correctional department may want to avoid some risk by terminating a program like "Boot Camp", because it is too costly and prisoners are frequently injuring themselves during physical exercise. The department may terminate the program to avoid further risk exposure. A department, however, may not shift the transportation of prisoners (e.g., from a prison to a court house or to a hospital or to other institutions) from its own responsibility to that of other agencies, such as the local police. Such a task cannot be avoided, so risk management strategies must be developed in order to perform the task while reducing the degree of risk to the officers involved and the prisoners being transported and at the same time ensuring safety to the community.

A more frequent risk control strategy used in many situations is policy development and training of corrections personnel which address the risk issue. The importance of policy has already been reviewed and training should be considered as the next most viable risk-control response. The United States Supreme Court has determined that a governmental entity maybe held liable for failing to train its personnel in *City Canton, OH v. Harris* (1989). This is the most common claim filed by a plaintiff, followed by claims of failing to supervise, direct (i.e., through policies), and discipline. The Court ruled that ongoing training must be provided on a regular basis concerning common tasks routinely performed by the officer. For the purpose pf implementing the risk control strategy, "routine tasks" will be defined as those which the officer performs frequently. This definition can then form the basis upon which to address regular training. For example, such tasks may include prisoner/cell searches, learning policies, responding to disturbances, use-of-force measures and force equipment, medical/psychological responses to prisoners, cross-gender supervision, understanding the legal issues of the job, crisis intervention, report writing, officer safety, responding to special-needs prisoners, and so forth.

An ongoing commitment to the training of officers and supervisors should be a departmental priority, and such training should be directed to the tasks that are unique to the department. Some training issues may be the same in a detention facility as they are in a prison, but because the purposes of these two facilities are different, the training should reflect the differences unique to the needs of the agency as identified through the risk assessment. Training is an administrative responsibility and an important component in risk management. Training which addresses supervisory competencies should include legal issues, leadership and motivation of employees, supervision and discipline of officers, management strategies, employee performance, and implementing policies. Training can increase officer skills in decision making, as well as organizational effectiveness and officer safety, and can therefore be useful in reducing exposure to the risk of liability.

An emerging area in corrections, which is unsettled in the law but has an made an important impact on detention facilities and prisons, is the issue of cross-gender supervision and sexual misconduct. While they compose two distinct issues, they involve multiple factors. Part of the issue involves the equal-employment opportunity rights of correctional employees to perform all assignments within the facility. These rights allow employees to supervise prisoners of the opposite gender. Prisoners complain that such supervision deprives them of their right to privacy under the Constitution and many have filed lawsuits which challenge this practice. There is no universal consensus by the lower courts regarding the degree of a privacy a prisoner possesses during confinement. Some courts grant more restrictive practices concerning cross-gender supervision, while other courts grant more authority to correction officials, holding that prisoners have very "limited" or "no" privacy rights and that employee employment rights outweigh the rights of prisoners. These decisions have created more than just confusion in correction officials, since they influence policy decisions, assignments and training of officers, and security practices. This issue bears close observation since the United States Supreme Court may address it in the future.

The spin-off of cross-gender supervision has resulted in some allegations of sexual misconduct, when indeed the correction officer was guilty of such misconduct. This is not to suggest that sexual misconduct is strictly related to cross-gender supervision, but some cases of it have emerged when a male officer has been assigned to supervise female prisoners. Sexual misconduct can be full of complex issues and in many situations involve "she said, he said" allegations. Such allegations can detract from the full and effective delivery of correctional services and can cause a breakdown in the secure operations of the facility. Correction officials should provide training which addresses cross-gender supervision, supervising/treating prisoners, sexual harassment, sexual misconduct of employees, and the officer's prescribed code of conduct. Administrators must make known that the agency has "zero tolerance" regarding sexual misconduct of correction officers with prisoners. Officials must take all such complaints seriously and conduct an investigation when a claim of misconduct has been made. Officer employment rights must be protected, and appropriate discipline commensurate to the offense should be implemented, including termination if warranted. Correction administrators should pursue the prosecution of officers involved in such sexual misconduct as the circumstances warrant.

Prison Litigation Reform Act

Perhaps the most significant impact on correctional litigation since prisoners won the right to file Section 1983 lawsuits was the enactment of the

Prison Litigation Reform Act (1996). In Chapters 1 and 3 of this text, trends of prisoner filings were noted which reveal that Section 1983 lawsuits have almost been cut in half since 1997, while petitions of habeas corpus have increased. The purpose of the act was to curtail prisoners from filing frivolous lawsuits. The act does not prohibit prisoners from filing lawsuits but places restrictions on filing lawsuits. A prisoner must first exhaust administrative remedies prior to filing a lawsuit, and if a prisoner files what the court deems a "frivolous" lawsuit, the prisoner may lose earned good-time credits. It is unclear, however, what constitutes a "frivolous" claim.

Since the enactment of the PLRA, the United States Supreme Court has reviewed two cases which challenged the provision of "exhausting administrative remedies" prior to filing a lawsuit. The challenge ostensibly claims that such a requirement deprives a prisoner of his First Amendment right to access to courts. In *Booth v. Churner* (2000) and *Porter v. Nussle* (2001), the Court held that such a requirement does not violate the filing prisoner's constitutional rights, that the requirement applies to all prisoner rights claims and not to selected issues of confinement. The requirement also applies to detention facilities and prisons. Consistent with other areas of correctional litigation, future challenges of the PLRA are anticipated, and correctional personnel should continue to monitor how the Supreme Court and lower courts interpret and apply the PLRA to the correctional setting.

The PLRA has also impacted consent decrees. For over forty years, detention and prison personnel have experienced consent decrees and have been placed under court order to correct certain practices and reduce overcrowding, to mention a few. The PLRA terminates consent decrees, unless there are ongoing violations of the decree. The PLRA only permits a consent decree when the court finds "harm" occurring in the facility. Such harm could be failing to adhere to the provisions of the decree by continuing practices which violate constitutional requirements and by continuing patterns or practices of excessive force and of the abuse of prisoners—to highlight a few. This component of the PLRA is also being challenged, and close observation of how the courts rule on such challenges is warranted.

First Line of Defense

While correctional administrators are faced with many managerial tasks in operating a correctional facility and supervising employees, correction officers are on the front lines and are therefore the "first line of defense" in reducing personnel's and their agency's risk of liability. As previously mentioned, when a prisoner prevails in a lawsuit, he or she may be awarded compensatory and punitive damages. Punitive damages are levied strictly against the officer, and some rather large awards have been levied against officers in the past. Officers are encouraged to review their agencies' policies on a regular basis, to maintain competency in implementing their agencies' policies correctly, to keep abreast of legal decisions impacting their job performance, and to maintain proficiency in all job skills.

Efforts to avert future lawsuits require a mutual partnership between officers and administrators. Administrators must equip officers with the knowledge, skills, equipment, and training to perform their sworn custodial duties. Officers must make sound decisions and perform their duties within the law, within agency policy, within their training and experience, and within the totality of circumstances. Because officers closely supervise prisoners throughout the correction facility, they are "first line of defense" in reducing legal claims made by prisoners. Research in many areas of correctional litigation reveals that officers and supervisors are prevailing at a higher rate in a significant percentage of prisoner claims than in past years. Success in this prevailing pattern will continue as long as the "front line" officer works to keep the risk of liability exposure to a minimum by performing his or her job within the established court standards.

Cases Cited

Booth v. Churner, 532 U.S. 731 (2001)

Bryan County Oklahoma, Board of Commissioners v. Brown, 117 U.S. 1382 (1997)

City of Canton, Ohio v. Harris, 489 U.S. 378 (1989)

Farmer v. Brennan, 511 U.S. 825 (1994)

Estelle v. Gamble, 429 U.S. 97 (1976)

Helling v. McKinney, 509 U.S. 25 (1993)

Hudson v. McMillian, 503 U.S. 1 (1992)

Pennsylvania Department of Corrections v. Yesky, 524 U.S. 206 (1998)

Porter v. Nussle, 534 U.S. 516 (2002)

Turner v. Safely, 482 U.S. 78 (1987)

Wilson v. Sieter, 501 U.S. 294 (1991)

About the Author

Darrell L. Ross, Ph.D. is a Professor in the Department of Criminal Justice at East Carolina University. He has taught legal, correctional, and managerial courses at ECU since 1992. He has been teaching and/or training criminal justice students and practitioners for over 25 years. He has authored 3 books and numerous articles regarding criminal justice issues.

He worked for the Michigan Department of Corrections for 13 years, working as a correction officer, cell block supervisor, probation officer, and a departmental instructor. Since 1988, Dr. Ross has provided expert witness services, testifying in federal and state courts, in civil and criminal matters. He has provided testimony regarding police and correctional issues in the subjects of: use of force, custodial restraint deaths, security issues in prisons and jails, custodial suicides, medical care issues, and administrative policy and training issues. He has served as a consultant to numerous police and correctional agencies, reviewing policies, designing policies/procedures, internal affairs investigations, excessive force complaints, custodial death investigations, training issues, and wrongful employee discharge incidents.

Table of Cases

INDEX